CW01046375

# A Brief History
## of Argentina

# FELIX LUNA

# A Brief History of Argentina

Translation by Judith Ravin

PLANETA

Diseño de cubierta: Carolina Schavelzon
Diseño de interior: Osvaldo Gallese

© 1995, Félix Luna

Derechos exclusivos de edición en inglés
reservados para todo el mundo:
© 1996, Editorial Planeta Argentina S.A.I.C.
Independencia 1668, Buenos Aires
© 1996, Grupo Editorial Planeta

ISBN 950-742-658-2

Hecho el depósito que prevé la ley 11.723
Impreso en la Argentina

# Prologue

Reader, friend

This book is written in the colloquial tone of my lectures and conferences. I preferred to do it this way so that those who might read the book could imagine that I was talking with them face to face, as I would truly like it to be. Because of this, you will have to make an effort to imagine my voice, my inflections, and my gestures; you will also have to pardon the reiterations that inevitably occur when one expounds verbally. And you may even, if you wish, reconstruct a laugh here and there or a murmuring in the audience... For this, in short, is narrated, recounted, spoken history.

It is possible that the attempt to summarize the course of four Argentine centuries in fifteen chapters is too ambitious. But we already know that history is infinite: just as one can delve indefinitely into it, so, too, can one synthesize it, extracting fundamental tendencies from the past in order to show them in their enormous contrasts.

In this book there are not many names, nor many dates; neither do battles, pacts, or political incidents abound. It is more about describing how our country began to be formed, since its founding substructures and on through the great phases of its formation. The purpose, the same that has animated the majority of my work, is to make our past known. Rather than being a detailed history, it is an exposition of the fundamental tendencies that Argentine society and institutions articulate. Rather than an erudite piece, it is a talk without pretensions, in order to clear up some doubts and to establish certain periods. A revision or, if you will, an introduction to the incredibly vast and fascinating territory of our history.

F.L.

# Making history

This work tries to encompass different situations that in the analysis of a given historic moment seem significant to us, and which, in addition, will allow some light to be thrown on the present; for history, in the last resort, is useful to better understand the country of today. Should this not be the case, it becomes mere entertainment.

In the course of these pages we shall try to answer certain questions that the community at times poses; the same ones that we, individually, ask ourselves at some point in our lives: What are we, why are we here, what is happening to us, why are we like this and not like others? Obviously, history does not answer all of these questions; it does not even answer them exhaustively, as it cannot give infallible answers. But without a doubt it helps us to feel that we are standing more securely on our roots, on our reality. For this reason, throughout these chapters we shall try to select significant events, trusting that we are casting light on the appropriate historical moments. And because it involves selecting, it is fitting that we make a brief methodological introduction.

When I say "I am selecting," it is because I am using that fascinating power that the historian has upon asserting: "History is as I tell it." Which is to say that I make use of that faculty which he who makes history has in order to establish that certain events are relevant and others are not. Perfect history would be that which might speak about life, about events, about problems of all of humanity during all eras. Naturally this is impossible; not even were we to limit ourselves to a specific era could we accomplish this. The historian, then, finds himself of necessity forced to select and discard events as they may or may not be useful to him. His choice is relative and also arbitrary, because it always depends on an ideology, on a table of values, and on a way of regarding the past, all of which lead some to think that certain events are relevant and others, by contrast, disposable.

Nevertheless, these limitations are precisely that which makes history enthralling. It is never exclusive; it is never one version that must establish itself discarding the others. There is always another possibility; there is always another point of view; there is always another way of looking at the past in a different manner, and consequently, of extracting other teachings, other fruit.

Another element of judgment to keep in mind is the idea of continuity. History is made through diverse factors —this we already know—, and there are moments in which it seems to speed up. Generally, when this occurs and historical events begin to gallop, it is because confrontations —ideological or otherwise— have occurred. We could say that these clashes form the preferred raw material of historians, above all, the younger ones. It always proves to be exciting to describe a confrontation between two personalities, two ideologies, or two forces, which at a given moment wage battles where one triumphs and the other does not and where, perhaps, the vanquished force amalgamates with the vanquishing one. It is really a very wonderful spectacle, but underneath these great confrontations, which at times are not as harsh as they appear, are the continuities, those processes through which, in a silent way, generally peaceful, the material that forms the plot of history begins to be woven.

Let us take as an example the figure of Juan Perón. It can be said that, at a given moment, his figure signified a rupture against the established order. And along with Perón, certainly, other values, another language, other personalities have prevailed in Argentine politics. But this same Perón, who arrived with a new language, also took a series of elements from the past, such as for example, the economic plan of Miguel Miranda, of 1947, which contained various elements from that of Pinedo, established in 1940 by a conservative regime. It is fitting to bear in mind that the historian takes a situation and reflects on it, but that between this situation and another there may have begun to occur changes —perhaps anonymous, perhaps imperceptible—, which shape an infinite amount of historical processes and define them in the course of time.

## CHAPTER I

# Humble origins

To begin with our topic, it may be useful for us to consider a historical moment of great importance for what would later be Argentina, one which, at that time, also influenced what today we call the Southern Cone of America: the founding of the city of Buenos Aires in 1580. We are assuming as common knowledge that America was discovered in 1492; that the River Plate and the Paraná River were navigated for the first time in 1517; that in 1536 the settlement of Mendoza was founded (it lasted but a few years).

We also know that in the following decades a wave of colonization originating from Peru and *Alto Perú* [Upper Peru] began to populate what is now the northern and central regions of Argentina, while another, with its point of origin in Chile, was in the process of founding San Juan, Mendoza, and San Luis; a third, issuing from Asunción, had already founded Santa Fe and Corrientes. We find ourselves, then, on the eve of the decade of 1580, an important period for Argentina that culminates when Juan de Garay founds the city of Buenos Aires.

## Buenos Aires, the gateway

What meaning does all this have? In the first place, let us keep in mind that when the Spaniards began to settle —we cannot say "conquest" because there were practically no wars of conquest in this first stage—, they had a very indefinite idea of the geography of this part of America. The immense plains, at times interrupted by mountain ranges (which, with the exception of the Andes, were not ominously inexpugnable), and the enormous rivers that came from the heart of America and flowed into the River Plate and then the Atlantic, exhibited an ungraspable geography, difficult to establish on the basis of reference points. So much so, that until well into the 18th century, in order to traverse the pampa, one had to take a compass along, for it was virtually impossible by sight alone to get one's bearings. But the Spaniards were good cosmographers and geographers and, above all, they had a sure-fire intuition that was proven true as they got to know the territory better.

On the eve of the foundation of Buenos Aires there already existed three cities. They were, in reality, very poor settlements, and temporary; but already back then they showed a natural calling to become cities, with all the bureaucratic red tape inherent in the Spanish way of functioning and all the hunger for governing and power that characterized the Spanish captains. These three cities were Córdoba de la Nueva Andalucía (founded in 1573), Santiago del Estero (1554), and Tucumán (1565).

If one looks at them on the map, they are three small points in the mediterranean interior of Argentina, facing northward or southward like post stations on a highway that led out from Alto Peru and, basically, from Potosí, a place that had already won the reputation of being the richest in America. It was the hill from which silver was extracted and it had generated great wealth within very few years, aside from creating a major center of consumption with significant purchasing power that needed goods to maintain the lifestyle to which not only the newly wealthy miners but all the people that profitted from the mining industry aspired.

The Spanish settlers, as we said, were good cosmographers and had good geographic intuition. An *oidor* of the Tribunal of Charcas, don Juan de Matienzo —*oidores* were like today's councilmen, members of a collegiate tribunal of the second instance; all of this land was judicially dependent upon the Tribunal of Charcas—, said in 1566 that it was necessary to open "a gateway to land"; that is, to provide a way out to the Atlantic, for the enormous extension that, from Potosí southward, already had post stations in Tucumán, Santiago del Estero and Córdoba. Matienzo postulated (from the solitude of his desk in the Tribunal, without ever having left there, but well informed by the people who had been in these regions) that it was essential to establish another settlement, more or less in the same place where don Pedro de Mendoza had founded the first Buenos Aires.

This is the primitive meaning of the foundation that Juan de Garay, sent by the last governor-commander of the River Plate, carried out: the idea of creating a gateway to land; the idea of opening comfortably and amply the entire route that that ultimately emptied into Alto Peru and into the city of Potosí.

Thus Buenos Aires was born in 1580 with several rather curious characteristics. The foundation, which at the time seemed to be transcendental, had little repercussion; what's more, over time one notes that Buenos Aires was to become, as one royal bookkeeper said only a few years later, "the poorest city of the West Indies." Within the Spanish empire, where the idea that wealth consisted of gold above all, and silver prevailed, Buenos Aires lacked both and was a small settlement where prior to 1610 there were, in the best of cases, some 500 inhabitants —if that—, shipwrecked in an immense double sea: that of the pampa (from where they were not inclined to leave, unfamiliar with practically all but the very bordering towns of the city) and that of the River Plate, which from there feeds into the Atlantic Ocean. Such was the sad situation of the proto-*porteños*, who depended on the arrival of registered ships to survive.

Having reached this point, it would be useful to give a brief description of what the Spanish commercial system was in those times. The Spaniards, due to fear of pirates and corsairs, established in the mid sixteenth century a system that consisted of sending two convoys (that is to say, expeditions), escorted by warships, that comprised thirty, forty, and even fifty units, which would leave two times a year from Spain and would return from there with the same interval.

They had a very precise itinerary; in general they travelled from Cádiz to the isthmus of Panama. They unloaded their merchandise in Portobello, carried it by mule through the isthmus until the city of Panama; they reached the Pacific, transported it once again on yet other ships and then, after passing Guayaquil, disembarked at the port of Callao, a short distance from Lima. There the merchandise was unloaded again, loaded onto mules, and distributed to diverse points of Peru and Alto Peru.

It was an extremely long route, and consequently, the value of the sale of the merchandise was very high: factored into the cost were the expenses of the trip. This, however, was the only system that Spain had found to defend itself against the attacks of the corsairs, most of all the English ones: by not allowing unaccompanied ships to transport merchandise, but rather dispatching it in convoys from port to port by way of the North Atlantic.

The elected system also indicated that Spain didn't have any point other than those privileged ports of Cuba and the isthmus of Panama in mind. For this reason, Buenos Aires as a port was totally marginalized and received only those so-called registered ships, specially authorized on the order of one per year, or one every two years. There were even lustra during which no registered ship arrived from Spain.

The *porteños* of that era suffered necessities. They didn't have any of the items they needed to survive and they couldn't manufacture them in a city and in a landscape such as that of Buenos Aires, where the type of production that could be carried out was very limited. They as yet had neither the custom nor the technique to explore the resources that the enormous pampa offered them and at whose edge they were located. Thus it was that the inhabitants of Buenos Aires began to make a living from contraband. It was the only form of survival.

## Mocking the law

Contraband came in from Brazil above all. It happened that (just when Buenos Aires was founded) Felipe II, because of a rather complicated dynastic problem, annexed the Portuguese Crown to the Spanish and became the king of Portugal, as well, though the two Crowns remained separate. The Portuguese took advantage of the benefits of this type of double citizenship and tried to trade with Buenos Aires. This exchange, nevertheless, was illegal, because it didn't consist of authorized, registered ships but rather of ships that, loaded with the merchandise that Buenos Aires needed desperately, entered any point in the enormous coast of the River Plate or the Paraná.

In time, in ten or fiteen years, an organization was formed that made its livelihood from contraband, but Buenos Aires continued to be a very poor city, practically wretched; the extremes of poverty in which one lived are legendary. The exception was the small group of people tied to contraband. There are some very entertaining stories, such as what Raúl Molina has recounted regarding the ostentatious form of life of the few who had billiard tables, concubines, and wealth that contrasted with the destitution of the rest of the inhabitants of the city.

In spite of the fact that a few governors, such as Hernandarias, tried to fight contraband, the force of necessity was so great, that *porteños* acquired the habit of mocking the law: they knew that in this way they could live under much better conditions, because the law was absurd as far as the interests of Buenos Aires were concerned.

In any case, each community, at some point, begins to find its *raison d'être* from an economic standpoint, what the meaning of its existence is, and what it is best suited for. Already, during the first years of the next century, the 19th century, there had been founded (besides Córdoba, Santiago del Estero, and Tucumán) Santa Fe and Corrientes, which formed the river route Asunción-Corrientes-Santa Fe-Buenos Aires. The land route, on the other hand, was Buenos Aires-Santa Fe-Córdoba-Santiago del Estero-Tucumán-Salta-Jujuy; as cities or marginal jurisdictions, La Rioja and Catamarca remained, while the province of Cuyo depended politically on the General *Capitanía* of Santiago de Chile.

With the passage of time, then, there formed a populational structure and with it, a certain differentiation, as well, in terms of work. Each jurisdiction slowly began to specialize, according to its climate and land, in a particular type of production.

There is a letter in the Archive of the West Indies known to be addressed to the king from a neighbor of La Rioja. (A nice aspect of the West Indies' organization was that a subject could address the king directly by letter, with a salutation that simply said "Sir:" and continued with requests, denunciations, or reports.) This letter is anonymous and it says why the writer fears that, because of the accusations set forth, he could be killed.

This unidentified neighbor of the city of La Rioja demands, in 1680, that every city of Tucumán and of the government of Buenos Aires have its own activity and be prohibited from carrying out any other in order to avoid competition between jurisdictions. For example, Buenos Aires should concern itself with mules, clothing, and furniture. La Rioja, should only produce wine and brandy; Catamarca, woven goods; Santiago del Estero, woven goods and mules; Córdoba, clothing; and so on. This outline of the interprovincial division of labor is evidently based on the existence of a productive differentiation in the activity of each region.

In this context, what is Buenos Aires to be engaged in? It was involved in contraband, which meant it became a gateway for all illicit commerce that then would spread throughout Tucumán, a jurisdiction that comprised the present-day provinces of Córdoba, Santiago del Estero, Tucumán, Jujuy, Salta, La Rioja, and Catamarca. The territories taken together (much larger than the government of Buenos Aires, which was created in 1617 and encompassed the entire province of the same name and part of Santa Fe and the *Banda Oriental*) was under the orders of a governor who resided in Santiago del Estero.

How did the inhabitants of Buenos Aires pay for the contraband they received? The source of wealth that was most accessible began to establish itself in the first decades of the 17th century: it revolved around the enormous quantity of ownerless flocks that roamed the pampa. Not far from Buenos Aires, in the same province, also to the south of Santa Fe and Córdoba, cattle had reproduced extraordinarily. The neighbors from Buenos Aires would set up societies to carry out so-called *vaquerías*, or hunting of cattle by lance point.

In order to do this, some ten, twelve, fifteen energetic peasants, willing to endure a hard life as well as to earn a few *reales*, would get together. When they found the unclaimed cattle, they would cut the clawed feet of each beast with the tip of a rod similar to a sharpened hacking knife, and the animal would fall to the ground immobilized. The second part of the task was to slit the throat of and skin the hundreds of fallen cattle.

The only part of the beast they took advantage of was the leather, loaded onto huge carts and brought to where it was cured and later exported. That was the great export product from Buenos Aires. The rest was lost: the meat, horns, tallow... One can imagine the pampa covered with rotten cattle, food for wild dogs and mice, the plague of the fields of Buenos Aires.

The *vaquerías* were important for several reasons. They

were Buenos Aires's first industry, no matter how coarse, primitive, and dissipating it may seem to us. Today we would define it as an ecological outrage, but in those times it was the only element of barter with which the people of Buenos Aires could pay for the imports that they in turn would introduce into the markets in the interior.

The cattle hunts then, constituted the first product of Buenos Aires. And how different from the modern-day cold storage industry. Nevertheless, from the cattle hunt to the salting house, to frozen meat, to refrigerated meat, and to Hilton cuts, there isn't more than a degree of difference. Growing technological progress made it possible for the primitive and crude *vaquerías* to become what is today not only an important industry but sophisticated, as well.

Another significant consequence of the cattle hunts was to begin to outline the political limits of what would later be some of the Argentine provinces. Frequently, neighbors of Santa Fe entered the jurisdiction of Buenos Aires to hunt cattle, to which the Cabildo of Buenos Aires reacted in anger, accusing the cattle hunts of usurping foreign land. There followed a series of disputes, not only with Santa Fe, but also with Córdoba.

Finally, about 1720, the *cabildos* of Santa Fe and of Buenos Aires agreed to the definition of a border, the Arroyo del Medio [Stream in the Middle], which still continues to divide the province of Buenos Aires from the province of Santa Fe. In the same way it was agreed where the province of Buenos Aires ended and that of Córdoba began. It could be said with a fair amount of certainty, therefore, that the *vaquerías* contributed to the establishment of limits for the jurisdiction of each province.

## Envy and rivalries

Another aspect of the primitive Buenos Aires is that ever since the moment of its foundation, Buenos Aires provoked a series of envy and rivalries. In spite of being very poor and living off of contraband, it was very well situated geographically: it was the "gateway to land" that Matienzo had dreamed of. The first rival to arise, due to Buenos Aires's good location, was Lima.

It was obvious (and many public officials said so at the time) that that the shortest and simplest itinerary for merchandise was to ship it across the Atlantic to Buenos Aires and then to transport it to Alto Perú, travelling over roads that were generally flat and without obstacles such as mountain ranges or great rivers. From Buenos Aires to Potosí, in fact, there is a perfectly transitable road. By contrast, the other itinerary (the port of Cádiz, Portobello, the isthmus of Panama, unloading, loading once again in ships that would travel by way of the Pacific Ocean, El Callao, Lima, and from there to cross the entire range of the Andes from Peru until reaching Alto Peru) was an extremely expensive nuisance.

In 1778, when the Edict of Free Commerce was passed, one could count on selling a rod of linen cloth that was to reach Potosí by way of the long route, for approximately thirty pesos a meter [1 meter equals 1 yard, 3.3 inches], whereas, if it came in through Buenos Aires, in Potosí it would be worth, at the most, five pesos. The geopolitical and geoeconomic superiority of Buenos Aires was undeniable.

Lima, realizing this, faced up to it from the beginning. For example: the commerce of Lima controlled the introduction of black slaves. When in 1720 the South Sea Company is set up because of the Treaty of Utrecht, England opens an overseas trading post in Buenos Aires to introduce slaves, causing the inhabitants of Lima to be up in arms. The same reaction occurred previously, with the support of the viceroy of Perú, who accused Buenos Aires of being not only the gateway of contraband, but the illegal backdoor for silver from Potosí, as well, all of which caused an uncontrollable drainage of foreign currency. The accusation was justifiable; all this formed part of the mechanism of contraband on which the survival of Buenos Aires depended.

Due to the rivalry with Lima, around 1620, an inland customhouse was installed in Córdoba. This meant that the admission of merchandise into the city of Córdoba was to be controlled, an operation that certainly was rather difficult. A road that crossed territory belonging to Santa Fe and joined Buenos Aires and Córdoba, without entering into the city, existed; by taking this route, one eluded the checkpoint. Residents of Lima, after much polemics, moved the customhouse to Santiago del Estero and, finally, after further polemics and discussions at the bureaucratic level, established that same customhouse in Jujuy, toward 1680 or 1690 .

Thus an internal market was created that would later define the borders of Argentina. With the exception of the customhouse of Buenos Aires, which was completely involved in contraband, the introduction of merchandise through Jujuy constituted almost an exclusive market. And, as we already know, markets tend to be a prerequisite for forming a nation. History provided the framework for what would be the territory of the future Argentina.

Buenos Aires competed with other cities as well: with Santa Fe, due to the aforesaid matters of cattle hunting, and —getting a little bit ahead of ourselves— let us mention in advance that from approximately 1730 onward the rivalry would be with Montevideo. When this latter city was founded, many noted that its port was superior to that of Buenos Aires, whose entrance suffered the serious obstacle of the tufas and the shallowness of the river. Montevideo began to be considered the true gateway inland, despite the fact that, to penetrate the interior, it was necessary to cross two large rivers, the Uruguay and the Paraná.

The competition between Buenos Aires and Montevideo was to such a degree that in 1804 the consulate of Buenos Aires (that is, the meeting of the merchants of Buenos Aires) opposed the building of a lighthouse on the eastern port. The tense relations between the two cities also explains why later Montevideo was one of the *realista* bulwarks against the May Revolution. In Montevideo, a counterrevolution was established that lasted four years, until 1814, when Alvear succeeded in taking it by storm. One could say that furthermore, the ancient rivalry with Perú also had a certain political expression during the period of·Independence, for Lima became the last of the *realista* bulwarks in South America; perhaps because it truly cultivated a feeling of fidelity to the king of Spain, perhaps a sort of projection of past rancor.

Let us summarize what has been said thus far. The city of Buenos Aires, founded in 1580, had first of all a permanent association with illicit commerce; that is to say, it practiced mockery of the law. Secondly, its production was based on a sort of ecological catastrophe —as is the indiscriminate annihilation of the wandering rodeos— to such an extreme that in 1715 the Cabildo prohibited *vaquerías* because "if things continue as they are we will be left without hide and stripped naked..." And, so it was.

## Power of assembly

Despite the fact that it inspired rivalries and competition, Buenos Aires was, at the same time, a city that had a remarkable power of assembly, as the confrontation with Portugal demonstrated. In 1680, a Portuguese expedition that founded a settlement appeared in Colonia del Sacramento (across the way from Buenos Aires; the River Plate dividing the two). Only a few years earlier, the Crowns of Portugal and Spain had separated.

Portugal aspired to have under its jurisdiction the entire southern portion of Brazil up until the River Plate. Thus, it established this expedition in Colonia, a very strategic location. On the one hand, it is a key to the River Plate, the Uruguay River and the Paraná, and on the other hand, it is the only place on the coast where there is stone, in other words, where one can construct fortifications, indispensable during that era.

The governor of Buenos Aires, José de Garro, found out about the settlement and sent a very strict ultimatum to Don Manuel de Lobo, head of the Portuguese expedition, advising him that the *Banda Oriental* belonged to the king of Spain and that consequently, they had to leave. Lobo responded by asking that they had let him settle there and that the diplomatic question be debated in the courts later. He said that his intentions were entirely peaceful, that what they wanted to do was to trade with Buenos Aires. Garro, who was an extremely obstinate Basque and patriotic, as well, insisted that the settlement be founded, giving origin to a very curious phenomenon.

Garro assembled what we might call today "the principle powers" of Buenos Aires (the secular *cabildo,* the eclesiastic *cabildo,* the most important merchants, the royal functionaries, and the men of greatest significance) for a consultation. All agreed that the Portuguese settlement should be attacked and the usurpers expelled. Garro, then, sent a circular to his colleague, the governor of Tucumán, so that he would mobilize the corps or milicias from the cities of Tucumán to Buenos Aires and thus undertake the initiative to expel the Portuguese.

And, in effect, from Córdoba, from Tucumán, from La Rioja, contingents were brought together by feudatory neighbors —as those who had *encomiendas* were called—, one of whose obligations was to come to the service of the king, at their own cost, whenever their military strength was needed. José de Garro, furthermore, asked the Jesuits to send Guaraní Indians as reinforcement. Thus was formed a sort of army of three thousand Indians. At the head of the entire force a *criollo* was placed, Antonio de Vera y Mujica, born in Santa Fe.

With that military appartus prepared, Garro once again convoked the principle powers of the city of Buenos Aires and asked them if despite the peace that prevailed between Portugal and Spain and the mandatory expulsion of the Portuguese, which could provoke a serious diplomatic incident, this plan should still go into effect. The principal powers agreed that it should, and the attack, which resulted in a horrible massacre, was carried out. The Guaraní Indians harbored a special rancor toward the Portuguese due to the expeditions of the *bandeirantes* against them (this is another story), and they killed almost all the poor settlers, many of whom were farm workers. Manuel de Lobo himself was taken prisoner; he died one or two years later.

The importance of this episode lies in the fact that Buenos

Aires, a city with one hundred years of existence, without the qualifications of Córdoba, for example, which already had a university; or those of Santiago del Estero, which was the oldest city in the country; without those of Asunción, which had been the mother of cities during the earliest period of colonization; Buenos Aires, with all its poverty and its burden of illegitimacy due to contraband, succeeded in convoking an event that was practically the equivalent of the first Argentine war: one fought against an outside enemy, who was usurping a clearly Spanish possession; plus, the majority of those who participated were *criollos*. The infantry of the city of Tucumán were grandchildren or great-grandchildren of Spanish conquerors, as well as Guaraní Indians; all of whom were under the command of a *criollo*.

Buenos Aires suddenly acquired a kind of prestige that later —when the Viceroyalty was created, when the residents of Buenos Aires repelled the English, and during the May Revolution— would be very important. A city that was born and lived in illegitimacy, that depended economically on something as strange as the vaquerías, that inspired rivalries and competition, had as well and nevertheless, sufficient assembly capacity to throw out a usurper from its environs and, in the effort, to obtain the cooperation of sister cities from the rest of this part of America.

Meanwhile, the interior was also growing and was specializing in some things. Tucumán, for example, in the manufacturing of wagons, taking advantage of the good wood. In Santiago del Estero, the abundant indigenous manual labor force allowed for a textile industry of a sort, very basic of course, but of certain importance. Córdoba specialized in the breeding of mules, which afterwards were sent to Salta, where they were sold to work in the mines of Alto Perú and Perú.

The interior was permanently besieged by problems with the Indians of Chaco, which in reality occupied part of Salta, Jujuy, present-day Formosa, and above all, Santiago del Estero and Santa Fe; the problems were a constant danger for the cities of Tucumán. For this reason, all of the governors required the services of the cities's neighbors to make incursions against the Indians, to subjugate them, and to instill fear in them. Córdoba responded almost always; Santiago del Estero, with great enthusiasm because its own interests were at stake; Salta and Jujuy, also; those of La Rioja and Catamarca, with greater reticence, as Chaco was very far away for them.

But those who never came to help out were the *porteños,* provoking indignation on the part of the cities of the interior. Within that context of solidarity, the *porteños* always had some excuse: they had seen pirates along the coast, they were having some problem.... This attitude created a differentiation as far as the political interests of each side went.

## Political organization

It would be appropriate at this time to describe briefly the political-judicial organization of this part of America, an organization which, to be sure, was no different from the rest of the Spanish empire. It was made up of a series of authorities, some of which had been instituted as an act of mechanical transference of Spanish authorities to the New World.

Take the *adelantados,* for example. During the eight centuries of the *Reconquista,* that is, during the fight of Castilla and León against the Moors, the kings, many times for lack of money, appointed *adelantados* so that they could extend the Christian frontier at the expense of the Moors. They would award these governor-commanders a certain amount of privileges, as they would do for those who would colonize future settlements in the new territories. Once Spain laid its gaze upon this sort of immense lottery that was America, the first thing that occurred to the authorities was to automatically relocate some traditional Spanish institutions to America. The *adelantados* were one of them.

The first governor-commander of the River Plate was don Pedro de Mendoza; likewise, in other regions of America other *adelantados* were appointed. The arrangement involved a contract by which the *adelantado* agreed to pay all the expenses of the expedition in return for the title of Captain

General and judge, as well as for a series of privileges of command and power, and a certain quantity of land that, once discovered, he would have the right to the natural resources that it yielded. In relatively little time, in less than a century, the system proved that it didn't work, that it was dangerous. The governor-commanders, because of the enormous distance that separated them from the authorities of the metropolis and because of the nature of their temperament, tended toward absolute autonomy. There had already been the question of Pizarro and Lope de Aguirre in Perú, for example.

The institution was therefore annulled and in its place the bureaucrats arrived; first the governors, then the viceroys. The governors were in charge of extensive territorial jurisdictions, such as Tucumán, Paraguay, or that of Buenos Aires, although these were in turn subject to the authority of a viceroy; in the case at hand, to the viceroy of Lima and the viceroy of Perú.

The Viceroyalty of Lima was established shortly after the Conquest, as in Mexico, and it consisted of a direct representative of the king, generally a gentleman, a nobleman of illustrious lineage; these were largely men who were quite capable and efficient. As of the establishment of this institution, there existed what we could call an Executive Power that sometimes also spilled over into judicial jurisdictions and had, over time, certain authority about which we will speak shortly.

The other very important institution, apart from the viceroy, was the *Audiencia,* a sort of chamber of justice or Supreme Court that, if all else failed, was in charge of judicial affairs. Its members, what's more, as in the case of don Juan de Matienzo, were informers; they performed a planning role of a sort, and they were obliged to report to the king all of their concerns. The *audiencias,* then, apart from their judicial function, worked as a form of control.

Then there were the *cabildos,* on the level of the municipal government organization. It should be remembered that here all the foundations of cities were made by the Crown in the name of the Crown. In North America, on the other hand, the colonists arrived freely and later founded a city; or a settlement company arrived and would sell lots and found a city. Here, where everything was done in the name of the Crown, the founder designated the first group of constituents of the Cabildo (six, eight, ten, according to the importance of the city), each one of whom would be in charge of a particular duty and would be granted great honors for serving in the Cabildo. They served one year, at the end of which they themselves would choose their successors; that is, there would be no popular election as in some states of North America.

In theory the Cabildos fulfilled municipal functions, but given that cities such as Córdoba, Santiago del Estero, Tucumán, and La Rioja were so far from one another, in reality they carried out all the functions of the government: in the case of a drought, they had to take measures to see that the population was provided for; if there were Indian attacks, they had to take military action; if there was any abuse on the part of the governor, they would complain to the viceroy. So that they were, in effect, not only a municipal government but a truly important political government.

Within the power structure of the West Indies there was also the Church, which fulfilled a religious function of course, but also a political function: it controlled, oversaw, complained, entered into conflict (almost always with the governors and with the viceroys) and, basically, established a certain balance between the different powers.

In the organization of the Indies, no power was too clear. We would be scandalized if the Judicial Body were to interfere with the political arm; nevertheless, in those days, the *Audiencia* could replace the viceroy, as occurred in Buenos Aires in 1806. The *Audiencia* could take political action, the viceroy could take judicial measures because he was president of the *Audiencia,* and the *cabildos* had a function that exceeded that of a municipal entity.

This situation was not accidental. The Spanish Crown tried to maintain a certain state of confusion in order to control the whole so that, in the face of abuse, infraction of a law, or an excess of independence, another organism could set things on the right track. It was a very delicate system of counter-balances, governed by the laws of the West Indies, which in addition were casuistical; that is to say, not general, but rather of a particular type, and what's more, shaped by a concept difficult to define, though very interesting.

The organization of the Indies was the offspring of the old Spanish law, whose fundamental principle was the idea that everything should be done to benefit the community, for the common good of the people. This was not only a concept of a philosophical nature, it also carried the weight of very concrete and transcendental practical applications. If when the viceroy or governor received a royal letters patent, sent from the very monarch installed in Madrid, and upon reading it considered it nonsense, he would solemnly convoke the functionaries, the *cabildo,* the *Audiencia,* the bishop and say: "The royal letters patent is respected but will not be carried out." In other words: "It's not that we disavow the authority of he who says this, but as it is not designed for the benefit of all and will do more harm than good, I will not apply it and will file it away in a drawer."

This procedure was common, a fact that indicates the existence of a sort of veto power on the part of the authorities of the West Indies as concerns the decrees of the royal authority, which although respected as the supreme authority, could be poorly informed as far as the reality of America. As a consequence, the representatives of the king who were in the new lands would say, for the sake of the common good: "This is not acceptable." After the May Revolution this principle is substituted by popular sovereignty.

## The indians

The administrative organization and the events that occurred in these territories had a very important backdrop, which permeates, justifies, and sets in motion the whole picture: the Indian presence. The existence of an indigenous population in the New World troubled not only Spain but Europe, as well. The fact that a "new" continent might have been discovered in which there were also living beings —recognized after some years had passed as human beings— brought on a series of enormous problems of the theological, philosophical, juridical, political, and naturally, scientific order.

Suddenly questions arose such as, if they are human beings, did Christ redeem them? Do we have to convert them to Christianity? Are we obliged to baptize them? Is it part of our mission to do so? And, fundamentally, in the case of Spain, do we have the right to wage war against them, or take their possessions from them, to enslave them, to take advantage of them? These issues were discussed in Spain time and time again; there were meetings among theologians and many books written on the subject. Under what circumstance can Spain make war against a group of Indians who have done nothing to us? We have landed here as invaders, what right have we to fight them?

During the first years of the conquest, the problem was relatively theoretical, but when, in 1519, Hernán Cortés landed off the coast of Mexico and encountered, for the first time in the history of European civilization, another culture, unknown up until then and perhaps more brilliant and more opulent than that of the Europeans, the Indian phenomenon appeared in all of its harshness to be quite a different problem. What are we going to do with the Indians, how are we going to profit by them? Because obviously, the conquest was the conquest and one couldn't stop it.

What's more, how should we go about taking advantage of them without this being tantamount to sin, something that would weigh heavily on our conscience and the conscience of our monarch? Thus was invented the institution that would defend the entire settled population of America (with the exception of Buenos Aires, where there were no subjugated Indians) and, especially, Tucumán: the *encomienda*. This consisted in entrusting a group of Indians, a tribe, or a few families to a Spaniard. What was being entrusted to him was the salvation of their souls and a certain minimum of well-being. In exchange, the Indian had to work for him or, after 1615, pay him a tribute.

The neighbor who possessed such a privilege was obligated to come to the aid of the king whenever he might require it; slowly he acquired the status of a feudatory, almost a feudal lord. He had entrusted a group of Indians to him, who were not his slaves, who could not be transferred, sold, or relocated, and with whom he had certain obligations. But at the same time, the entrusted colonist had certain rights with respect to the Indians: fundamentally, that they would work for him or they would have to pay a fee.

In general terms, this was the panorama of Tucumán and of the government of Buenos Aires around the middle of the eighteenth century, the period during which this social structure and power structure that we have described was, shall we say, consolidated. The mid eighteenth century is also the moment when the idea of the wealth of the nations of Europe changes, when the Bourbon dynasty secures itself in Spain, when the concept of the value that the possessions in the West Indies have also changes. This is the eve of the creation of the Viceroyalty of the River Plate.

# CHAPTER II

# The colonial period

Before going specifically into the creation of the Viceroyalty of the River Plate and elucidating the historical significance it had, we will note some developments occurring in the middle of the 18th century that appear to be interesting. During the time that elapsed since we interrupted our chronicle at the end of the previous chapter —toward the beginning of the 18th century, when the death of Charles II; the War of Sucession; and finally, the coronation of the first monarch of the Bourbon dynasty, Philip V, in Spain—, during those years and the following ones, a series of circumstances occurred that, although they had originated during the previous century, took on at this point major significance.

# The estancias

Buenos Aires began to change, perhaps not as much the city itself as the territory that surrounded it. We mentioned previously that, basically, its inhabitants lived as if ship-wrecked between two enormous seas: one, the pampa; the other, the River Plate. By the middle of the 18th century, indigenous peoples —probably of Chilean origin—, who had discovered the horse, occupied the uninhabited areas of the pampa, constituting a greater danger for the Christians.

Consequently, the inhabitants of Buenos Aires tried to protect the few settlements that surrounded them by creating little towns, which when necessary could be defended by small clay constructions or by stockades in Mercedes, San Miguel del Monte, Chascomús, and Dolores. Thus was formed a line of fortlets through to Melincué that were manned by local peasants who were summoned as a sort of militia: the *blandengues,* or frontier guards. Despite the fact that they were poorly paid and poorly armed, it was to them that one had to resort in the event of an Indian attack.

The purpose of this small circle of fortlets was to protect from surpise Indian attacks the first *estancias* created in the vicinity of Buenos Aires. Up until then agricultural wealth, consisting fundamentally of cattle, was obtained directly through the *vaquerías*. But as stray cattle began to disappear by the beginning of the 18th century, a few *porteños* with ini-tiative and courage established places where they could be domesticated, where they could become acclimated. This way, when it came time to slaughter them, the cattle were right at hand and their exploitation didn't imply expeditions lasting many days, during which one had to press inland through the plains to find them.

In the new establishments the most common form for retaining the cattle was by *rascadero,* a rather notorious stick placed in the middle of the pampa, where the animals would go to scratch themselves (this is the *"palenque ande ir a ras-carse"* mentioned in *Martín Fierro*). There they could go to drink water and, if they were left any salted bread, to balance

Foundation of the city of Buenos Aires, by Don Juan de Garay in June 1580.

View of the Fort of Buenos Aires in the time of the colony. In the background, the River Plate.

The surrender of the English troops, commanded by Beresford. Here, the capitulation of 12 of August, 1806.

The power of the Spanish King is over.

their diet of grazing. Near the *rascadero* would be the ranch of the owner (or sometimes that of his representative or overseer), who, needless to say, led a very solitary and savage life. He was a distance of many days from the city of Buenos Aires, where he could stock up on the necessary elements of life. In reality, as far as the type of relationships that he could have and the type of work that he could carry out, it was a life very similar to that of the Indians.

Despite so much precariousness, thus was the start of the incipient *estancias* of Buenos Aires. From these, leather primarily was obtained, which had already been the principal objective of the *vaquerías* and now was exploited by way of more refined methods. One tried to tan them on the premises and ship them off with relative regularity. In some cases people sought to include some subproducts such as the horns or hooves.

For historians and readers of history, we find it difficult to imagine how daily life was fifty, one hundred, or two hundred years ago. As a result, we have to make an effort in order to grasp to what extent leather was an extremely important commodity in the life of Europeans and Americans. By the mid eighteenth century, leather formed a part of a variety of objects of everyday use that today have disappeared or are manufactured in a different way.

Among other things, there was the axle lining of wagon wheels; it was with leather that the harnesses for horses and the cartridge belts of uniforms would be fashioned or made: not only cartridge belts but shoes and boots, as well; with leather many pieces of furniture were finished as were wagons of a certain quality; and, among many other uses, it was used for toiletry articles.

Leather was a commodity for which there was increasing demand in Europe, above all when there was a war and it was needed to pack and line cannons. Consequently, the *estancias* that began to form near Buenos Aires, proteced from the Indians by a cordon of fortlets, responded to the demand that was on the upswing for the River Plate.

And so the physiognomy of the Buenos Aires described in

the previous chapter gradually changed, that Buenos Aires whose inhabitants made their livelihoods exclusively from contraband, waited for a registered ship that arrived every one or two years, and felt abandoned by the hand of God. In this new Buenos Aires of the mid eighteen hundreds, by contrast, there existed a sort of local industry that basically consisted in the exploitation of leather.

On the other hand, toward the latter decades of the 18th century, there began to form in Buenos Aires with increasing intensity a society where people were valued for what they were and what they had. Social worth was not obtained by either a name or by pertaining to the aristocracy (incipient or not), but rather from the success that one might have attained in life.

In the interior, meanwhile, some other differentiations began to occur, such as, for example, a greater local identity in the cities of Córdoba, Mendoza (that still pertained to the General *Capitanía* of Chile), La Rioja, and San Miguel de Tucumán, among others. Each city began to focus on a particular type of production that was associated with it and in a certain way created a connection among its inhabitants. There was, for example, a distinct style to the wagons fabricated in Tucumán and a whole different style to those from Mendoza.

## The jesuits

The political-philosophical framework of the Bourbon dynasty was absolutism, a conception that maintained, among other things, that nothing that is within the State should be set against the State itself or its representatives. In the middle of the 18th century this ideology had repercussions with respect to two events in the part of America that concerns us here. One is the expulsion of the Jesuits in 1767.

The Jesuit order had succeeded in constituting a very curious enclave within the Spanish empire and one worthy of analysis; it was spread over part of what is today Paraguayan territory, the province of Corrientes in Argentina, and the

Brazilian and Uruguayan littorals. It comprised approximately seventy towns, whose inhabitants were Guaraní Indians who had abandoned their nomadic habits and were directed by Jesuit fathers, who in turn had been rigorously trained by the Company of Jesus to become administrators of each one of these towns.

I believe we should render homage to the intentions of these priests, who were heroic. They attained such a strong identification with the Guaraní Indians that they even adopted their language in place of Spanish, saved the Indians from their nomadic destiny, urbanized them, taught them métiers, unified their language, and ultimately turned them into authors of a great quantity of cultural expressions that even today continue to be important and continue to have beauty and usefulness.

At times I have thought that it seemed that about the mid seventeenth century, the Jesuits must have said to themselves: "In Europe we no longer have anything more to do; this civilization is corrupted by money, greed, cruelty. Let us look for a place where we can try out a totally different civilization, one where the spirit of profit doesn't exist, where people work in solidarity, where no one has money because there is no need for it, where people live as brothers." From a certain point of view, one could say that the Jesuit towns had a socialist economic system of government. No one had anything of his own, except domestic items, and all necessities were provided for by the community: "Each according to his capacity; to each according to his need."

The presence of the Jesuits in Argentine territory, furthermore, had a political significance. They defended the Spanish territory from the *bandeirantes* and they opposed the barter of seven Guaraní towns in exchange for Colonia del Sacramento; only with a great deal of difficulty were they persuaded to abandon them and leave them under Portuguese jurisdiction.

One of the problems that the Jesuits presented to the Spanish Crown was precisely their political power. In the towns lived thousands of Indians —some with military training—, who could make up quite a significant force. As a result, in 1767, King Charles III sent a secret order to the authorities of all the Spanish colonies throughout the world, ordering them that on a certain, predetermined date they should take under guard all existing Jesuits in the jurisdiction, establishing by inventory the assets they possessed.

In effect, by mid year 1767, with an interval of a month between the time of the order and its execution, various armed pickets knocked on the doors of Jesuit residences in present-day Argentine territory (these were not only in Misiones but in almost all the cities of present-day Argentina), arresting priests and seizing their possessions. From that moment on and for almost a century thereafter, the Company of Jesus disappeared from Argentine territory.

The incident had infinite consequences. The cultural activities developed by the Jesuits were suddenly cut off, not only in the missions but in the rest of Argentine territory. Other religious orders tried to fill in the void. The worldly possessions left by the Company of Jesus were sold or auctioned off, causing the rise of a new class of proprietors, individuals from the provinces who thus achieved higher status. An example is the splendid *estancia* in Santa Catalina, in Córdoba near Jesús María, which, having been acquired by a Cordobian gentleman by the last name of Díaz, formed one of the most important cattle exploitation industries of the time.

The Jesuit settlement in this territory couldn't last very long, among other reasons, because its prosperity tempted the avariciousness of certain Spanish functionaries who supposed that the settlements (called *reducciones*) were part of a patrimony that should be in the hands of the Crown. The error of the Jesuits was probably in not having taught their pupils to govern themselves. The proof that they didn't form a ruling class was that when they were expelled, the missions were left in total ruin. Although the Franciscan fathers took the missions over with the greatest determination, their cultural patrimony fell apart relatively quickly. From what had been an emporium of industriousness, practically nothing was left standing fifteen years later.

In any case, what was achieved during the one-hundred-and-fifty-year period that the Jesuit experiment lasted was truly admirable. The evidence lies in the many chapels and churches that can still be seen: in Córdoba, the church of the Company, the *estancias* of Jesús María and Santa Catalina, and the chapel of Candonga, among others, are demonstrations of what the experience in the missions was. What's more, the Jesuits succeeded in creating in the middle of the jungle a printing press with types of wood that allowed them to print books that even today are a marvel for their graphic quality. The press was later moved to Córdoba and from there, when the Jesuits were expelled, to the press in Buenos Aires responsible for so many publications, the Imprenta de los Niños Expósitos [the Press of the Foundling Children].

There were other factors, as well, that motivated the expulsion of the Company: the Masonic elements that were operating at the center of the government of Portugal and Spain at the time, the theories of the Encyclopedists, the liberal ideas that were already spreading in Europe. Furthermore, there were some financial scandals that caused the Jesuit order in France to lose prestige, and weaken. It would suffice to read *Candide,* by Voltaire, for example, to perceive to what extent the Company during that period was the object of calumny and to note the, at times, warranted criticism. The power of the Jesuits was too strong; therefore, it became suspicious.

When the expulsion went into effect, several European States, such as Russia and Poland, offered the Jesuits hospitality. Some went to Italy. Many of them lived in Faenza, and some wrote very beautiful things about their experiences in America. Others celebrated the advent of Independence, either because they abhorred the Spanish power that had expelled them, or because of their affection for America, where they had spent many years. There were even others, as for example, Villafañe, an Argentine from La Rioja, who returned to the River Plate after Independence. In general, their lives were very unfortunate after the Company was dissolved. They were accustomed to being part of a corps with great solidarity, and they were forced to become scattered throughout the world; they lived in poverty, generally taken in by some Italian principality, some dukedom, some earldom. Only in 1815 did the order reestablish itself.

# Changes

Another important change related to the absolutism of the Bourbons is, aside from the expulsion of the Jesuits, the beginning of a more strictly fiscal regime, something that created great resistence in these parts. There existed, on behalf of the Crown, the need to introduce reforms for the sake of a better government and a greater control of things, what lead to a more colonial type of regime: orders were even given to cut down olive trees and tobacco cultivations that competed with Spanish olive oil and tobacco.

Previously, during the time of the government of the Hapsburg dynasty, the only important contribution that America made to the Spanish Crown was the tribute of twenty percent —the royal *quinto*— of the metals that were obtained here; the rest was left for private enterprise. With the Bourbons, a more rational fiscal system was established. What's more, the idea of the wealth of nations had changed. Instead of believing, as in earlier periods, that this was based solely on gold and silver, goods and economic activity had begun to be regarded as wealth. Hence the importance of leather. As a result, the area of the River Plate, which had no gold or silver but did have other assets, increased in value.

The colonial regime never managed to flourish, as the Independence movement interrupted it. When the English invasions occcurred, the military impotence of Spain to defend its colonies in America became evident, but even before, it proved itself to be economically impotent to supply the colonies given the lack of a fleet. With relative success, Charles III and his successors set about reconstructing both Spain's military might and its commercial strength. Mercantilist economy demanded it.

Another important fact was the continuing advance of the

Portuguese in the River Plate. We have already recounted how Buenos Aires succeeded in convoking a sort of national expedition that expelled the Portuguese from Colonia del Sacramento, an event that gave rise to a series of diplomatic and military maneuvers. Several times the Spaniards took Colonia del Sacramento by force and then had to cede it due to diplomatic treaties. Finally the Treaty of Permuta was signed, according to which Spain was to give up seven mission towns in return for Colonia del Sacramento. In 1776, don Pedro de Cevallos arrived at the head of an enormous expedition, the biggest that America had seen, with the task of definitively taking Colonia del Sacramento and reaffirming the borders between Portugal and Spain. To the north of the present-day border between Uruguay and Brazil he founded the fortress of Santa Teresa.

## The viceroyalty

In 1776, the Viceroyalty of the River Plate was created. Up until then Buenos Aires was one government and Tucumán another, and both depended —at least theoretically— on the Viceroyalty of Lima. After 1776 the entire jurisdiction was to become part of the Viceroyalty of Buenos Aires, along with that of Paraguay and the region of Cuyo, which depended on the General *Capitanía* of Chile. Thus the outline of a great nation was established, conceived on the basis of a grandiose thought, which is apparent in the jurisdiction that was conferred to it as in the capital that it was given.

From an institutional point of view, the most important development was the designation of don Pedro de Cevallos as the viceroy of the River Plate, by way of a royal letters patent that granted him a jurisdiction that included Alto Perú, the government of the former Tucumán, and the government of Paraguay. In these regions there were several cities that had more than sufficient attributes to warrant their aspiring to be the capital of the new viceroyalty. There was Córdoba, that since 1615 was the headquarters of the most prestigious university of this part of America. There was Potosí, whose legendary wealth had fed the coffers of the Spanish State during more than a century and that, although in decline, continued to maintain its legend. There was Asunción, Paraguay, which had been the first Spanish settlement in this part of America.

Nevertheless, the Spanish court decided in favor of Buenos Aires because, in spite of its peripheral location, it was the ideal place from which to resist the advance of and an eventual attack by the Portuguese, and furthermore it had the easiest access to Spain by way of transatlantic navigation. Most assuredly a good lobby on the part of the *porteños* in Madrid also contributed to the city being raised to the status of head of the Viceroyalty, the last in America. Its jurisdiction comprised the present-day republics of Argentina, Bolivia, Paraguay, and Uruguay.

Though Buenos Aires was the capital, the other cities had of their own jurisdiction. These municipal governments, or *cabildos*, were communal and had as responsibilities a variety of things that they did for the common good and that exceeded municipal concerns: in 1810 there was already fairly significant political activity. In large part the *cabildos* were made up of *criollos* of several generations back.

Later in fact, the municipal jurisdictions began to establish the rough limits of each one of the modern-day provinces and countries on the basis of *uti posidens,* one of the legacies of Spanish civilizations. It is a principle of American international law, whose translation from the Latin is: "As you possess, you will continue to possess." When there is a border question between American countries, the first thing that is done is the Spanish archives are looked at to see what the Spanish jurisdiction was, and if it is clearly marked, it is accepted as an international border. Thus, for example, Bolivia and Peru have their border in the Desaguadero River, because it was there that the Viceroyalty of the River Plate ended and the Viceroyalty of Perú began.

The Viceroyalty of the River Plate had an exit to the Pacific Ocean (through the Puno region, where the Chilean-Bolivian border exists today) and to the Atlantic. Its extension was enormous. It had two great rivers, the Paraná and the Uruguay, and huge prairies where one could carry out all sorts of agricultural activity. As far as its economic possibilities, one might add that in the zone that encompassed the north of Buenos Aires, the south of Córdoba, the south of Santa Fe, and continued on through Entre Ríos, forty thousand mules were reared that, yearly, were taken to Salta to be sold to the miners of Perú and Alto Perú. In Misiones, Paraguay, the north of Corrientes, and Tucumán, there were splendid jungles that permitted all kinds of woodworking, during a period when this was a highly valued material for construction. In the region of Alto Perú there were mineral deposits and, in that of Mendoza, silver and other minerals, as well.

The new Viceroyalty had sufficiently ample dimensions to it so as to be able to maintain itself and, in effect, lasted for about thirty years. But it included regions that were too heterogeneous, inevitably creating a political association between territories whose inhabitants, among themselves, had very different ways about them, were of distinct ethnic origins, and had conflicting interests. Alto Perú, for example, which for centuries had had a social, commercial, and political association with Lima, was suddenly incorporated into Buenos Aires. A similar situation was that of the region of Cuyo, which had been a dependency of Santiago, Chile, and suddenly belonged to a capital that was a distance of more than 620 miles from it; or that of Montevideo, founded thirty years earlier, whose aspirations were to be the only port in this part of America.

The conception, at any rate, was grandiose. The Viceroyalty of the River Plate had the breadth of a country of the dimensions of the United States. Its two outlets, to the Atlantic Ocean and to the Pacific, gave it the possibility to connect itself with the whole world. Patagonia and the *Malvinas* (Falkland Islands) were included within the jurisdiction, creating an entire perspective of maritime exploitation, fishing trade, and manufacture of oil from seals and whales, among other very promising productions during this period. Nevertheless, the Viceroyalty probably needed some years more to forge ahead.

The elements that it comprised were so diverse and heterogeneous that, after 1818, the moment in which the central dependency on Spain was interrupted, there appeared, apart from the Argentine Republic, Bolivia, Paraguay, and Uruguay, in an irrepressible explosion of nations.

## Prosperity

From 1776 onward there began a period of prosperity for Buenos Aires and to a certain extent for its outskirts, as well, including the former government of Tucumán, which profited by the Decree of Free Inland Penetration and the Free Trade Regulation (1777 and 1778, respectively). Immediately following the creation of the Viceroyalty of the River Plate, essentially, a type of commerce was possible that was much more open, flexible, and liberal than that which went on before.

The Free Trade Regulation allowed the port to have direct links to the ports of Spain and to almost all of America without the need for prior authorization. Furthermore, they could introduce merchandise not only into the former government of Tucumán, that around that time pertained to the Viceroyalty of the River Plate, but also into Alto Perú. Thus, the dependency that tied this jurisdiction to the Viceroyalty of Lima was definitively curtailed, something that provoked very bitter protests not only by the inhabitants of Lima but also by the viceroys of Lima themselves, who went so far as to ask the Crown of Spain to annul the Viceroyalty of the River Plate.

With the new regulation, the introduction of merchandise through the port of Buenos Aires increased, and in 1780 and 1800, the city experienced a boom of progress (similar, on the other hand, to that which it would experience one hundred years later, between 1880 and 1910, and which today still remains in the collective memory of the Argentines). Many immigrants, Spaniards mostly, but Italians, French and other nationalities as well, settled in Buenos Aires. The port received North American ships, whaleboats that carried wheat, and a rather active exchange began. The houses of commerce, then a trademark of the city of Buenos Aires, were on the rise and gave life to an entire bourgeoisie who decades later would have political importance.

There were many cases of young boys, practically adolescents, sent from Spain by their families, consigned to some house of commerce in Buenos Aires. Martín de Alzaga, for example, who didn't know how to speak Spanish when he arrived in Buenos Aires (he spoke Basque), or the founders of such traditional families as the Lezicas and the Anchorenas, among others. All of them came to Buenos Aires consigned to a house of commerce; they worked as clerks for several years; they got married —generally to the daughter of the owner—; they acquired status, at some point were elected as members of the *cabildo*, and received honorary privileges and wealth; their sons would become officials of the national army; their grandsons, emphyteutas along with Rivadavia and friends of Rosas; their great-grandchildren would do quite well with Roca and, as in Argentina the family fortunes don't last more than two generations, from Roca onward they would all be penniless...

Let us return to the final years of the 18th century. Buenos Aires as we have said, attracted a large quantity of merchants and apprentices in the houses of commerce. Perhaps it would be useful to recall the first chapter of *The Age of Enlightenment,* by Alejo Carpentier, when he describes the arrival of the main characters in Havana, as they enter the paternal grocery store and note the smells: that of dried fish, of salted cod, of individual pieces of merchandise. Certainly not the smell of *mate* tea, because it was unknown in Cuba, but here, yes. We can imagine then what the neighborhood near the docks of Buenos Aires, near the Plaza de Mayo, might have been like. The warehouses were there, and it was there that the trade took place which would then branch off to Córdoba, to Mendoza, to Salta, and so forth, in wagons.

At the same time, or as a result of this, a society arose in Buenos Aires that perhaps had a certain aristocratic impetus, though it was essentially plebeian: a society of merchants and, eventually, of *estancia* owners who gradually became rich or who were rich but continued living on their *estancias* the hard, arduous, and savage life of forty years earlier, when the lines of fortlets had just begun to be built.

In any event, the society of Buenos Aires was formed in such a way as to be lacking in the aristocratic prejudices of Cordobian society, for example, where there were no exceptions made to the rigidity that characterized the Spanish colonial society of the period. Concolorcorvo (pseudonym of a mestizo whose color was that of a crow; the self-referential name means "with the color of a crow"), in charge of travelling the Buenos Aires-Lima route to establish where the different post stations could be erected so as to set up a postal system, records these differences in his book *El lazarillo de ciegos caminantes*.

Concolorcorvo recounts there how the prejudices of caste that he observes in other cities of the interior do not exist in Buenos Aires. He points out that in Córdoba, for example, when a young female mulatto put on clothes that belonged to women of another social stratum, the ladies created a sort of conspiracy; they gave her a beating, made her get undressed, and they made her make a fool of herself so that she would learn well where her place was. In Buenos Aires, by contrast, it was possible for an immigrant such as the father of Manuel Belgrano who had come from Genoa to make a bit of money by dint of hard work and be able to send his son to study in Spain; and that he himself would receive the honors that corresponded to a social position obtained through economic success. This distinguished Buenos Aires from the interior, where lineage and one's antiquity were still taken into account; where *criollos*, descendants of the conquerors, made a living off *estancias* aged in their conception and barely capable or yielding profit. There existed other differences, as well. Buenos Aires found itself favored by the organization of the viceroyalty, since naturally, such an enormous territory would have to be looked after in some cities by respresentatives of the viceroy so that the distant authority could have some effective power. Thus the so-called *gobernaciones-intendencias* [intendancy governments] were established in Córdoba, in Salta, and among others, four more in the territory of Alto Peru and Asunción, Paraguay.

These intendancy governments, looked after by functionaries (some of whom were fondly remembered for the activities they carried out, such as the Marquis of Sobremonte in Córdoba), had in turn subordinate cities that were dependent on them, a fact that produced certain consequences. Cities such as San Juan, Mendoza, La Rioja, or Catamarca, that depended on Córdoba; or Tucumán, that depended on Salta, felt their rights diminished and tried to circumvent the cities where there were intendancy governments. They appealed, then, directly to Buenos Aires, which became a sort of de facto protectress of small cities and the rival of, for example, Córdoba and Salta.

In some way this explains why the events of 1810 were received with a counterrevolution in Córdoba, and why the adhesion to the Junta of May on the part of Salta took a long time. There existed not only political but also commercial contradictions between Buenos Aires and the interior. Buenos Aires had finally achieved its foundational ambition: to be the gateway to land, to become responsible for controlling the port and opening the way to those who entered or left the house.

It exercised this control in such a way that many times, when too many imports entered, the small industries of the interior (the weaving mills of Catamarca or of Córdoba; the textiles, wines and alcohol of Mendoza or Catamarca) suffered from the foreign competition. This was to be seen more acutely years later, but by then one could give warning in Alto Perú, which was an important source of homespun cloth and of thick woolen fabric.

## Criollos

In any case, the most important development of the period as far as the society of the times is concerned is the apparition of a human category that acquired more and more importance and greater ambitions: the *criollos,* sons and daughters of Spaniards, who were not mestizos (for they didn't have mixed blood, at least seemingly) and who were preceded by three, four, five generations who were born on American soil.

During this period, provinces such as La Rioja or Catamarca were virtually governed by the *criollos* through the *cabildos*. Studies have been made of the composition of the *cabildos* of the cities of the interior where one can see that, with the exception of a Spaniard here and there —almost always a merchant integrated into local society—, the *cabildos* were controlled by descendants of the conquerors or of the old families of each province. This leads us to think that the politics carried out in the country after 1810, so subtle, so complicated, had their antecedent in those *cabildos* where the *criollo* and the Spaniard vied for political power; it also leads us to believe that the *criollos* and their descendents were given considerable training in these disputes.

The very existence of the *criollo* already constituted in itself a very special human category: he was active, jealous of the Spaniard, who he would ridicule and whose importance he tried to attenuate, and he had an indubitable love of the land where he had been born. In Santiago del Estero one finds the capitular minutes from one thousand seven hundred and seventy something, where it is reported —naturally, in the language of a notary, as all official records were entered— that a rather inflamed dispute occurred regarding a problem of a ceremonial nature of precedence, of an accusation in the Cabildo, between a Spaniard and a *criollo* by the last name of Bravo. All of this ended in such a large dispute that the very records state that this *criollo*, Bravo (who must have been as brave as his name indicates), said to the Spaniard: "Go, Your Grace, to hell." We can see that the fights and rivalries reached even this extreme.

## The English invasions

The existence of the *criollo* was a new fact that also signified an element of pressure within this Viceroyalty that had been created, within this Buenos Aires that had begun to refine itself. Viewed from a historical perspective, the city amounts to almost nothing, but for that time it was quite important: theater; a press; the Alameda promenade; a viceregal court that, although rather plebianlike, small, and very poor, could be compared to that of Lima or New Spain.

Between this Buenos Aires and the interior there was, we said, a passive contradiction without great manifestations of hostility, except for some picturesque cases. Within a few years it acquired significant superiority in addition to a degree of wealth that defined it and showed it to be to the Spanish American empire an example of a new social class, of a new type of wealth and other factors that, as Ricardo Levene says, were explosive if one looks at them in the light of a possible revolution, such as the one that, in effect, occurred in 1810.

We should highlight another event connected to the creation of the Viceroyalty that added to this explosive situation: the English invasions. They occurred in 1806 and 1807, although it was really only one invasion. The English established themselves in the *Banda Oriental* [Eastern Shore] of the River Plate; from there they invaded Buenos Aires, occupied it, were ousted, held firm in the Banda Oriental, obtained reinforcements, and finally, attacked again only to be defeated in the reconquest. These are the facts that are more or less known and we are not going to go into detail about them. The question is: what were the direct consequences of the English invasions with respect to the increasing power of Buenos Aires, to the contradictions of this city with the interior of the country, and to the creation of a new consciousness that we cannot call national but that begins to be embodied in the new caste of *criollos*?

The consequences are very important for several reasons. In the first place, it emphasized the administrating power of Buenos Aires, that centralized all the jurisdictions of the Viceroyalty. Although the city fell in the hands of the English, it was able to reestablish itself and recover, and its administrative structures did not suffer any damage: the cities of the interior continued to offer their compliance.

In the second place, Buenos Aires acquired a new power,

the military, previously nonexistent. Up until 1806, Spain maintained a regiment in Buenos Aires that was called the Fixed Regiment; it was a corps of troops stationed in Buenos Aires, that came from La Coruña, in Galicia. After one year, the soldiers and the officials disappeared, whether it was because they devoted themselves to commerce, because they married women from the area, or simply because they deserted. So that the Fixed Regiment was practically of no use at all, and during the English invasions, Spain proved that it didn't have the strength to avoid an attack. What on the other hand was demonstrated was that Buenos Aires had the military power to resist, to recover, and to defend itself against invaders, who furthermore, were not rookie solders but the best in the world, those who had confronted Napoleon. The victory was obtained thanks to the enthusiasm of the population and the courage of Liniers, also thanks to the errors committed by the English.

After the first invasion, and anticipating a second, corps were formed that quickly armed themselves, were outfitted into uniforms, and proceeded to elect their head command according to an old statute of the Spanish militias that permitted the soldiers themselves to designate their commanding officers when new military forces were created. Thus Saavedra was elected as chief of the Patricios Regiment after an internal struggle that he had had with Belgrano. The corps were formed on the basis of the regions of their constituents: the *arribeños,* that is to say, those from the provinces up north; the *patricios,* natives of Buenos Aires; the gallegos (Galicians), *vascos y catalanes* (Basques and Catalonians), and *pardos y morenos* (mulattos and Blacks), among others.

It happened, then, that the military corps that were made up of Spaniards were generally formed by individuals of relatively good social position, in large part commerce clerks who, when they had to show up at the barracks, participated in doctrinal or firing exercises, marches and maneuvers, became not only very bored but also had to leave their jobs. As this didn't suit them, they would gradually abandon these obligations. The *criollos,* by contrast, who in general were

poor, assumed their new jobs as soldiers with great enthusiasm as well as the money it provided in the form of a salary.
These corps of *criollos* slowly molded what today we would
call a considerable fire power, which up until that time no
one had, and a military power of their own that, virtually,
was not dependent on the Spanish Crown but rather on their
own resources.

Finally, after the English invasions Buenos Aires acquired
an enormous prestige in all of America because it had not
only repelled an invader, but had also been capable of being
the protagonist of an event without precedent within the
Spanish empire: the overthrow of the representative of the
King. Essentially, Sobremonte appears as chicken-hearted in
the eyes of the *porteños* for having followed instructions that
dated from the time of Cevallos, according to which, if there
was an outside attack, the first duty of the viceroy was to
secure the royal treasury and the money of private enterprise
and to escape, placing these funds under safety. He did this,
and from a historical standpoint, he came out as a coward.

After the reconquest of Buenos Aires, there was an outcry
and demand on behalf of the population for his overthrow
and the *Audiencia,* in the presence of such unrest, ratified
popular decision and suspended Viceroy Sobremonte, despite
his protests, and designated Liniers in his place. Although
Liniers never managed to be appointed by the Crown, he
was for all practical purposes a temporary viceroy appointed
by the people. This is a fundamental precedent: the people
of Buenos Aires overthrew a viceroy, something never seen
before in the Spanish empire.

But furthermore —it is worth reiterating it— the feat of
expelling and making prisoners out of the most valiant soldiers in the world granted Buenos Aires an enormous prestige before all of America and, of course, in the eyes of the
cities of its own viceregal jurisdiction. It gave it a character of
older sister, something that has extreme importance, as will
be seen in the next chapter.

Summarizing the aforesaid: the Viceroyalty, which was
created in 1776, established a huge jurisdiction that, in the

end, benefited basically the city of Buenos Aires. It gave it prosperity and an administrative power that would increase only a few years later when, after the English invasions, the city not only strengthened its administrative power through the loyalty of the small cities of the interior and the rivalry with Córdoba, Salta, and Montevideo, but also acquired a frightening military might and an enormous moral prestige. Such was the panorama of this part of America on the eve of the May Revolution.

## CHAPTER III

# 1810 and its effects

*The subject of this chapter is the May Revolution, a foundational situation full of significance and consequences. We will not be concerned with the facts in themselves as much as in trying to comprehend what their meaning was and what their consequences were; what changes were introduced in the society of the River Plate and what new problems it created, because of its own dynamics; that Revolution which sought to confront old problems, fundamentally that of the dependence with Spain.*

The Revolution of 1810 was an event that, when viewed from its historical perspective, seems inevitable, for things happened in such a way that an occurrence of this kind in this part of America was almost necessary. Let us sum up briefly the national context of the period, since it is important that we see why at a given moment the inhabitants of Buenos Aires resolved to adopt such an extreme and scandalous attitude as was that of deposing the representative of the king and appointing a junta in his place.

## A new dynasty

England and Spain had been at war since 1804, and not for the first time; in reality, we could speak of a long war that had begun toward the end of the 18th century. But this war in particular had special importance, among other reasons because in the battle of Trafalgar (1805) —where the Spanish fleet along with the French, was left practically destroyed—, the struggle that Napoleon and the British empire were engaged in at the time was resolved.

The war between France and England provided a framework for the political developments happening in Spain. There, Charles IV reigned but Manuel Godoy, prince of La Paz, prime minister of Charles IV, and favorite of María Luisa, governed. Despite the fact that, according to rumor, he was not all that bright, within a few years Godoy succeeded in a sensationally rapid career and acquired wealth, power, and influence. His politics consisted of total backing for France, which was logical: if Spain was at war with England, the most sensible thing to do was to stand by and uphold Napoleon, with whom it had a common enemy.

Nevertheless, when the favorite of the queen allowed Napoleonic troops to go through Spanish territory in order to attack Portugal, many Spaniards thought Godoy to be exaggerating in his support of the French. Napoleon, who had a global conception of war, believed in the efficacy of the continental blockade, a sort of alliance of all the countries of the European continent against England in order to keep it from exporting its increasing textile production, asfixiating the country and causing it such an economic chaos that it would facilitate its surrender. One of the basic points of the continental blockade, whose goal was to align the whole continent against the islands, depended precisely on not allowing Portugal to continue being the traditional ally of Great Britain.

So that with Spanish support, the French troops reached Portugal almost without encountering resistance; what's more, as they approached Lisbon, the Portuguese court set sail and moved itself to Rio de Janeiro. The fact that the court of the king of Portugal, including his relatives as well as the bureaucracy, should install itself in Rio de Janeiro, was very important and had repercussions in the River Plate.

Meanwhile, pro-French politics continued in Spain until finally, because of a popular protest demonstration in Aranjuez —the summer resort of the kings of Spain— pronounced in a rather disorderly fashion against Manuel Godoy, the prime minister was forced to resign. Charles IV was forced to abdicate and his son Ferdinand VII ascended the throne in March of 1808 to Napoleon's disgust, who no longer had in Spain instruments as malleable as Godoy and Charles IV.

By making use of his power, Napoleon convoked the royal Spanish family to Bayonne in May, of 1808. There, during a session that was nothing but a farse, Ferdinand VII was made to return the crown to his father, Charles IV, and Charles IV, in turn, to relinquish it to Napoleon. As for Napoleon, he handed it over to his brother Joseph Bonaparte, whom he appointed king of Spain. This is to say, that in a span of a few days, Spain saw the Bourbon dynasty expire and another rise to power, that of the Bonapartes, new, plebeian, and usurping. Ferdinand VII was confined to Valençay, in Talleyrand's castle, and Charles IV and his wife retired to Italy along with Godoy.

In Spain, Joseph Bonaparte, in the name of his brother and supported by the force of the battalions and the French regiments, began to govern. This provoked a tremendous reaction on the part of the Spanish people, who after 1808 rose up spontaneously in rebellion throughout the entire peninsula, and popular and regional juntas were formed and at some point sent delegates to a central junta.

International alliances changed. Spain, which previously was at war with England, aligned itself with the latter in order to fight against Napoleon, the common enemy. The Bonapartist forces had some setbacks in Spain, but after 1809, when following the battle of Wagram Napoleon put an end to the military problems that he had had with Austria, he sent large reinforcements to the Iberian Peninsula and succeeded in occupying most of it. Only Andalusia resisted (where the Junta of Seville was, which practically summed up the powers of the remaining juntas).

Meantime, in the River Plate there was great restiveness. Loyalty to the Bourbon dynasty caused the French dynasty to be greatly opposed but, by unfortunate coincidence, at that moment the Viceroy of the River Plate was a Frenchman, Santiago de Liniers, appointed by the people of Buenos Aires as a replacement for the Marquis de Sobremonte. Although Liniers was never appointed titular viceroy, though he was in any case accepted by the Junta of Seville as provisional until things became settled, the fact that he was French sparked suspicions. It also turned out that Liniers was not a very political man and he made some errors —more of form than of content—, due to which suspicions about him increased.

On the other hand, in the Portuguese court of Rio de Janeiro was the Spanish Infanta Carlota, sister of Ferdinand VII and married to the heir to the throne of Portugal. Because she was the most direct heir to Ferdinand VII, in that captive moment, Carlota was considered the virtual titulary of a sort of protectorate on the River Plate. All factors, no doubt, helped to complicate the situation.

About mid 1809, the new viceroy arrived, sent by the Junta of Seville. He was a Spanish marine, Baltasar Hidalgo de Cisneros. Despite the fact that some friends of Liniers urged him not to cede power, Liniers, loyal to the Crown, complied and retired to Córdoba. Some months later, in May of 1810, the news arrived that the Bonapartists had occupied Andalusia, where the last popular junta existing in Spain against the French functioned. The news caused great commotion and exploded in the events of May, the meeting convoked by the Cabildo, with the knowledge of the viceroy, so that the residents of the city could openly discuss what should be done in this situation.

## The revolution

Let us situate ourselves in the case at hand and in the times. Buenos Aires was a viceroyalty that depended on Spain. The legitimate king —who, obviating the farse of Bayonne, was Ferdinand VII— was being held prisoner. The populace opposed the usurping king, Joseph Bonaparte. The popular juntas that fought militarily against the French had been demolished. What to do, then? Surrender to the Bonaparte dynasty? Follow the game of the usurper who controlled almost all of Europe? Wait to see what happened in the battle fields of the Old Country?

In May of 1810, various sectors converged with different ideas regarding the destiny of these lands. It is possible that some of those who participated in the May Sessions —for example, Moreno and Castelli— might have wanted to initiate a day's run toward independence. It is possible, as well, that others, Spaniards or those close to the Spaniardist party, might have thought it most advisable to form a junta and wait.

Some remembered what had happened a century earlier, during the Spanish war of succession, between the Hapsburgs and the Bourbons, that lasted almost fifteen years. Throughout the course of this interval, the colonies had remained hopeful with respect to what might be decided in Spain, willing to recognize the legitimate king. Once Philip V, the first Bourbon, installed himself in the Spanish throne, the colonial functionaries of the Crown recognized his legitimacy and the issue proceeded ahead without any major problems.

It is possible, then, that in 1810 many might have thought that something similar to this would happen.

The fact of the matter is that a junta was formed as a replacement for the viceroy, and this provoked important consequences. Some factors had been put into motion in the past and the situation of 1810 gave them force. For example, the capacity of assembly attained by Buenos Aires when, in 1680, it took Colonia del Sacramento with the cooperation of the infantry regiments of Tucumán, Paraguay, and the Guaraní Indians. Also, the prestige that the city won more than one hundred years later, when in 1806 and 1807 it repelled, all by itself, the most valiant soldiers of the world.

So the prestige consolidated by Buenos Aires acquired a new institutional and juridical projection in the May Sessions of 1810. It happened that one of the adherents in favor of not making innovations and of maintaining the viceroy suggested in the open cabildo of the twenty-second of May that the neighbors of Buenos Aires didn't have the right to take an initiative as important as that of substituting a viceroy for a junta. As important as the city may be, it was just another city of the viceroyalty; the logical thing to do was to consult the opinions of the other jurisdictions. Let us not forget that there were intendency governments and subordinate cities that had the right to establish their positions at that time.

It was then that Juan José Paso, a skillfull and very distinguished politician, called forth the "older sister" argument. He said that Buenos Aires was acting in this emergency as an older sister taking custody of the property and interests of its siblings and that, naturally, it promised to assemble the delegates of the other cities so that they could homologate the decision to substitute the viceroy.

On the twenty-second of May of 1810, the almost rhetorical figure of the sister city was transformed into a concrete juridical projection. Buenos Aires obtained the right to introduce this substantial change in the structure of the viceregal power, under the condition that it later convoke the other jurisdictions and ask their opinion. It acted according to what in Law is called a *gestión de negocios* [commercial compact], something that you do for another person without his knowing it, and that ultimately averts greater problems for him. At the opportune moment, the beneficiary may find out, but in principle behaves like a good father of a family or an older brother.

As important, if not more important than this concept of the older sister, is another concept that is set forth during the session of the twenty-second of May: that of popular sovereignty. One of the juridical arguments that is wielded, in effect, is a theory according to which, power resides in the Crown because it was granted by God in some legitimate way. Nevertheless, the reasoning continues, it turns out that the Crown was snatched from its legitimate titulary. Given that even the juntas have been defeated militarily, who has the power? The people, who can temporarily delegate it to the person or persons that may desire it until the situation clears up.

The previous concept is fundamental. Today it appears to be common ground in Political Law, but in those days it was revolutionary. That the governed could elect their own rulers, even if it was temporary, was an explosive doctrine. Later we will come back to this idea.

Apart from the juridical innovations, the May Sessions demonstrate that the *criollos* had military power. It will be useful to remember that after the first English invasion and the reconquest of Buenos Aires, a series of organized military corps were armed urgently in accordance with the regions where their members were from: Galicians, Catalonians, Northerners, patricians (from Buenos Aires), mulattos and Blacks, et cetera. We said that the Spaniards, who in general were employees of commerce, and of good social standing, evaded military exercises because they represented a loss of time and money, while the *criollos,* the mulattos, the Blacks, for whom the rations and the small stipend were important, fulfilled the duties punctually, all of which caused them to acquire very respectable fire power. This was demonstrated when on the first of May, 1809, Martín de Alzaga led a sort of coup that tried to be military against Liniers, and Saavedra, at the head of the patricians, imposed order immediately and was left commander of the Plaza de Mayo.

## The revolution in the interior

In 1810 the military power of Buenos Aires was made evident not only because of the pressure of the *criollo* regiments, but also because a dispatching of expeditions to diverse points of the viceroyalty was ordered immediately. What had occurred in Buenos Aires, in effect, was too scandalous to be accepted peacefully. The overthrow of a delegate of the king or of the Junta that claimed to represent him, and its substitution by a [popular] junta, was really something difficult to swallow in the more loyalist regions of the viceroyalty.

In Córdoba, a counterrevolution broke out that was presided over by Liniers; it concluded with his execution and that of his counterparts. In Mendoza there was quite a bit of reticence to accept the junta of Buenos Aires. In Salta many debates took place. And in three points, above all, the resistance turned active: in Alto Peru, Paraguay, and Montevideo. The eastern port, as we know, had an old rivalry with Buenos Aires. This antimony grew while Liniers was viceroy because he was not acknowledged as such in Montevideo, precisely because he was French; a junta was formed, then, that was dissolved upon Cisneros's arrival, but the seeds of the anti-Buenos Aires attitude remained. And when in Buenos Aires the Junta members were designated, military resistance that was to last four years broke out in Montevideo.

The expeditions, which were not simultaneous, set out from Buenos Aires. The one to Paraguay had the purpose of trying to convince or vanquish the Paraguayans. One lived a different sort of life there, more Mediterranean, and their interests conflicted with those of Buenos Aires, gateway before which they had to render homage in order to carry out their imports and exports. Belgrano, chief of the patriotic expedition, encountered resistance therefore. A battle was fought, and lost; there were negotiations. Finally, Paraguay maintained a neutral attitude toward the war of independence, without hostilities toward the authorities of Buenos Aires.

The expedition that was sent to Alto Perú, by contrast, managed a triumph at first, Suipacha, but after a few months suffered the disaster of Huaqui, on the shores of the Desaguadero River, the border between the Viceroyalty of the River Plate and that of Perú.

It remained clear that the troops had been sent to establish recognition of the authorities of Buenos Aires, but not to extend their power to another viceroyalty. Buenos Aires considered itself an heir of Spanish power up to its borders only.

The expeditions of Alto Perú were taken up again afterward by Manuel Belgrano, with the triumphs of Tucumán and Salta, and the defeats of Vilcapugio and Ayohuma. Command of the army was then assumed by General Rondeau, who continued on up through the interior of Alto Perú and suffered the defeat of Sipe Sipe, in 1815. From 1815 onward, there were no longer expeditions to the northern frontier set in motion from Buenos Aires, but there was on the other hand a permanent state of guerrilla warefare, urged on, above all, by the caudillo Martín Miguel de Güemes, who more or less froze the situation with a war of guerrillas that prevented the *realistas* from advancing toward the south.

The other military problem was Montevideo, who assigned a flotilla to harass Buenos Aires. The *orientales* [those of the eastern shore] even bombarded the city and carried out several raids against the populations of the Paraná River. The Spanish resistance in Montevideo endured various circumstances. There was a spot where the *realistas* were fenced in the city; Artigas, transformed by popular election into the caudillo of the Banda Oriental, participated in the patriotic fight, backing the junta of Buenos Aires, but then, due to some difficulties he had with the latter, he retired; in 1814, nevertheless, the patriotic troops succeeded in taking Montevideo and this triumph permitted José de San Martín to vary the military strategy of the Revolution and to conceive and carry out the campaigns of Chile and of Perú.

Just as important as this military aspect are the events that broke out in Buenos Aires and in the interior from the time that the viceroy is substituted by a government that begins to call itself *patrio* [native]. There are, of course, several wings: the more radicalized, such as those of Moreno and Castelli; the more conservative, such as that which Saavedra led; and the diverse factions that follow one another in the titularity of power during the ten years that transpire between 1810 and 1820, when the central government falls.

Up until this moment, there existed in Buenos Aires a government that —call it the First Junta, Great Junta, Triumvirate, Second Triumvirate, Directorate; whatever their juridical form and regulations might have been— resided in the city; considered itself the inheritor of Spanish power; and collected funds, fundamentally through customs, which were allotted in large part to the national cause for independence: arming and dressing the native army, sending diplomats abroad, creating propaganda for the Revolutionary cause, and so forth. Its characteristics were those of a central government, and though, embodied in the Directorate, it fell in 1820, throughout the course of its ten years of existence, very important changes were generated within that society that already began to call itself Argentina.

## The changes

In the first place, a change was produced in the collective belief system. We said that the common good was one of the fundamental concepts of Hispanic juridical norms in America. "Common good" meant that measures taken by the State (that is, the Crown, the viceroy, the governor) had to be directed toward the good of all, not toward that of a particular sector. We also said that this conception permitted that an ordinance or royal letters patent, though it came countersigned by the king in Madrid, be respected but not carried out if the viceroy believed it would cause more harm than good here: it simply would not be put into effect.

The concept of the common good was left aside from 1810 onward and substituted by that of popular sovereignty, a banner that theoreticians of the Revolution, such as Moreno, Castelli, and Monteagudo, rallied behind. The revolutionary concept took a century to be implemented through elections, but it was already a governing principle in this new society.

Popular sovereignty, which borrowed from the idea that the people can designate their representatives when the legitimate authority is absent, was replaced by the Rousseauian thesis, according to which the majority rules —at least in theory— the various elections, appointments, and assemblies that occur. Naturally it was a gradual change that began to take hold through government measures and the thinking of some leaders, yet a change that was aimed at the formation of a society that was both republican and democratic.

In the second place, and no longer in the theoretical realm but in that of concrete facts, the disintegration of the viceroyalty had an impact on its inhabitants. Let us not forget that the viceroyalty had been the outline of a great country, a conception whose grandeur resided in the vast jurisdiction that was attributed to it, from which four nations arose afterward. Its great defect, nevertheless, was related to the magnitude of its territory: the viceroyalty was made up of very heterogeneous elements, whose climates, manufactured goods, peoples, mentalities, and interests were very different among themselves and, in some cases, contradictory. As the viceroyalty lasted only thirty years, there wasn't time for its elements to forge, thereby transforming it into a nation with self-awareness.

We know that after 1810 the points of resistance to the Revolution were in Alto Perú, Paraguay, and Montevideo. It was specifically these regions that tended to separate themselves from the viceroyalty. The process lasted some twenty

years but was irreversible. Alto Perú, situated within the jurisdiction of Buenos Aires in 1776, continued to preserve its link
with Perú and maintained its distance from the capital as
always. The resistance to the patriotic troops was, then,
authentic, even popular; it was the last place in South America where Spanish resistance continued, until 1824, when the
battle of Ayacucho put an end to it. On the other hand, this
battle wasn't waged by troops from Buenos Aires, but rather
by those of Simón Bolívar, sent from the north, a fact that led
one to presume that he would protect the new path to independence of these regions. Hence, Bolivia was born.

Paraguay took a few more years to become independent;
it was only in 1846 that it declared its independence. As for
the Banda Oriental, who since 1815 had endured the meticu-
lous and permanent advance of the Portuguese, it was the
scene of a war between the Argentine Republic and the
Empire of Brazil that concluded in 1827 with the proclama-
tion of the independence of the Banda Oriental as the
*República Oriental del Uruguay* (present-day Uruguay).

All of these factors of disintegration began to operate as
soon as the Spanish authority ended, which in a peaceful
way regulated life in such diverse regions; the uncontrollable
revolutionary process began separating them.

## The military

Suddenly, after 1810 there were military needs. That city
of anchoring grounds and merchants that had formed battalions and regiments following the English invasions found that
it had to make a great military effort in order to be able to
propel the revolutionary idea. It was Buenos Aires, essentially, who carried forth the Revolution. We said before that in
the interior there was reluctance, resistance, delays. Little by
little, not the capitals such as Salta or Córdoba, but the intendancy governments and the subordinate cities began to
acknowledge or recognize the Junta.

In any event, because of the rigid and traditionalist character of the societies of the interior, the new conceptions that

came from Buenos Aires took a while to be accepted; as a result, the major weight of the Revolution was carried by Buenos Aires. Although in Córdoba and in Tucumán mothers handed over their sons so they could form part of the native armies, the revolutionary dynamism was provided by Buenos Aires.

Despite its new needs, Buenos Aires began to assign to everything military —to the uniform, to the language, to style— an importance, which it previously did not have. These changes occurred mostly after 1812, with the arrival of José de San Martín and of Carlos de Alvear, the first military professionals at the service of the Revolution. Officers previously were improvised; Belgrano, for example, was a lawyer and was appointed general because there was no one else. The only brigadier —and not a very efficient one— was Miguel de Azcuénaga.

San Martín and Alvear urged the boys of high society to join the army as officials and, in effect, it became fashionable to be a soldier. The sons of families such as Escalada, Balcarce, and others of the sort, began forming themselves as officials, and this activity, up to now performed by amateurs, became a professional and serious occupation in view of the fact that the war, also, was going to be serious and, in addition, long.

The militarization of society altered the foundation of the traditional order. José María Paz, who served in practically all the native armies that existed from 1813 onward, tells in his memoirs how he doesn't remember that horses were ever bought: whenever they were needed, they were requisitioned. At best, the owner was given an I.O.U.; after, he would demand payment from whomever he could. The difference was remarkable: with the previous order, for better or for worse, the Spanish authority maintained respect for property through its various structures or solicitations.

The new state of things favored the appearance of military caudillos. When society allocated a portion of its wealth to those who had arms because it was they who would defend the Revolution, this prefigured the idea of the triumphant military caudillo who, at some point, would knock on the table with his saber and say: "I command here!"

Another novel idea, very interesting, as well, is the anti-Spanish sentiment. From 1810 onward, when the rupture with ties to Spain became more notorious because the Revolution continued to progress in spite of the fact that Ferdinand VII had returned to the throne; when the envoys of the Spanish government couldn't come to an agreement with the government of Buenos Aires; in short, when independence showed itself to be something inevitable, there reigned an enmity toward all things Spanish. The Spaniard was an adversary and one had to be hostile toward him. This sentiment appeared in a wide range of contexts; for example, in literature. Though the romantic movement would still take some years to arrive, there already existed a rejection of Hispanic arts and classical forms.

There were cases where the rejection was quite concrete. For example, the First Junta was already demanding the expulsion of all unmarried Spanish men in Buenos Aires; naturally, this caused a mess of broken engagements and destroyed families, to such an extent that there was great pressure on the Junta to revoke the measure. Then, as usually occurs in our country, the decree was completed by another that created an exception for those unmarried men who demonstrated solidarity with the Revolution, who had written guarantees, and so on. Finally, the measure was left without validity.

Now, the question is, how is it possible that there was so much antagonism against the Spanish, if ninety-five percent were Spaniards or children of Spaniards? I believe that this new society needed to find an identity for itself in some way, and to achieve this, it had to rebel against its father and convince itself that he had been tyrannical, despotic, evil, et cetera. It is a rather comprehensible psychological mechanism.

The feeling of rebellion of *criollo* sons and daughters against their Spanish parents and grandparents was perceptible. An English traveler, Brackenridge, wrote in 1819 that

General Belgrano at the command of the Northern Army swears loyalty to the national flag.

Crossing of Los Andes by General José de San Martín and his army on their campaign to Chile.

The National Anthem played for the first time at Mariquita Sánchez de Thompson's house.

The formal declaration of independence in San Miguel de Tucumán, 9 of July 1816.

along the fashionable promenade of Buenos Aires, the Alameda, phantasmagoric groups of large men, poorly dressed, could be seen talking sadly among themselves; these were the Spaniards who in earlier times had been rich and respected merchants in Buenos Aires and who now found themselves marginalized because of the revolutionary process and impoverished because the link that joined the merchants of Buenos Aires to those of Cádiz had been interrupted.

The anti-Spanish sentiment manifested itself in many ways. In some cases, as concrete measures against those who could be enemies. The conspiracy of Martín de Alzaga (1812), for example, marked a high point in the anti-Spanish mood. Alzaga was shot and his property expropriated: he had led what could have been a really dangerous revolutionary movement, in large part financed or directed by elderly and rich Spaniards who had seen their power weaken.

The ill-treatment of the Spaniards was extended to prisoners of the same origin. In the battle of Tucumán —not in that of Salta, because Belgrano made a pact with the Spanish general and all were set free— many Spanish prisoners were confined to prisons in different cities of the viceroyalty. The majority remained in prison. This author, in fact, descends from, among others, a Spanish prisoner of Tucumán, Tomás Valdés, who settled in La Rioja, married, and many years later died. He was always very respected.

General San Martín sent many Spanish prisoners to Mendoza to work under the orders of the *criollo* proprietors in replacement for the slave labor force, which had been recruited by the native armies. In other cases the treatment with respect to the Spaniards was harsher; during several years there existed a concentration camp near Dolores called Las Bruscas, where Spanish prisoners had a very rough time. There are many prisoner notebooks, wherein they complain of the conditions in which they lived, the climate, the food. Some tried to flee.

Don Faustino Ansái, for example, a very respectable man from Mendoza, had a difficult life, about which he has left a most interesting account. He was one of those who in 1810 headed the position against recognition of the Junta of Buenos Aires. They defeated him in the *cabildo,* arrested him, and sent him to prison at Las Bruscas, which had only recently come into being. Ansái escaped and took refuge in Montevideo; when the patriots took Montevideo, they took him prisoner and sent him back to Las Bruscas. Only in 1820 or 1821 did he manage to be set free.

The anti-Spanish sentiment changed the lifestyle of Buenos Aires. Breeches —truly the mark of a Spaniard from a well-to-do family— began to fall out of use and were replaced by trousers that North American sailors brought with them. There are portraits of Mariano Moreno that show him in knee-breeches and white socks, and in his famous honors decree he himself talks about the use of tails in order to be admitted into any offical function. But all of this was abandoned shortly, thus too, the salaam and the ceremonious greetings of Spanish protocol; instead, the Anglosaxon handshake was simply adopted. In the same way, chocolate was replaced by tea.

These cultural changes, what's more, were due to the fact that, accompanying the free trade that the new Junta established, little by little an English colony settled; to a lesser extent, the French also arrived. The patriot authorities, in general, were very liberal as far as commerce went. There was no type of restrictions: anyone could bring in the goods he wished if he paid the resulting custom fees; and he could also take them out —buying them, of course. This policy did not arise from liberal thinking but a necessity of war. To the extent that there was a good deal of trade and many customs fees were paid, the generous amount collected permitted the government of Buenos Aires to arm, feed, and clothe the native armies.

English merchants, as a consequence, began to settle in Buenos Aires. Because of the Napoleonic wars and the continental blockade, England had an overstock of goods that it found difficult to place. Many English merchants, looking for new markets, traveled to Buenos Aires because Viceroy Cisneros, even before 1810, had begun to allow a certain commercial openness. This meant that not only might English merchants settle in the city, but also that many of them would travel throughout the country in search of markets and new and convenient forms of commerce. At the same time, they imported customs, manners, and words; and, while the interior of the country continued to maintain a more closed position on the matter, Buenos Aires was a window to the outside world.

Commercial liberalization and the war brought about a series of effects. As most of Alto Perú was in the hands of the Spanish, the traditional mule trade, typical of the colonial era, came to a halt, as did the influx of coins that came from there. Previously, the miners from Alto Perú traveled to Salta, where they purchased the mules with cash, and the muleteers and local producers would pocket a fair amount of silver coins. But the war ended this exchange, and currency began to be scarce.

The English merchants, furthermore, demanded that their goods be paid for with money, basically with silver, and thus they helped to reduce available currency. They brought mostly textiles (of good quality, attractive, and inexpensive, better than those that could be produced here), as well as household goods, knives, pots, and other objects of immediate use. The furniture mostly came from the North Americans. These sales were paid for with metal coins, so that within a few years, the population of the former Viceroyalty began to be left without money, a circumstance that occasioned a series of economic and monetary complications.

## Toward a certain democracy

Among the novelties associated with the May Revolution is the notion of equality; that is, that there should not be privileges, that each citizen is equal to the other, that all have the same right, et cetera. In those days it was still a very abstract idea, but it later permeated very deep into Argentine society and had a very concrete projection some decades after. The anti-Spanish sentiment, the liberalization of commerce, the concepts of popular sovereignty and equality are all changes that made the way for a transformation, so direct, so abrupt as the May Revolution itself.

Along with the aforementioned, there are in addition two other rather important factors. After the Revolution there began to be conceived something we could call "public opinion," generalized through cliques, fractions and *tertulias,* and expressed in the newspapers by means of editorials, critiques, or articles with a conceptual exposition, such as those of Mariano Moreno. For the first time —rather than their tiresome publication of commercial-type news, news about some scientific development, or something that was happening in Europe, as would be published during the viceroyalty—, the newspapers brought under discussion revolutionary ideas, stimulating ideas, in many cases shocking for a public opinion that had only recently begun to appear in this kind of debate.

Elections were another novelty. Each time that some representative body was convoked from Buenos Aires —such as the Assembly of the year 1813, or the Congress of 1816 in Tucumán, plus others that never managed to assemble—, people got together in all the cities of the former viceroyalty and appointed someone who would represent them in Buenos Aires in the associated bodies that would be formed. Naturally, the people who would gather were of the same sort as those who, during the colonial era, would participate in the open *cabildos.* "The principal and most sound part" they were called; that is, the residents who had a house set up, a family, and respectable work. The general public did not vote.

Just as the slaves and the mestizos could not vote, so too, the Whites who didn't carry out an honorable profession — be they Spaniards or *criollos*— were not able to vote. The butchers, for example, did not vote; neither did the shoemakers. Suffrage was reserved for an elite that previously had not exercised the right of assembly, the right to form part of the cabildo, to opt for one or for the other, to draw up a document, sign it, and, eventually, to give instructions —such as those of the Banda Oriental to the representatives of the Assembly of 1813, where among other things they requested that Buenos Aires not be the capital of the new government.

There was, then, a movement of public opinion and a use of the intellect, of the imagination, and of the views that began to appear by way of the newspapers; by way of these restricted elections; through the transformations that the diverse national governments would undergo, from the Junta to the Directorate; through military events, some victorious, others unfortunate; through, finally, the openness toward a trade that linked this part of America with the rest of the world. Between 1810 and 1820, the May Revolution marked a profound transition. Things occurred that had never occurred before; there was a real transformation of society, whose manifestations acquired a freer and self-assured, even youthful tone. In this context some revolutionary leaders began to distinguish themselves who in the former colonial period would not have had the slightest possibility of appearing on the political scene.

## CHAPTER IV

# The search for a political formula

*All nations that plan a transition to an era as new as that which was begun in 1810 pose a series of questions, some overtly, others implicitly. The first question to resolve was what kind of relationship would we have with the former metropolis. There were those who thought it wasn't worth entering into an armed struggle for independence, rather, it was more advisable to establish a sort of association with Spain; but the very dynamics of the war made this an impossibility. On the other hand, after 1815, when Ferdinand VII returned, an absolutist policy was implemented in Spain that rejected the liberal ideas in vogue in Buenos Aires at that time.*

The second question, evidently more important, was what political framework would be given to this new entity, the United Provinces of the River Plate *(Provincias Unidas del Río de la Plata).* One possible model was the United States. Thirty years earlier the English colonies of North America had declared their independence, sanctioned a constitution, and set in motion a very novel political plan, the democratic republic, in an era —the end of the 18th century— when the progressive option seemed to be a constitutional monarchy. The English colonies, liberated from their former metropolis, decided to choose the republican system which, though it had been in use two thousand years earlier in Greece and in Rome, was not contemporaneous.

The republican sentiment, also, was very much present in what had been the former Viceroyalty of the River Plate. The natural ability of its inhabitants, a freer life, the type of skilled farm work, the enormous distances, all contributed to make the future political model a republican design and federal,· moreover. Nevertheless, in these lands there was also a centralist tradition that was strengthened during the viceroyalty with the predominance of Buenos Aires as capital. Let us remember that the intendancy governments —Córdoba and Salta in present-day Argentine territory, for example, and others in Alto Perú and Paraguay— were subordinate to Buenos Aires, and that there were also subalternate cities that maintained an almost permanent rivalry with the principal ones.

## Juridical developments

We could say that these questions began to be posed from 1810 onward. What political system do we apply? Republic, monarchy, federal republic, centralist republic...? Aside from the antecedents of the *cabildos,* of the intendancy governments, and of the viceregal centralism, one must keep in mind that during the May Sessions two juridical concepts that would have enormous political consequence in the years to come were utilized. In the first place, the doctrine of retroversion; in the second, that of subrogation.

The Junta that substituted the viceroy, in effect, *subrogated* the powers of the latter; that is, it substituted him in the prime of his powers, his duties, his legal authority. For this reason, the Junta of May and subsequent governments (the Great Junta, the First Triumvirate, the Second Triumvirate, the Directorate) thought they possessed the totality of powers that had belonged to the viceroy and, consequently, aspired to govern these lands. This is to say that, although there was an enormous difference of political signature between the viceregal governments and the native ones, not so with respect to the aggregate powers that they each attributed to themselves.

The concept of subrogation permitted Buenos Aires to justify the central power that it exercised over the rest of the territory of the Viceroyalty, after 1810. This, for example, explains why the first expedition to Alto Perú, sent in June of 1810, had instructions to stop at the Desaguadero River, which separated the jurisdiction of the Viceroyalty of the River Plate from that of the Viceroyalty of Perú. If the Junta of May subrogated the powers of the viceroy, it could not exceed the jurisdictional legal authority that this latter had had at the time.

The other doctrine, that of retroversion, held that should the legitimate authority not function for whatever reason, the people had the right to provide themselves with their own authorities. In 1810, for instance, the legitimate king, Ferdinand VII, was being held captive; it was thought, moreover, that the Central Junta of Seville had been captured by the French.

This theory was raised on many other occasions by legal experts from Buenos Aires and from the interior of the country, where it quickly became popular. So much so, that the inhabitants of Jujuy, for example, had recourse to it in order to refuse Salta the power to send them legal authorities: the inhabitants of Jujuy wanted to govern themselves. Thus the federal sentiment, which exploded after 1820, also began to take hold.

The use that the concepts of subrogation and retroversion

had shows that juridical theories are not abstractions, rather than they tend to have, when they take root with force, great juridical and political repercussions; it shows that theories are not exclusively elements that are employed ideally, but that they have a very concrete practical application.

## Buenos Aires and the interior

The relationship between Buenos Aires and the interior of the country began to turn tense following the government of the First Junta. The capital, after the First Junta subrogated the rights and powers of the viceroy, tried not only to continue to manage the government, but also to appoint intendancy governments, to send armies so that its authority would be recognized, to establish diplomatic relations with other countries, and, of course, to collect fiscal fees, which fundamentally were customs duties. By means of the treasury collection, we said, Buenos Aires defrayed the costs of the need for native armies, public administration, propaganda for the Revolution, sending of diplomatic representatives, et cetera.

Meanwhile, in the interior, the feeling grew rapidly that the May Revolution had merely substituted the despots of Madrid, a situation which brought on a series of consequences. The strongest enmity —though far away— arose from Lima, which was in the hands of the *realistas*. Within the composite totality of the former Viceroyalty, it was in the Banda Oriental where the rivalry with Buenos Aires had always been the most acute. Let us recall that Montevideo, which had a better port than Buenos Aires, aspired since the colonial era to be the port of entry and issue for this whole part of America.

It was, then, in Montevideo (which at that time was in the hands of the *realistas* anyway) and in the campaign that surrounded Montevideo, through Artigas —a caudillo with obvious popular charisma, very headstrong, with some culture, and some knowledge of what North American federalism was— that one began to question seriously the centralist regime of Buenos Aires. The confrontation became evident during the Assembly of the year 1813 and during the Congress of Tucumán, to which Artigas did not send delegates.

The thinking and political-military activity of Artigas did not only influence the Banda Oriental, but also the provinces of the littoral (Entre Ríos, Corrientes, Santa Fe) and, at some point, in Córdoba, too. His was an important opposition viewed from all perspectives. Quantitatively, because he had sufficient power to remove from the effective jurisdiction of Buenos Aires a part of the former viceroyalty as important as were the aforementioned provinces; and qualitatively, because his dissidence implied resolved political thinking, inspired by North American antecedents.

One has to consider, of course, whether the politics of Artigas were appropriate at the time, since in these lands elements were missing that in the United States, on the other hand, existed. In the former North American colonies, for example, there was —aside from the governor, generally sent by the English Crown— local legislative sessions, made up of important residents, that colegislated with the governor; there existed, therefore, a practice of pseudodemocratic government. And what is even more important, the populational structure consisted of small cities and towns where a population, generally literate, made up a sort of public opinion by reading local newspapers. That's the way things stood before and after the North American revolution: conditions that created the foundations for that democracy that would be born after the presidency of Washington.

Here, by contrast, cities were scarce and they were situated hundreds of miles from one another; a generalized public opinion did not exist; nor did a largely literate population. Hence the huge difficulties in setting up a power structure that would respond to a sort of rough draft of democracy, such as the one that existed in the United States at that time. There didn't even exist elements that might make the development of political parties possible, such as those that were formed in the United States and slowly began to give rise to North American democracy as we know it today.

Artigas, at any rate, expressed an important localist sentiment that, besides reacting against the, at times, abusive centralism of Buenos Aires, made evident the existence of regional peculiarities. We mustn't forget that the former viceroyalty was composed of totally different territories: Neither did Alto Perú have anything in common with Paraguay nor did the provinces of the present-day Argentine Northwest have anything in common with Buenos Aires. The ethnic composition, the landscape, the production, the idiosyncrasy, all were different in each case, and there were jealousies, loves, and a respectable localist sense of roots that ultimately was embodied in the figure of the caudillos.

Following the time of the May Revolution, this federalist sentiment that began to sow the seeds of opinion arose in what today are the Argentine provinces, and it was incarnated, above all, in the figure of Artigas. But it had in addition characteristics very typical of these lands. Whereas in the former British colonies of North America there was respect for the law inherited after a century of British tradition, the Argentine colonial past, from the mid 16th century on (as soon as these lands were settled) was marked by countless instances of unrest, insurrections, rebellions, and struggles against the powers considered authoritarian and tyrannical. The second governor of Tucumán, Jerónimo Luis de Cabrera, was beheaded by his successor, Gonzalo de Abreu, who in turn was also beheaded by his successor, Hernando de Lerma, and so forth and so on. This tradition did not exist in the United States, all of which gave the political struggles there a certain sweetness that here just didn't exist.

In 1815, when in the interior a sort of general rebellion against the appointment of Alvear as Supreme Director broke out, the first national revolution against a central power took place. Two or three months later, Alvear was deposed. In reality, already in 1812, with the implicit support of San Martín and of Alvear, the First Triumvirate had been removed and the Second Triumvirate formed. Before this, on the fifth of April of 1811, the Great Junta that Saavedra presided over had been strengthened by a popular movement. So that the custom of resolving disputes concerning the central power existed not only by means of reasoning and polemics, but also by means of armed recourse.

## Independence

In 1815, a violent change of government occurred. The circumstances created a need to infuse a new cause for fervor into the Revolution, which was going through a critical period both militarily and politically at the time. Politically, because Ferdinand VII returned to the throne that year. Militarily, because after the defeat at Sipe Sipe the troops of the auxiliary army of Alto Perú had had to retreat and were almost at the limit of Salta; Paraguay remained neutral, and although Montevideo had been taken —that was the great triumph of 1814—, practically all the revolutionary movements akin to that of Buenos Aires in the rest of America had been suppressed.

Thus arose the urgent need to declare independence, a matter which up until that moment had not been expressly mentioned, despite the fact that the former viceroyalty already began to take on the appearance of a country. After the Assembly of the year 1813, it had a flag, an anthem, currency of its own; it legislated with the laws of the times, such as those that abolished of slavery for those who were born as of that date onward, the slave trade, titles of nobility and primogeniture, and the law that established freedom of the press. However, it was necessary to homologate these developments with a formal declaration of independence, which took place in Tucumán, in July of 1816.

It was at that opportunity that the second great question was also defined. The first, as we saw, was, Do we depend in any way on Spain? The nature of the process made this impossible, and Independence was declared. The next question was, What form of government to choose? At the Congress of Tucumán, the possibility that this country might be a monarchy was seriously proposed. Napoleon had been vanquished and the Holy Alliance, a union of very reactionary nations —the czarist empire of Russia; the Bourbons in France; Austria, run by Metternich—, prevailed in Europe. In this context, the republics suggested subversion, chaos, Jacobinism.

Several important men, Manuel Belgrano among them, advised that a monarchy be set up. The proposal had a chance to crystallize through some very complicated diplomatic procedures in Europe; the idea of restoring an Inca to the throne was also thrown into the shuffle. Nevertheless, these options were never more than soundings of a public opinion that, as minimal as it might have been, repudiated the possibility of a monarchy in Buenos Aires: that would have been the end of the Revolution. The people, in spite of being an undefined, vague entity, rejected that possibility and preferred a more open, freer, more democratic one.

So then, the monarchic initiative was discarded, Independence was declared, and the Congress of Tucumán, which moved to Buenos Aires, continued in session to prepare a Constitution. It was the Constitution of 1819 —planned in case there was a decision in favor of the monarchic alternative at some point—, and it had practically no effect. It was an aristocratic constitution, with a Senate formed by delegates of the provinces —but that, at the same time, included individuals appointed on the basis of character: university presidents, generals, bishops, et cetera. In the text the word *republic* is never mentioned. The Constitution of 1819 didn't function, because the federalist dissidence was already great and the distrust of the people vis-à-vis monarchic intrigues, very profound. And so things stood; after a series of political events and while San Martín was occupied emancipating Chile, in February of 1820, the battle of Cepeda took place.

# The informal organization

The battle of Cepeda was waged by two authentic caudillos of the littoral, Estanislao López and Francisco "Pancho" Ramírez, who confronted the rest of the National Army, defeating it at Cepeda not far from San Nicolás, on the first of February, 1820.

Several weeks prior to this, the army of Alto Perú, brought in by the Directorate to face the caudillos, had revolted in Arequito. It refused to continue fighting against its compatriots and retreated to Córdoba. The Directorate was rendered defenseless and it was thus that subsequent to this battle a federal system was created, in an inorganic but nevertheless very deliberate way. Present historiography refers to that year, 1820, as the year of anarchy.

*Anarchy* comes from the Greek *an arkos,* which means "without government, acephalous," and, essentially, in the battle of Cepeda the national government collapsed: the Directorate and the Congress fell. From 1810 onward there had existed in Buenos Aires a government whose authority was national; a government that, one presumed, subrogated the former power of the viceroy. After Cepeda, Buenos Aires became a province: a Legislature was elected and the Legislature elected a governor.

During 1820, Buenos Aires endured countless political misfortunes, including the previously mentioned day of the three governors, but toward the end of that year its political situation strengthened. At the same time, thirteen provinces —the true founders of nationality— began to become established. Thirteen because Jujuy separated from Salta only in 1833, completing thus the fourteen traditional provinces.

What was the meaning of the formation of the provinces? In the first place, it should be mentioned that after the battle of Cepeda, Estanislao López and Ramírez didn't impose upon Buenos Aires terribly onerous conditions. They asked only that a treaty be signed which would establish what they considered to be two major principles: that of nationality and that of federalism. The first consisted in expressing concretely the idea that the former viceroyalty wanted to be a country, a nation. Although it was going through a period of anarchy and turbulence, it had the desire to become a country and, when conditions would allow, it would do so.

With a little bit of optimism, the Treaty of Pilar established that, within sixty days of its signature, a congress would meet in the convent of San Lorenzo, near Santa Fe —where San

Martín won his first battle—, to set down the forms in which the country would organize itself under the federal system. Although the events violated this term, the Treaty of Pilar remained as proof of the desire of the provinces to become a nation.

The second principle that López and Ramírez wanted Buenos Aires to recognize was the federal principle. The nation would not be a monarchy, but rather a federal republic; that is, a republic where some authorities were delegated within a central power, but where each one of the provinces would be able to govern itself. This came from an old tradition that can be found recorded since the colonial era.

We said that the cities of Córdoba and of Salta were the seats of the intendancy governments on which the so-called subalternate cities depended. (Córdoba, for example, had La Rioja, San Luis, Mendoza, and San Juan.) But the subalternate cities detested the seats of the intendancy governments. They considered themselves despoiled and regarded Córdoba and Salta as abusive authorities, and —we have said— they tended to appeal to Buenos Aires to save them from this supposed tyranny. Each time they had some economic problem that was more or less grave, an exaction, a tax; each time that an appointed governor or some lieutenant governor was sent to them, the subalternate cities would appeal to Buenos Aires which, confronting the corresponding seat of the intendancy government, would "bridge" it [i.e., bypass its authority]. The *cabildos* that were in the city, subalternate or not, were the centers that fought against denounced extortions of the indendancy governments and were focal points of subsequent federalism.

When in 1820 the national authority fell and there were no longer intendancy governors appointed by Buenos Aires, nor lieutenant governors appointed in the subalternate cities by the intendancy governors, those former *cabildos* converted their region into a province. A legislature was appointed; a governor was appointed; in some cases a constitution was written up; some provinces established a fiscal system to find out about the necessities with which, one presumed, a government should concern itself.

While this occurred, in Córdoba governed Juan Bautista Bustos, who had been a soldier in the war of Independence and who had attained power with the help of a revolution —backed, specifically, by the Army of Alto Perú that had rebelled in Arequito some days before Cepeda. Bustos regarded with preoccupation the number of provinces that, according to him, did not have viability in order to practice good government. Although he was a federalist, he had believed that the provinces should be formed on the basis of the former intendancy governments and he began to realize that many of them did not have the money to conduct their government, nor a respectable class of men who could manage it, neither did they have a clergy who could represent it. In short, as he saw it, the minimal conditions to function as provinces were lacking.

Bustos, as governor of Córdoba, would have naturally wished for his province to comprise Córdoba, San Luis, La Rioja and Cuyo, but the provinces that had been set up from the *cabildos* wanted to have their own autonomy, although in some cases they truly had barely the means to subsist in a dignified manner. Take the province of La Rioja in 1820: What were its fiscal revenues? Minimal taxes that it would collect on trappings, or troops, or the goods that passed through its territory every so infrequently, or the installation fee that would be collected from a bar. There was no fiscal system; they lived in extreme poverty. And, with the passage of time, this characteristic was accentuated to an even more dramatic degree. At any event, the provinces responded with a respectable localist sentiment and, at that time, the only thing that could be done was to give them some type of satisfaction.

In the years following 1820, a dual experience unfolded. On the one hand Buenos Aires felt excused from its role as older sister, seat of the national government. It no longer had national obligations. The customs duties that it collected —the most important category in matters of fiscal revenue— were dedicated exclusively to its necessities: to better the streets, to create the university, to establish all that made

Bernardino Rivadavia famous as a progressive governor. The funds that previously had been allocated to the armies and to diplomatic missions, were now applied to local needs. In the rest of the provinces, by contrast, the lack of resources made it so that the provincial governments steered their way through failures, frustrations, mini revolutions, insurrections....

On the one hand, then, Buenos Aires carried out what at that time was called "the happy experience," that of a peaceful government, which year after year presented before the Legislature its budget, drew up a rendering of accounts as was appropriate, created new institutions, bettered the quality of life of the inhabitants, and permitted a prosperous trade. On the other hand, there were the provinces whose situation had not improved in any way with independence, rather quite the contrary: it had deteriorated. After 1824, with the battle of Ayacucho —the final battle of Independence— the region of Salta, Jujuy, and Tucumán, which previously made its livelihood from the commerce with Alto Perú, suffered from the lack of currency and, above all, the lack of a market where it could offer its production. In Cuyo, something similar occurred, though the liberation of Chile permitted a certain expansion of its economic activities. Other provinces of the interior that did not have their own resources had a hard time.

Thus the need to create some type of constitutional organization in the country began to be noticed. The provinces demanded a constitution, while in Buenos Aires they loitered about, because they knew that a constitution would imply once again a central government to which Buenos Aires would have to subordinate itself.

## War against Brazil

The situation would have gone on indefinitely had it not been for a new development that hastened a constitutional form of organization: the war with Brazil. Although the Banda Oriental was at one time under the hegemony of Artigas, the Portuguese, who had always coveted it, began a gradual, but progressive and steady invasion, which ended in 1820 with the occupation of Montevideo. One year later the Banda Oriental was declared Cisplatina Province; that is to say, one more province of the Portuguese empire —and, after independence, one more province of the empire of Brazil. This was unacceptable.

The Banda Oriental had always belonged to the Spanish Crown, and let us not forget that one of the juridical notions that was sustained during the native governments was the principle that new nations would maintain the same frontiers as those of the colonial jurisdictions. That is, that just as the Viceroyalty of the River Plate extended as far as the Desaguadero River in Peru, Bolivia, already transformed into a republic, did not try to go beyond the Desaguadero. In the same fashion, the Banda Oriental had always belonged to the Spanish Crown and its occupation by the Portuguese was an usurpation.

The ruling class of Buenos Aires understood the need to make a great effort to avoid this and convoked all the provinces to send delegates to a congress, which met in Buenos Aires in 1824. After several negotiations before the emperor of Brazil, and faced with his refusal to vacate the Banda Oriental, plus pressed by the expedition that thirty-three compatriots from the Eastern Shore made to head the liberating crusade, the government of Buenos Aires, with the authority of all the provinces, declared war.

In a certain sense, the meeting of the congress of 1824 in Buenos Aires with delegates from all of the provinces responded to the urgency that the Argentine Republic, as it was called during that period, put forth the effort to oust the Brazilians from the Banda Oriental.

The congress, however, had a pure unitarian bias. Regardless of the fact that the provinces sent their delegates —some through great effort— so that the federal constitution could be sanctioned, the constitution that was sanctioned was unitarian, and Bernardino Rivadavia, head of the unitary faction no less, was elected as President of the Republic. This arrangement was short lived.

After a war that was almost tied with Brazil —in Ituzaingó the war on land was won, but the Brazilian blockade was very strong and it asfixiated the United Provinces economically—, a peace treaty was reached, by which the Banda Oriental would constitute an independent republic. Thus the fragmentation of the former viceroyalty was complete: Bolivia had declared itself independent with the approval of Congress, Paraguay continued in a state of neutrality and confinement, and the Banda Oriental became the República Oriental del Uruguay.

From that moment onward, the frontiers were defined for what later would be the Argentine Republic, but the war with Brazil and the utopian aims of Rivadavia terminated the presidential system: the unitarian experiment was thwarted by the renunciation of Rivadavia and the country returned to its former situation. That is, the thirteen provinces that were each governed by their institutions, but who entrusted to Buenos Aires the management of foreign affairs.

Buenos Aires, because it had been the viceregal capital and because it had the necessary administrative body, was acknowledged as the province most qualified to carry out negotiations with the rest of the world. In fact, since 1822 the most important nations recognized the existence of the United Provinces of the River Plate as an independent nation. The government of the province of Buenos Aires thus took on a double responsibility. On the one hand, that of being concerned with foreign affairs; on the other, that of taking into account the national tendency, which had been expressed in the Treaty of Pilar and which at some point had to be fulfilled.

## Civil war

The governor of Buenos Aires, Manuel Dorrego, a federalist who held the trust of the caudillos of the interior, was unfortunately brought down from power by a corps of former combatants of the war with Brazil, headed by Juan Lavalle. This development introduced once again a period of civil war, which had two focal points: Buenos Aires and the interior.

In Buenos Aires it was Juan Manuel de Rosas, the commander of the campaign, who took on the responsibility to fight against the insurgents who had overthrown Dorrego. After a few battles and more or less confusing encounters, it was agreed upon with Lavalle that Rosas would be the governor of Buenos Aires; the Legislature that had governed with Dorrego was restored, and peace in the province was reestablished.

But in the interior —where General José María Paz, who immediately overthrew Bustos and set himself up as governor of Córdoba, was sent— a unitarian league was created that deposed the federal governments that were in the interior. In spite of being called a "unitarian league," most likely it did not have a unitarian ideology. It opposed the power of Buenos Aires, a circumstance that gave rise to the Federal Pact of 1831.

The Federal Pact was an agreement made between Buenos Aires, Santa Fe, and Corrientes. It had as its objective the establishment of an offensive-defensive commitment: whoever might attack any of the three provinces would have to face all three. Moreover, as in the earlier Treaty of Pilar, the pact implied a commitment to organizing the country under the federal system once the indispensable conditions of peace and tranquility were achieved.

At the time of the signing, a delegate of Corrientes, Pedro Ferré, proposed furthermore the need to design an economic program for this new country. Was it going to continue to be free-trading? Was it going to continue to permit that all foreign goods enter and that the local merchants be condemned to absolute poverty, having to sell off their small businesses? These questions were posed by Ferré, who had a small shipyard and was familiar with the problems created by the insane free trading that the provinces had experienced since 1810, when the native governments opened up trade because they needed money from customs to help pay for their necessities.

The free-trading policy had meant a total invasion of goods, especially British; and the annihilation of the few homegrown industries that were in the interior; plus, an extraction of coined currency that had subjected these provinces to a great shortage. Ferré asked that before signing the treaty the parties make an agreement so that local industries —wine, wheat, leather goods— would be protected by reasonably high customs tariffs.

Buenos Aires, governed by Rosas, opposed this proposal, and in the end, in January of 1831, the Federal Pact was signed without any type of provision regarding the economic policy that would ensue. The only thing stipulated was that a representative commission of the three signatory governments would be formed and that, once there was peace and tranquility in the country, the other provinces would be invited to form part organically.

At that time, however, the Federal Pact signified a military power set against the unitarian league of General Paz. The civil war ended in that year with the imprisonment of General Paz, who by chance was lassoed with a *bolas* by a soldier from enemy lines. Thus his army was left without a head and General Juan Facundo Quiroga ended up with the last remaining unitarians in the interior.

## The Letter from the Hacienda de Figueroa

Within the search for political forms that had been going on since 1810, in 1834, a very important document was signed that, along with the Federal Pact, would be the skeleton of the more or less pragmatic organization that sustained the country until the battle of Caseros.

Rosas, who following the agreement with Lavalle was governor of Buenos Aires from 1829 to 1831, governed correctly and put things a bit in order. His government coincided with a terrible drought that affected Buenos Aires and the provinces in the area; it also signified the end of the civil war in Buenos Aires.

After having carried out the conquest of the desert,

Rosas refused to be governor, because he wanted to govern only with extraordinary authority. In his opinion, the state of things did not permit a ruler to control the situation if he didn't have the sum total of public power..., if he wasn't a dictator. As the Legislature of Buenos Aires did not want to give him these powers, Rosas did not accept to be reelected.

Various provisional governors succeeded one another and, toward the end of 1834, the news reached Buenos Aires of a civil war between two federalist provinces: Tucumán and Salta. Rosas summoned the most prestigious man of the interior, Juan Facundo Quiroga, who at that time was living in Buenos Aires, and asked him to go as a representative of the government of the province in order to pacify the situation. After several days of meetings, Quiroga headed north; Rosas stayed in an estancia of San Andrés de Giles, the Hacienda de Figueroa, where he wrote a long document, dated the twentieth of December of 1834, which reached Quiroga's hands when the latter was in Santiago del Estero.

This is the famous letter from Hacienda de Figueroa, one of the few documents where Rosas explains his political thought which, in essence, is the following: the country is not yet in a condition to organize itself constitutionally under a federalist system. Not even the basic elements to do it exist. The country has just come out of a civil war, the provinces are wiped out, the scars are still very deep. If a congress is convoked, it will be filled with unitarians, "with freemasons and scoundrels" and the result will be a new downfall. Furthermore, money is needed and there isn't any. On the other hand, Where would the congress meet? In Buenos Aires, no; that would immediately arouse the distrust of the interior, as always occurred. And, what type of constitution would be drawn up?

Let's let things straighten themselves out over time, said Rosas. Instead of imposing an organization of the country from top to bottom, it's preferable that matters be put in order from bottom to top: that the provinces settle their issues, that they become accustomed to living in peace, that they set up their institutions, and only then will we be able to think about a national constitution. Until then, let's try to live in harmony.

Although some historians, rather pro-Quiroga, sustained that this letter betrayed the vision of Quiroga, who wanted a constitution, it is very probable that the caudillo was in agreement with Rosas. The letter is in the General Archive of the Nation, stained with blood: Quiroga was carrying it with him in his suit when he was assassinated in Barranca Yaco. The death of Quiroga signified the postponement, perhaps indefinitely, of the country's yearnings for a constitutional organization. From that moment (1835) on, the country endured a de facto confederation, under the pragmatic thinking of Rosas.

To summarize: The Federal Pact, signed in 1831 by Buenos Aires, which was governed by Rosas; Santa Fe, governed by Estanislao López; and Corrientes, governed by Pedro Ferré, was a pact in which the three provinces promised to defend themselves in the case of external or internal attacks, to not allow the disintegration of the country, and to convoke a constitutional organization when there was peace and tranquility. The terms of the commitment were upheld by Facundo Quiroga who, although he did not sign the treaty, was the military and political power in the interior.

Joined after a fashion to the alliance of littoral provinces, then, was the power of Quiroga, who confronted the unitarian league, under the predominant influence of General Paz. Only months later, the unitarian league was dispersed on the occasion of General Paz's capture as well as the struggle by Quiroga, who ended up with the remains of the unitarian army.

The unitarians, moreover, after the disastrous experience of Rivadavia, ceased to believe with such assuredness in a centralist type government. They realized that reality was much stronger than their theories and that to think about this kind of organization of the country was utopian. The only thing they wanted, once and for all, was an organization of the country. Anyway, the unitarians disappeared from the scene, above all after the second government of Rosas; and the political hegemony of the country was, through different figures that went about occupying the governments of the various provinces, federal.

## Chapter V

# Toward national organization

*We said that as part of the search for a political formula that would give reasonable unity to the provinces, two agreements were signed. One was the Treaty of Pilar (1820), which defined the national and federal calling of the signatories (Buenos Aires, Santa Fe, and Entre Ríos) and even outlined some steps to achieve a constitutional organization of the country that, ultimately, was not realized. The other agreement was the Federal Pact (1831), which established for the signatory provinces (Buenos Aires, Santa Fe, and Corrientes, to which the remaining provinces were incorporated successively) the commitment to meet, once there was peace and tranquility, in a congress destined to adopt the federative system. Finally, we mentioned, as well, the Letter from Hacienda de Figueroa (1834), a doctrinal piece which reflects the thinking of Juan Manuel de Rosas on the subject. It says, in short, that conditions were not ripe for the country to organize itself constitutionally and that only time would begin to settle things.*

# Rosas

We left our story in 1835. So, it is now appropriate to talk about Rosas, whose second government began in the early months of that year and continued on for seventeen more months, until the battle of Caseros, in February of 1852. We will not treat the topic at length, because the polemics surrounding Rosas are so repetitive that they have ceased to be of interest to me. It's that when the issue is discussed, what is really being discussed is the sense of values, such as liberty or national sovereignty, that continue to be important in the collective and even private life of Argentines today.

Rosas had a very particular idea of liberty: he thought that governments should be authoritarian and should exercise implicit or explicit repression. He didn't have the slightest notion of tolerance or of pluralism in relation to his opponents; he believed in the need for a paternalistic authority that would rule over even the most minute details of the life of the community. On the other hand, he inexorably defended Argentine sovereignty (in that era it was called "independence"), he valiantly opposed the pretensions of countries such as France and England, who were the most powerful nations of the world, and he fought against their advances.

Given that Rosas is criticized or lauded for facets of his personality that are so distinct, there is no longer room for discussion about him from the historiographic point of view. It is very unlikely that some document be found that sheds new light on unknown aspects of Rosas as a person or as a ruler; that is to say, the critical material with which the historian works has been practically exhausted. On the other hand, controversy does exist surrounding these values that, even today, trouble people, and it is around this controversy that the discussions about Rosas revolve. For those who value liberty as a fundamental category of collective life, Rosas will never be likeable; those who believe in sovereignty as an argumentative element of the national community will speak well of him. And so his detractors and defenders will go on for years and years.

Independent of these polemics, we will examine some characteristics of the government of Rosas. It was, fundamentally, a conservative government. That is, a regime that did not try to modify anything, and that in a certain way revived the practice of the colonial system with respect to not permitting debates that could lead to the fragmentation of society; with respect to the absolute preeminence that was given to the judgment of authority; and even with respect to certain ideas, such as those that Rosas disclosed in 1836, on the occasion of the celebration of the Ninth of July. It is a little known speech, whose thesis was that the May Revolution had come about because of loyalty to the king of Spain, in order to maintain his sphere of control, and that only the incomprehension of the *realistas* led the patriots to a series of steps, after which there was no choice but to declare Independence.

In many aspects, then, Rosas lived in the colonial era. He awarded great importance to the religious question and to that of paternal authority and, undoubtedly, he gave his government a direction that today we would call reactionary. There were no initiatives, for example, for important public works; the university practically stopped functioning because subsidies were cut, and the very few lectures that were given in Buenos Aires were due to the fact that the students themselves paid their professors.

During the government of Rosas there was little opening abroad, although foreigners in the country lived without being persecuted or discriminated against, and there even existed a moderate immigratory current. But there was no interest in opening a window to the world, nor in the ideas that could come in from the outside. On the contrary, a certain distrust of things foreign was perceived, coincidental with the sentiments of Rosas, who was very *criollo,* very nationalist, and attached to things of the land —however primitive or barbaric they might be.

The conservative attitude, with regard to the country, with regard to what already existed, began to develop a sense of national unity which up until that moment was not mature.

The long Rosas regime, with the reiteration of bureaucratic ceremonies, was beginning to create an integration that the provinces did not previously have. For although Rosas spoke of the Federation and consecrated his motto as a federalist, in practice, he headed an absolutely centralist regime.

Thus, Rosas began to create a de facto national government. On the eve of his overthrow, he had accumulated as governor of Buenos Aires a series of powers that today are practically the same as those that the Constitution grants the President of the Republic and, in certain cases, they even went beyond what one today might expect from the National Executive Power.

Apart from handling foreign affairs, for example, he maintained careful watch on the provinces that had borders with neighboring countries in order to impede clandestine trade of gold coins —foreign currency drain, we would say today—, and to impede as well that there be any kind of propaganda in those countries that might effect the federalist regime.

The governor of Buenos Aires had under his direction, in addition, a sort of Ministry of Economics —insofar as it collected taxes through the customhouse of Buenos Aires—, and in some cases he would graciously send subsidies to provinces that might be very needy. It thus came to pass with Santiago del Estero, to which he sent money to extract the province from its economic prostration.

Rosas also operated a kind of War Ministry, as he controlled what today we would call the National Army, which at various moments fought against Bolivia; part of the Banda Oriental; Brazil; and France and England, with whom there was no declared war but yes, hostilities.

He intervened in the provinces that were rebellious toward him, either with a simple letter, taking advantage of the fear that Buenos Aires inspired, or by military expedition, as occurred with the Northern Coalition.

Likewise, he controlled all that had to do with the ecclesiastical Trust; that is, the appointment of bishops, permits of bulls and papal documents. He also kept an eye on the religious orders and parish priests in order to detect whether they were sympathizers with the regime of the Federation or not. And, of course, he exercised extensive censorship of the press and control over newspapers or books from the opposition that might enter the country.

The fact that Rosas might bring together some of the powers that the Constitution would then grant to the national government, created the necessary conditions so that, after his long stay in power, when he was defeated in the battle of Caseros, the unity of the country might be able to be established by means of a constitution.

# Constitutions

Among the conservative attitudes of Rosas, it is worth pointing out, in addition, that of being unaware of the mood of the times, something which tends to happen with governments of this ilk. During a certain period of time, the rigidity that keeps things as they were can be useful, because it offsets discord or chaos. But later, the times set forward other demands, other necessities, and a very conservative government doesn't register them, doesn't absorb them. This happened with the Rosas regime.

In 1835, this rigidity could have been necessary in order to create a parenthesis for the ignoble wars that had seized Argentine society. But afterwards, society began to progress reasonably and in a self-sustaining way, and other demands began to materialize, even those of an intellectual and juridical sort. For example, that of counting on a written constitution. Throughout the decade of 1840, the popular revolutionary movements of Europe called for or imposed upon the kings a constitutional charter.

The idea was in fashion that in a book, in a written law, there be relationships established between an authority and its subjects, relationships between the different organisms of power and the guarantees and rights of the inhabitants.

The same need was felt in the River Plate, but Rosas was unaware of it. When in May of 1851, Justo José de Urquiza rose the flag of rebellion, Rosas, as an intellectual counteroffensive, limited himself to publishing the famous Letter from Hacienda de Figueroa, which he had written seventeen years earlier. For him, time had not passed and, in his judgement, it was necessary that there be a long parenthesis, for things to calm down and the constitutional organization to begin to occur from bottom to top.

His government had become an anachronism. What was useful fifteen years earlier, no longer made sense. Nevertheless, Rosas was still the chief of numerically important armies. All the provincial governors gave him their support and, apparently, so did the federalist masses of Buenos Aires. But in reality his government was in decay; it no longer had the justification that, in its time, it held.

In this sense, it's also worthwhile to point out that there were *several Rosas,* according to the Argentine regions where his activity made itself felt. There was a Rosas for the city and the province of Buenos Aires —probably loved by the masses and respected by the middle classes; a Rosas, guarantee of security, which had imposed order and established the conditions enabling people to work and prosper. In the province of Buenos Aires, for example, an English traveler in 1847, William McCann, gave himself the pleasure of traveling through the province during almost a month without ever stopping in a house that wasn't an Englishman's, a Scotsman's, or an Irishman's. To this extent were these foreigners settled with all variety of guarantees and without anyone bothering them, even when Rosas, when the occasion arose, had resisted the hostilities of France and England.

On the other hand, in the province of Buenos Aires one had reached a certain level of coexistence with the Indians, who during the time of Rosas had organized practically no surprise attacks. There existed a system of bribery whereby the government of Buenos Aires would send them mares, tobacco and *mate* tea, and keep them calm and peaceful, in a more or less friendly state. This was the Rosas of Buenos Aires.

But in the littoral, there was a Rosas with a different meaning, and it is the Rosas who provoked that state of

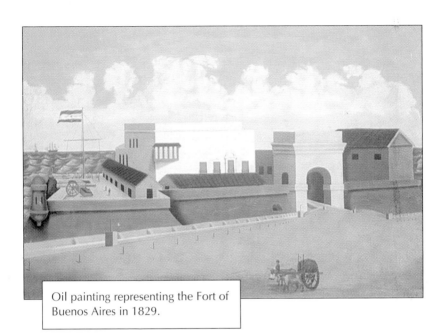

Oil painting representing the Fort of Buenos Aires in 1829.

Sea battle between Argentina and Brazil over the possession of the Banda Oriental.

Battle of the Vuelta de Obligado.

Urquiza's soldiers in front
of San José Palace, his manor house.

affairs which would culminate in the insurrection of Urquiza. It was a Rosas who unlawfully maintained a monopoly over the navigation of rivers, for he would not permit foreign vessels to navigate the rivers of the interior, thus smothering a flourishing economy such as that of Entre Ríos, where salaries equal to the province of Buenos Aires were paid and where there was intense trade with the Banda Oriental. This Rosas was no longer so pleasing, moreover because, faced with the continual uprisings of Corrientes, the repression had been very severe.

And finally, for the interior there was a Rosas feared and hated: he who ordered the terrible expeditions of Oribe, that for a long time left the mark of great cruelties; he who ordered the execution of José Cubas in Catamarca, that of Marco Avellaneda in Tucumán (1840); and other repressions. Things such as these, plus the economic prostration in which the provincial governments found themselves, greatly worried the latter, already reduced to a state of destitution vis-à-vis the increasing prosperity of Buenos Aires. This state of affairs had to come to an end before the country could organize itself; give guarantees and rights to its inhabitants; and establish, along with a definitive political scheme, a more equitable distribution of the wealth of the Nation than what had been offered up until then.

## Caseros

After the battle of Caseros, Rosas disappeared from the political scene; he went into exile in England, and Urquiza was left as the protagonist of the new phase. Caseros was not a battle between enemy parties where one won and the other —that of Rosas— lost: Caseros was an internal fight within the federalist party, where the old caudillo was forced out and a new caudillo, Urquiza, took a step forward.

A series of factions that also hated Rosas had united with Urquiza: the former unitarians; those who called themselves unitarians but were liberals and lived in exile, such as Sarmiento or Mitre; and the Brazilians —against whom Rosas had declared war a year before—, who reinforced the expedition of Urquiza, facilitated the movement of troops by river, and, ultimately, made possible the victory of Caseros.

The action of Urquiza in the province of Buenos Aires was moderate. Here there began to form a center of political power made up, above all, of liberals and of former unitarians. There existed a pro-Buenos Aires sentiment damaged by the fact that Rosas could not be taken down by the *porteños* themselves, but rather by an expedition that came from the interior, something akin to what had happened in 1820 with Ramírez and with López, but this time in a more spectacular way.

After Caseros, Rosas resigned as governor and the Legislature dissolved; under the regime of Urquiza new elections took place, in which the *porteñistas* [those who were pro-Buenos Aires] triumphed; a new legislature was elected; and Vicente López y Planes was appointed provisional governor. Urquiza, then, who had a commitment with the country to call for a constitution, assembled in San Nicolás de los Arroyos the governors of all the provinces and reached an accord, the Accord of San Nicolás, which, along with the Treaty of Pilar and the Federal Pact of 1831, formed the set of preexisting pacts to which the Preamble of the Constitution alludes.

The Accord of San Nicolás, established by ex-governors of Rosas incorporated into the order founded by Urquiza (who did not want to face them but rather to utilize them as instruments for this new institutional phase), was truly very important. In the first place, it established a mechanism to put into practice a Constituent General Congress, formed by two deputies from each province who were to meet in Santa Fe. This clause was very disturbing to Buenos Aires, who was going to have the same representation as Jujuy or La Rioja.

In the second place, it paved the way for a future constitution by abolishing the customhouses in the interior, declaring free of all duties the people or goods that should pass through Argentine territory, and declaring the open navigation of the rivers, a step forward in the direction toward giving constitutional staus to a freeing of trade that, until then, did not exist. Along with this virtual creation of a common market within the Argentine territory, it was established that the customhouse of the province of Buenos Aires, henceforth, would be shared by all the provinces.

The third order of intentions that the Accord of San Nicolás included was the creation of a provisional government, to which the name Directorate was given. Urquiza was appointed Director and received specific powers; among them, to be commander of the existing militias in the country, and to manage national funds, fundamentally, the revenue from duties at the customhouse of Buenos Aires.

The Accord of San Nicolás was rather risky, because none of the governors had the mandate to subscribe such an agreement. But it made clear an intention to organize the country, despite the hostility of certain interests, in particular those of Buenos Aires. As for the *porteños,* they had opposing arguments, even of a juridical nature, that were expounded by Bartolomé Mitre before the Legislature of Buenos Aires.

To begin with, the governor of Buenos Aires —said Mitre— did not have the authority in San Nicolás to dispose of the assets of the province, as were its resources or its troops. Secondly —it wasn't said but it was implicit in the words of Mitre— Buenos Aires did not have any interest in nationalizing its assets, such as its customhouse or its city, which could be declared the Federation's capital.

The allegation of Mitre caused the Legislature of Buenos Aires to reject the Accord, which, on the other hand, was approved by the rest of the provinces. Facing the resignation of Governor López y Planes, who felt deprived of his authority, Urquiza effected a coup d'état and assumed control of the principal province of the country. But the opposition within Buenos Aires was very great: in September of 1852 there was finally a revolution that permitted the inhabitants of Buenos Aires to retake control of the city. Urquiza tried to lay seige to it but did not succeed, and finally, he had to retreat.

Some months later the delegates of the provinces met in

Santa Fe without the attendance of Buenos Aires; they sanctioned the National Constitution of 1853 and elected Justo José de Urquiza as president. From that time on, and for ten years hence, a very dangerous situation was prolonged. On the one hand there was the Argentine Confederation, an entity made up of thirteen provinces that tried to be the Nation in its totality; it had a National Constitution sanctioned by the congressmen in Santa Fe, a Congress, and an Executive Power with headquarters in the city of Paraná. There went the ambassadors and the foreign consuls whenever they had to, but whenever they could they escaped, because it was a terribly boring city and they preferred to live in Buenos Aires.

On the other hand, there was the State of Buenos Aires, whose situation was ambiguous: it did not proclaim either its sovereignty nor its independence. It did not claim to be a free State, but neither did it form part of the Confederation. One presumed it an autonomous State that recognized itself as belonging to the Argentine Republic.

## Segregation

This secession —that could have been definitive, thus thwarting forever the desire for national unity— set a national entity with headquarters in Paraná against another entity with headquarters in Buenos Aires. Both competed, antagonized one another, and attacked one another, including militarily. What were the real obstacles that prevented them from uniting? Fundamentally, the difference in economic development that existed between Buenos Aires and the rest of the country. There was a huge gap, as there had been during the time of Rosas, between the progress of Buenos Aires and the manner in which the remaining provinces developed their economy and their political life.

In the Buenos Aires of 1857, for example, there was already gas lighting in the streets, a railroad that reached San José de Flores and a Customhouse, built to serve the necessities of increasing trade. The development of Entre Ríos, the province that could come the closest, had no means of comparison with that of Buenos Aires. Much less, that of Santiago del Estero, Córdoba, Tucumán, and so on, which, on the other hand, were controlled by caudillos from the period of Rosas and did not have a ruling class as enlightened as that of Buenos Aires, nor institutions as firmly rooted and important as the University, the Legislature, or the press of Buenos Aires. The difference was so great that it made it very difficult to work out formulas that would make the union of Buenos Aires with the interior possible.

The Argentine Confederation, what's more, had almost no sources of permanent revenue, while the Customhouse, by contrast, sustained the government of Buenos Aires. It also allowed one, for example, to bribe the chief of the fleet of the Confederation that was besieging Buenos Aires, or to recruit an armed National Guard to face the cavalry of Urquiza, which, though it was made up of civilians from Entre Ríos and was very colorful, had a rather limited offensive capability. On the other hand, in the Confederation there were extremists willing to incorporate Buenos Aires by force, and in Buenos Aires there were also those who suggested that the province declare itself an independent republic. But in the end good judgment prevailed over both parties.

What prevented this state of segregation from continuing forever? The comprehension that Buenos Aires alone was not and could not ever be a country, and that the rest of the provinces, without Buenos Aires, were inviable. The idea had been around since the times of the former Viceroyalty: Buenos Aires and the interior were two distinct realities, though complementary. Each one of them taken alone was not viable, reason for which a formula had to be sought so that the great differences that separated them could be pared down.

The patriotism of some leaders also contributed to national union. It is clear that Urquiza wanted the definitive organization of the country and, though he was a man from the interior, he understood that this organization was impossible without Buenos Aires. This explains in part his attitude at the battle of Pavón, as we shall see.

And, finally, what also influences matters is history, which demonstrated that it had already been half a century (since 1810) that the Argentines, be they from the interior or from Buenos Aires, were looking for a formula in order to live harmoniously. Common past events, common national leaders and heroes, the memory of the great exploit of Independence.... The presence of several men of that period who were still alive transformed into a terrible sin this division that, if prolonged, could become definitive.

The sum total of these factors led one to believe that, beyond the conflicts, confrontations, and differences, it was possible to achieve some sort of permanent formula, which, in effect, happened following two great battles. One was that of Cepeda (1859), where the Confederation triumphed over Buenos Aires. Urquiza advanced as far as the city but, once again, he showed himself to be very moderate. He didn't enter Buenos Aires, but rather encamped in San José de Flores, and asked only that the governor, Valentín Alsina —raging *ultra-porteñista*—, be removed from office and be replaced by someone with whom one could converse.

Thus they agreed to what would enter history as the Pact of San José de Flores, by which Buenos Aires pledged to enter the Confederation and the latter, to recognize the reforms that the province of Buenos Aires might wish to make to the Constitution. There was, essentially, a very conflictive issue: that of the Capital. The Constitution of 1853, in its first draft, said that the Capital of the Argentine Nation would be the city of Buenos Aires, a stipulation that the inhabitants of Buenos Aires could not tolerate, as this signified the surrendering of their city to the national authorities, which, possibly, they could not control.

For this reason, among other minor reforms, it was finally established that the Capital of the Argentine Nation was going to be the city declared as such by a law of Congress, upon cession made by a special law of the Legislature of the province that would have to cede it. So that if Buenos Aires was declared Capital by the Congress of the Nation, the city in turn could sanction or not sanction a law wherein the city of the same name might be ceded to the Nation.

The Pact of San José de Flores, which is along the same line as the Treaty of Pilar, as the Federal Pact, and as the Accord of San Nicolás, was the final step taken in pursuit of national organization, the final agreement in order for Buenos Aires to be able to enter the Confederation peacefully.

But after the province had examined the National Constitution, suggested some reforms, and sent its delegates to the Congress that met especially, certain political events occurred that brought about a new rupture between the Confederation and Buenos Aires.

Their troops were brought face to face once again, more or less in the same spot where the battle of Cepeda had been fought, and finally, in 1861, the battle of Pavón took place. From a military point of view, it was a fight without definition, because although the cavalry of Urquiza won, the infantry of Buenos Aires, commanded by Mitre, remained virtually intact, and Urquiza retreated from the battlefield. Mitre took advantage of the circumstance and advanced with his army to Rosario, while Urquiza returned to Entre Ríos and went into seclusion, passively.

The government of the Confederation, located in Paraná, seeing that no aid was coming from Urquiza, declared itself in adjournment, and dissolved. Mitre sent army corps toward the interior, as well, to change the positions that were opposed to him, and succeeded in getting the different provincial governments to delegate as his charge foreign relations and the temporary direction of national affairs —just as Urquiza had done after Caseros, despite Mitre's criticism.

In 1862, elections were held, and on the 12 of October of that year, Bartolomé Mitre assumed the Presidency of the Nation. Buenos Aires was already reincorporated into the country and was its provisional capital according to a law pronounced by the Legislature, wherein the city was not ceded but rather it invited the national government to install itself as a guest: a juridical subtlety to avoid the capitalization of the city.

# A national government

After this long story —of necessity confusing, because the circumstances were confusing and it is very difficult to summarize them—, we achieved a national government. A government that had to suppress the rebellions of the interior by force (above all, those of Chacho Peñaloza, who came out in defense of the defeated Confederation with the little funds that he had and was crushed first and assassinated years later). But, for better or for worse, there was a national government installed in Buenos Aires whose meaning and jurisdiction were national. For the first time since 1820, there was a formal government and a truly national one.

The solution that had been reached lasted only two decades. But regardless, it was appropriate at the time. The provinces had a Constitution, the Customhouse of Buenos Aires went about investing its revenue and expenses at the service of objectives of national import, there were constitutional guarantees and a separation of powers, and in the country an ideological plan —to put a name to it— was in effect.

It was a plan that Juan Bautista Alberdi, most of all, had outlined in his book *Bases y puntos de partida para la organización de la República Argentina* [*Fundamentals and Points of Departure for the Organization of the Argentine Republic*]. When Urquiza assembled in Santa Fe the Congress that would sanction the Constitution of 1853, its members began to look for models in order to create the first draft. Even though there was a rather concrete idea of what was wanted, the operative, practical aspect was missing. And so a little book arrived in their hands that Alberdi prepared, an Argentine lawyer established in Valparaíso who, having left Buenos Aires some twenty years earlier due to disagreements with Rosas (although he was never persecuted), had achieved in Chile an outstanding professional career.

In his book, Alberdi put forward a project for a Constitution and the theoretical foundation of this new country that was going to undertake its march forward, leaving behind the long dictatorship of Rosas and the long period of civil wars, and preparing itself to have a different role and new functions, including in the rest of the world.

What did Alberdi say, in essence? To sum it up in my own words: Let us draw up a Constitution where all types of guarantees are given to people who might want to come here to work, to conduct their industries, to educate and to become educated, to transmit their ideas. That is, a Constitution that would guarantee the creation of a prosperous society. But on the other hand, let us not be so liberal where politics are concerned. There is no electorate nor citizenship. Argentina, as yet, has no citizens. The native Argentines do not yet have customs related to work, respect for authority. They do not have anything of that which makes a regular government possible.

What do we have to do then? Foment immigration. Let many foreigners come, if possible Anglo-Saxons, and let them mix with the native population. Then, when with children or grandchildren of those immigrants a new type of man is forged, a new type of Argentine, it will be the moment to give not only civil but political liberties, as well. In the meantime, let the most capable govern, the best —us—, running things in such a way that with foreign investment, with the laying of railroad tracks, with the rational exploitation of the pampa, little by little, conditions are created that make possible republican forms with a republican content, as well. Meanwhile, let us uphold the republican form only.

In the final analysis, this was quite realist thinking, comparable, if you will, to what Rosas set forth in his Letter from Hacienda de Figueroa.

And, without anyone stating it in a direct way, it was thinking that was set in motion during the time of Mitre and, furthermore, during that of Roca, after 1880. That is: let us make a prosperous country, but let us try for it to have insertion within the contemporary world, let us open the border to immigrants, to capital, to ideas, and for now, let us postpone the political aspect a bit because the conditions are not yet ripe for a perfect republic. This is not the United States, nor Europe.

But in the meantime, as long as this society becomes wealthy, prospers, has the pleasure of the cultural and physical assets that civilization affords it, peace and order, we will be creating the conditions for there to be better politics, when the time is right. The people will not vote or will vote in fixed elections so that the natural ruling class continues to govern. I repeat, it was realistic thinking: it governed Argentine life until the sanctioning of the Sáenz Peña Law, in 1912.

## CHAPTER VI

# Institutional formation

Between 1869 and 1880 a process took place whose development made possible the definitive constitutional organization of the country. During this lapse of twenty years, which is very significant and very interesting, it is demonstrated, as perhaps during no other circumstance in our history, that communities are not created out of nowhere and that they are very rare those occasions when definitive changes or ruptures are produced. In general, we can observe certain tendencies that mark the continuity of a way of life, of work, of customs, of mentalities, of beliefs, even of prejudices, that in time become blended, but are not interrupted suddenly and, in any event, if they are exhausted, they tend to be the seeds of new forms that will become more defined in the future.

This happened during the time that we shall examine in this chapter. The confrontations and civil wars that occurred before 1860 were atrocious, and although between 1860 and 1870 there were also terrible struggles, the ferocity tended to be attenuated. Society was changing, evolving; new institutions were created that served to temper the brutal wars that characterized our country previously .

Argentina continued to be rather uninhabited, but at the same time, immigrations, colonies, and railroad lines were established; and political struggles were channeled through currents with some ideological definition. In this way, although the country did not change much, it continued to evolve along certain lines and situations that were already present and that in general tended to better things.

## The world

These two decades, so important in our history, cannot be understood if we do not make reference to the international context, because it was an era of great changes in the world: qualitative and quantitative.

The decade of 1850 witnessed the second-to-last great war of the 19th century in Europe, that of Crimea, between England, France, Russia, Italy, and Turkey, where new techniques and war strategies were put into motion. In the United States, during the early years of the decade of 1860, the Civil War was in effect, which in the final analysis signified the triumph of the industrialized north over the feudal and romantic (and pro-slavery) south of the cotton plantations. In 1870, the Franco-Prussian War took place, which ended with the defeat of France, the fall of the empire of Napoleon III, and the founding of the German empire, a new and tough political entity that arose in the old continent.

From that time on there was peace in Europe —with the exception of colonial wars, in general there was peace in the world—, and European societies expanded and developed on the basis of some inventions that affected the quality of life of people and that became known in these parts, as well, as for example, gas lighting, which was a very important innovation —not only in the streets but in the interior of houses—, because it made it possible for people to read more: this was one of the keys to the success of Dickens, who was read in English houses and promoted literacy in the population.

Furthermore, forged steel at high temperatures permitted a series of applications in construction. It was a time of great medical advances: bacilli and microbes that were previously unknown were detected. The railroad acquired an enormous importance throughout the world practically. This is to say that these years of peace between 1870 and —for us— 1890, signified a great advance in the quality of life of people, even for the working class of Europe, who benefited from the cheapness and rapidity of transatlantic voyages, all of which permitted them to emigrate to other continents with greater ease than before.

On the other hand, the industrial workers of England, Germany, and France lived much better than their parents or their grandparents, and they demanded then a series of products that afterward our country and other countries of America supplied. It was an international context marked by peace, by the availability of capital to invest abroad in the principal countries, and by scientific and technical advances, which had a direct repercussion on the lifestyle of the inhabitants of Europe.

## The political mechanisms in Argentina

From 1860 to 1880, three presidencies succeeded one another in Argentina; the founding presidencies, so to speak, those that established the solidity of the republican system —perhaps not as much in their content, but in their form at least. They were those of Bartolomé Mitre (1862-1868; although from 1860 on, after the battle of Pavón, Mitre practically exercised control of the country), Domingo Sarmiento (1868-1874), and Nicolás Avellaneda (1874-1880).

Already the mention of these dates indicates that there

was constitutional continuity; that is, that the phase of caudillismos, of governments overturned by revolutions or insurrections, and of dictatorships prolonged over time had been overcome. The dates under discussion are those of the six-year term that the Constitution stipulates for each president and, although electoral procedures may not have been very clean, the fact that the presidents could complete the constitutional term in that era was, regardless, a great improvement, one that upheld the validity of the Constitutional norm and established a certain respect for the law.

This improvement did not signify a brusque change, rather the affirmation of what had already been clear in coming. That is, of the need for the country to not be governed by the arbitrariness of a few rulers annointed with the sum total of public power, nor by caudillos who could represent the power of the provinces, but rather by presidents established during a period set forth by the law.

During these years, how were politics conducted, in what way were leaders elected, how was public opinion expressed? In general terms, it should be said that after Pavón, Mitre felt in control of the situation and built in the provinces and in Buenos Aires the power structure that would win him the definitive presidency in 1862. He based his ideas on a party called the Liberal Party, because he recognized that he had embraced the flag of liberalism, the ideology that began to spread throughout almost the entire civilized world.

Liberalism signified very little in the other provinces, but a fair amount in that of Buenos Aires: institutions founded, free press, parliamentarianism, opening of trade, freedom to carry out lawful industries. Nevertheless, the Liberal Party, found itself with serious inherited problems, as for example, that of the capital of the new nation, the same problem with which Urquiza had to contend in 1853; namely, the unwillingness of the *porteños* to surrender their city and convert it not only into the capital of the province of Buenos Aires but into the capital of the Nation.

We said that to resolve this problem, a sort of juridical

ruse was effected: the province of Buenos Aires became the host of the Nation's government, inviting it to install itself and remain there during a fixed period of time. By means of this Law of Compromise, Buenos Aires was the provisional capital. At the site of the Viejo Fuerte, where the Casa Rosada (the presidential palace) is now, the government installed its administration, while the province of Buenos Aires maintained its jurisdiction over the city. The legislative bodies, of the Nation as well as of the province, met in the same place where today the National Academy of History functions: there within is the space that pertained to the former Legislature of Buenos Aires and the former National Congress.

Upon agreeing to the Law of Compromise, the Liberal Party split up: the most pro-Buenos Aires faction, with Adolfo Alsina at the head, adopted the banner of autonomism, and called itself the Autonomist Party. The other faction comprised the liberals, or Mitreists [supporters of Mitre]. On the other hand, there was also the old Federal Party, which had supported Urquiza: it was composed of, finally, the unpleasant remains of that power structure that had maintained Rosas for so many years and that was still in force in the interior, though in Buenos Aires, barely so. These were not political parties in the modern sense of the term. They did not have organic bodies, nor the machinery to proselytize in an ongoing way. Federalism (with the figure of Urquiza at the head), Mitreism, and autonomism were simply currents affiliated with certain political leaders, and within whose framework these latter trammeled their alliances, ruptures, confrontations.

On the eve of elections there arose various curious institutions that were called "clubs" and that were in a certain way the antecedent of the committee. The Liberty Club and the Buenos Aires Club convoked the population to meet in a closed or open space —a square or a theater, for example. A directing commission would preside over the session, where a list of candidates were voted or a declaration, manifesto or whatever, would be ratified. Afterward, the club would dissolve until its reappearance. It was a very primitive democracy, if you will, very Athenian in style, and it lent itself to all variety of strategems.

Leopoldo Lugones recounts in his *History of Sarmiento* that the Liberty Club had to decide in favor of the candidacy of Sarmiento or that of Alsina. So, one summer afternoon, with a beating sun, the president of the club, who was pro-Sarmiento, asked those who supported Sarmiento to stand in the shade and those who favored Alsina, in the sun. Naturally, all went to the shady side and the Liberty Club voted for Sarmiento. Despite these anecdotes, this business of clubs was an incipient form of political activity, which up until then had not existed.

Similarly, the elections were as fraudulent as ever. The manner in which they were held always left a remainder of dead and injured. Without a civil register, nor permanent authorities, without a document of identification, anyone could vote four or five times, the authorities could throw someone out of the polls saying that he wasn't of the parrish, or a person could show up in five or six different parishes. But regardless, there began republican-democratic activity that in the time of Rosas had remained totally immobilized and, after the battle of Caseros, had been practiced in an extremely violent way. Now, it tended to be, if not diminished or pacified —because there were some pretty tough elections—, at least to establish a certain respect for the results, be these what they may.

This political system, though not that of organic parties, did prefigure it; the system was topped off by two practices, which at that time attained great popularity. On the one hand, *"diarismo"*, as it was called back then, due to the amount of newspapers [*diarios*] that published opinions and provided a forum for debates concerning any number of problems and in which anyone could participate. Paper and manual labor were very cheap, and every political leader who was more or less important had a newspaper at his disposal. Thus *La Nación* began, for example, as a personal newspaper, practically, of Mitre. Gas lighting, already installed in houses, facilitated reading, which in turn was a form of transmission of opinions, of selection of candidates, and of polemics regarding different problems that affected the communities, such as the problem of the Indians, that of where the port of Buenos Aires should be set up, or where this or that railroad line should be laid, and under what conditions.... This is to say that by way of the newspapers public debate was made commonplace.

The other democratic activity was parliamentarianism, or the habit of exercising the right to an opinion in the Legislature and in the National Congress, where there were certain rules of the game for debates, where one presumed the discussions should be orderly and reasonable and where oratory was exercised as a sort of sport of the period. During a historical period when there were no forms of mass communication other than newspapers, oratory, in effect, played an enormous role. There could be no political leader who wasn't a great orator. Some, according to legend, were very important and swept away the masses, such as Adolfo Alsina, José Manuel Estrada or, later on, Leandro Alem. As part of a parliamentary game that marked an improvement with regard to those eras when there was no citizen participation nor representation in the legislative bodies, one had to know how to complete paragraphs, one had to know how to stir the crowds.

During these three presidencies, then, constitutional continuity began to take hold, and the country began to grow accustomed to obeying the law. It's not that transgressions didn't exist; they did, of course, but it is curious to discover to what extent there existed a certain feeling of guilt each time a transgression was committed on too large a scale. When a scandalous electoral fraud took place or an unjustifiable intervention in a province, when there was excessive influence or interference in the politics of some other area on the part of the incumbent party, there was also tremendous interest in covering it up or justifying it.

This, obviously, was progress. Because one thing is a strike of the hand made without any type of justification: Lavalle's report to the representative government in Buenos

Aires ("I relay to you that I had Colonel Dorrego shot by my order"), indicated total arbitrariness, brutality in its purest form. Another matter is the type of journalistic and legislative debate that was engendered as a result of a situation such as, let's say, the intervention of Entre Ríos following the assassination of Urquiza by Ricardo López Jordán. In this case there was a series of justifications that we can find acceptable or not but that, at any rate, show a concern for demonstrating certain respect for the law. To all of this, one must add the presence of certain institutions, such as the National Supreme Court and, in the provinces, the federal judges, who in a way were the custodians of the Constitution.

## Immigration

At the same time that this political activity was beginning, some changes developed that, evidently, contributed to the progress of the country, to a better quality of life for the inhabitants, and to rational exploitation of natural and human resources. One of these changes was immigration. Alberdi, Sarmiento, and all of the men who, after Caseros, prepared themselves to run the country, had great faith in the possibility that thousands of Europeans would arrive to settle our pampa and to teach our inhabitants work habits, economy, and respect for authority, which still did not exist and whose absence made our people, in the opinion of these men, incapable of governing themselves.

The formula of Alberdi was to create a civil society that offered citizens all the guarantees to prosper, to work, to become educated, to move from one place to another, and to hold on to their property, free of whims or abuses; but that at the same time was a society where one would not yet vote, where one would not yet choose. Alberdi proposed that the republican form be maintained, but that in point of fact, the country be run by that small group of illustrious men —in which he included himself, of course—, who could carry things forward precisely because they knew how.

Immigration, one presumed, was going to produce over

time the forging of a new man, a different Argentine, hard-working, industrious, who had an understanding of machines, who didn't have that undisciplined, free, squandering nature of his fellow countryman. It is the period in which Martín Fierro appears as an archetype of the gaucho, who was already on the decline; it is the period in which Estanislao del Campo ridicules the gaucho in *Faust*. Immigration, then, was one of the elements that these men believed indispensable in order for the country to become settled, above all, by races that might better the ethnic level and the mentality of the Argentine *criollos*.

Nevertheless, the immigrants that arrived during the subsequent decades were not exactly those that Alberdi or Sarmiento had desired. The latter wanted, if possible, Anglo-Saxons who had the same type of mentality that he had seen in the United States: that of the small farmer who more or less was self-sufficient, who felt totally autonomous as far as politics, and who was not dependent on help from the government. Although not of this type, between 1860 and 1880, immigrants began to arrive in quantities that were not large but significant enough to warrant the creation of an immigration policy and, in some cases, to allow them property in the colonies that began to be established, in Entre Ríos and Santa Fe, above all, and, to a lesser extent, in Buenos Aires.

The railways began to be laid also in this period. In the opinion of Alberdi above all, this was the great instrument of communication and integration in a country where the enormous distances were tied into a factor of backwardness. From the outset, immediately following Caseros, the men of Buenos Aires as well as those of Paraná made an effort to try to get capitalists and technicians who were willing to lay railways to come: this is perhaps the reason for the unfair conditions with which the first contracts were written up.

The railroad from Rosario to Córdoba, the *Central Argentino,* stipulated a gift for capitalists within a league (3 miles) of each side of the track. The Central Argentino would remove the settlers all along its trajectory, and afterward, create subsidiary land companies that sold these large plots of land in huge lots to different people. It was a donation that today we view with horror almost —the richest land in the country given away in this manner— but it was commonplace occurrence in high-risk countries such as Argentina, and it was done, as well, in the United States and in India, for they desperately needed to unite the distinct regions that up until then had been very separate.

In 1870 the railroad went from Rosario to Córdoba; in the province of Buenos Aires there were also lines, above all, that of the *Oeste* [West], which reached as far as Chivilcoy, down to the south of the province, as far as Chascomús. That network so characteristic of Argentina, that later would converge at the port of Buenos Aires, began to be created. Some investors —British almost all of them— began to show interest in the advantage of constructing railways in the country.

Another characteristic of these years was a type of rural exploitation that today seems anachronistic to us, but at that time was a very apt way of extending the frontier of exploitable land, at least up until the Indian line. This type of exploitation was based fundamentally on the raising of sheep; the province of Buenos Aires was sheep producing by definition. Sheep rearing had the advantage over cattle rearing of rapid parturition times and with many young, and the wool as well as the meat (which was prepared at the saltworks and exported) could be exploited. Wool was an essential product, above all at a time when the standard of living tended to be on the rise and the common people were looking for better materials to protect themselves from the cold.

Among others who were involved in sheep exploitation, there were many Irish, who had come during the decade of the forties and a little after, in the fifties, having been displaced by famine. In that decade there had been a plague in Ireland that ruined several harvests of potatoes, a staple of the Irish diet. Many emigrated to the United States and to

Argentina, where there were individuals such as Father Fahy, who received them, guided them, took them to places where it could be worthwhile for them to work for a particular employer, and married them, eventually, to fellow compatriots.

One presumed that a shepherd who arrived without a cent in his pocket, could make himself, within two years, a rather important flock of sheep of two thousand or three thousand sheep. This animal, then, increased the advance of the animal husbandry frontier of the province of Buenos Aires, forcing out the cattle lead. Today it is thought of almost as an animal that pillages, but back then its type of feed allowed it precisely to remove the coarse grasses and to prepare the land for the more tender grasses that, at a later stage, the cattle would eat.

Immigration, sheep raising in the provinces of Buenos Aires and Santa Fe, and the colonies of Entre Ríos, Santa Fe, and the east of Córdoba began to define the economic activites of an Argentina that still did not have presence in the world circuits of production and consumption, but that was searching for what its role could be by means of the incipient agriculture industry and livestock —most of all, wool-bearing—, and the exploitation of the few natural resources that were known or could be produced with a certain amount of relative convenience.

## Difficulties

During the same period, a series of very negative events occurred. In the first place, the War of the Triple Alliance, a rather absurd war that broke out in 1865. It was a very complicated product from a problem of the balance of power in the River Plate; of the megalomania of Francisco Solano López, dictator of Paraguay; of the expansionist anxieties of Brazil; of the weakness of the República Oriental del Uruguay; and of the alliances of Mitre and his friends, the Uruguayan *colorados*. All these factors led to a war that lasted five years and produced no benefit whatsoever to the country, this in spite of having won the war; a war that brought terrible plagues to Buenos Aires and to the entire Littoral, and that, in the end, had only one beneficial result: having forged an army of a national character.

Up until then, in effect, there had not been a national army. There were provincial militias or national guards that, in spite of their name, were provincial. The War of the Triple Alliance compelled many young men of Buenos Aires, moved by a patriotic attitude, to join the Army, and in the interior, to send recruits, who were dispatched generally by force. Many young officers made their careers in the encampments of the War of the Triple Alliance, and there the sort of function that the National Army would have to fulfill in the future was defined: to place itself at the service of the governments, that is, to back up the National State. This was the only positive outcome of the War of the Triple Alliance.

On the other hand, during these years as well, there were three rebellions of López Jordán in Entre Ríos. In 1870 he led a revolution whose most spectacular action was the assassination of Urquiza in the Palace of San José. From then on, Sarmiento found that either he tolerated the situation or he intervened militarily in the province of Entre Ríos, seeing that López Jordán had the support of the population. He decided in favor of this latter option, and the intervention led to a very long war that would end toward the middle of 1871 —but that later would be repeated two more times with several other uprisings of López Jordán. It cost a large amount of money, effort, and armaments to completely destroy this insurrection that, although it wasn't against the National State, Sarmiento could not tolerate. So that this, too, is a negative note of those years, which in other aspects are obviously years of progress.

Finally, there was the problem of revolutions, which practically marked the arrival of a president to power. We know how Mitre came to power: aided by the bayonets of national regiments to eliminate the federalist positions and to erect governments that after would support his candidacy for president. Sarmiento's assumption of power was pacific, but when he left the presidency, the candidature of Alsina and Mitre, or between Avellaneda and Mitre, was transformed into a terrible confrontation. The struggle ended in an insurrection headed by Mitre that would last several months and be declared void by General Rivas in the province of Buenos Aires and by General Roca in Santa Rosa (Mendoza). This, which occurred in 1874, would occur again in 1880, when Avellaneda left power.

Permanent revolutions with each change of government, provincial uprisings, disturbances of all sorts. Nevertheless, the reason was different: no longer of total arbitrariness, rather, out of a certain respect for the law. In general, the pretext was that fraud had been committed or that there was unjust interference on the part of the national power, and word had it that it was against this that one was reacting. In some way, this meant a greater respectability for juridical norms.

Another problem was that of the Indians. During the time of Rosas, peace was maintained by way of a system —quite onerous— of bribes or tributes to the Indian chiefs. After Caseros, the Indians not only organized *malones* [surprise attacks] and entered into the Christian settlements, but in some cases participated in the civil wars, aligning themselves with one side or the other (with Urquiza, for example, or Mitre, as the circumstance dictated). They took an active part and became a political element to bear in mind. Furthermore, Calfucurá, who was a very intelligent man, succeeded in arming a sort of confederation of tribes in the pampa, giving strength to his entire power of attack.

In those years of relative prosperity, in which sheep were raised and some *estancias* and saltworks had been established, the presence of the Indians from the south of Mendoza, north of San Luis, south of Córdoba, west and south of the province of Buenos Aires, marked a territory that was a permanent threat against the Christian settlements or exploitation industries. Nonetheless, one could say that it was a prosperous era and one of settling, and the problem of the

Indians was resolved a short time thereafter with the conquest of the desert. Precisely at this time, 1879, two elements appeared, in a somewhat unspectacular way, that later would have enormous importance in Argentine life.

## Wheat and cold

Suddenly, wheat; the first export was made in 1878. It was small but up until then our country had only imported it, to make flour. In general it came from the United States. Following 1878, there was a small export toll, which thirty years later became the most important category of Argentine exports.

On the other hand, in 1879 a technological element that had major significance appeared. That year, a ship, *Le Frigorifique,* which produced artificial cold, transported to Europe several tons of frozen mutton. A part of the shipment was lost because a section of the machinery broke, but the rest arrived in France in good condition and was consumed.

Thus, the old problem, which had kept cattle breeders up nights since the colonial era and henceforward, began to be solved: how to preserve beef. During the era of the *vaquerías,* the meat remained as food for the rats and dogs of the countryside. After, came the salthouses: that meat, which previously was wasted, began to be macerated, dried, salted, and sent in medium-sized barrels to markets that, although they had reduced buying power, turned the salthouses into a category of export nevertheless, and permitted the foundation of some salthouses where up to several thousand people were employed in different tasks.

But what one was really searching for was how to preserve the meat in such a way as to not jeopardize its quality and have it please the European palate. Around 1870, the Rural Society of the province of Buenos Aires offered a very important metallic reward for the person who could invent a technique that would preserve meat in those conditions. A Frenchman, Charles Tellier, discovered the way to artificially produce cold. It was by means of cold, then, that meat began to be preserved and exported, and what in 1879 was an experiment, later had enormous significance within the Argentine economy.

Meanwhile, Mitre tried to achieve coexistence between Buenos Aires and the interior, and Sarmiento strove to scatter schools throughout the country and to begin to change the customs and mentality of Argentine society through education and colonization. As for Avellaneda, he tried to surmount the tremendous economic crisis that afflicted the country in 1874-1875, a crisis that obliged the government to restrict its expenses significantly but did not prevent it from paying the credits that the Nation had assumed. Avellaneda established, in addition, a sort of experimental protectionism, as he imposed some moderately high customs tariffs that, unintentionally, favored some of the incipient national industries, above all, those that depended on the raw materials that the country produced, such as leather and wool.

In the interim, the political struggles were considerable. The Liberal Party, already divided into liberals and autonomists, was contending for power, and in 1877, reached a conciliation to have Adolfo Alsina be the successor of Avellaneda when the latter completed his term, in 1880. Although the conciliation of the two parties did not make everyone happy and some elements within Mitreism and Alsinaism rose up against it, it nevertheless was a kind of civilized political pact that permitted the future to be viewed with optimism. But the death of Alsina cast this policy of conciliation down, and in the firmament a new star appeared: General Roca, who had successfully carried out the Desert Campaign and was beginning to be supported by some elements of former Alsinaism. Mitreism, by contrast, opposed him. Furthermore, Roca obtained the backing of certain sectors in the interior of former federalism —dispersed by now, following the death of Urquiza—, and from mid 1879, no sooner had he returned from the Desert Campaign, he prepared himself for the fight for presidency of the Nation. The candidacy of Julio Roca —national in a certain way, as he had the support of the provinces and was sponsored by his brother-in-law Juárez Celman, governor of Córdoba— clashed against that of the governor of Buenos Aires, Carlos Tejedor, backed by a segment of Mitreism and of Alsinaism, a situation that unleashed a very complex political process. This confrontation, instead of being a struggle between two political candidacies, turned into a struggle between the Nation on one side and the province of Buenos Aires on the other. The Nation backed the candidacy of Roca, despite the hesitations of President Avellaneda; and the city of Buenos Aires and surrounding countryside, that of Tejedor.

During the months of June and July of 1880, the opposition between both parties led to an armed confrontation (not a revolution, for the party that initiated the hostilities was the national government) between the Nation and the province that resulted in many dead; more than two thousand, almost all *porteños*. There was a sort of siege of Buenos Aires, until the provincial government surrendered at the hands of the national government which, having moved to the locality of Belgrano, expelled from there the delegates who had adhered to the position of Buenos Aires, and filled their positions with delegates elected ad hoc.

Finally, taking advantage of the moment in which Buenos Aires was vanquished and under government control, and its troops, unarmed, Roca decided to audaciously put an end to the problem of the capitalization of Buenos Aires. He forced the sanction of a law by which the city of Buenos Aires was declared the capital of the Republic. That is, what the Constitution of 1853 said back in the early stages and was later modified at the request of the province of Buenos Aires, was in 1880 realized with this law, homologated furthermore by a special law of the province, by which it ceded the common land of the city of Buenos Aires for use as the Nation's capital.

Thus ended this ongoing process of the balance between Buenos Aires and the interior, which had endured since the final years of the viceroyalty. Henceforth, the city —whose differences with the interior of the country were very great— was in the hands of the National Executive Power, whose jurisdiction over it was direct. As for the province of Buenos Aires, it had to build another capital, the city of La Plata.

## A foundational year

The year 1880 was a foundational year, then, for many reasons. Firstly, the conquest of the desert ended: the Indians were driven out of the land they occupied and 15,000 square leagues were left at the disposal of progress: in reality, it was the land holders who managed to acquire the land, to which they went about assigning varying destinies. Secondly, two important developments came about whose significance, at the time, was not perceived: the modest exportation of wheat and the successful preservation of beef through artificial cold. Thirdly —and very important—, upon the transformation of Buenos Aires into the capital and having been achieved, following the presidency of Roca, the true foundation of a National State, the institutional problem of the country was resolved.

Up until that moment, the National State virtually did not exist; it was a guest of the city of Buenos Aires. During the turbulent days that preceded the Revolution of 1880, President Avellaneda, in the face of complaints by provincial deputies who demanded guarantees, would point to the watchman at the corner of his house and he would say to them: "What guarantee am I going to give you, if I haven't even power over that watchman there?"

From 1880 onward, the National State acquired an importance and a strength that previously it did not have, subject as it was to the problems derived from its relationship to the government of the Province, which in many cases was stronger than it was. The Bank of the Province of Buenos Aires, for example, was much more solid than the National Bank which, although it wasn't exactly the bank of the national government, functioned a bit like its agent. Subsequent to 1880, the National State had a seat and sufficient resources to create certain structures that would be extended to the whole country: national schools, federal courts, Army garrisons, public health, the *Banco Hipotecario* [Mortgage Bank], and the *Banco de la Nación* [Bank of the Nation]. In short: what Roca called the duties and functions of the State.

The year 1880, then, was a very important one in the fullest sense, and the figure that incarnated this process was General Roca, a native of Tucumán, barely thirty-seven years old who, out of pure luck, went about ascending the ladder until he became General of the Nation at the age of thirty-one and succeeded in stirring a movement of opinion that united a small number of *porteños* and many provincial folk for the purpose of sponsoring his candidacy as a figure of national unity.

To summarize, we could assert that between 1860 and 1880 the model began to be defined, the plan of what would become the Argentina of the end of the century. Although in those times many former elements, positive and negative, continued to exist, the world context, the changes of the national society, and the will of some of the leaders converged toward the making of a country that would show genuine identity and would clearly determine its role in the world. I am referring to the Argentina whose history stretches from the assumption of the presidency of Roca (1880) to the sanction of the Sáenz Peña Law (1912).

## CHAPTER VII

# A shaping of modern Argentina

*One has taken to calling the period that falls between 1880 and 1910, when the Sáenz Peña Law was sanctioned legal instrument that defined the confines of an era, the Conservative Order, or the Conservative Regime. The adjective is used incorrectly, as the people who gave impetus to the political, economic, social, and cultural processes during this time were not, in fact, conservative, for their intention was not that of conserving anything, rather on the contrary, that of modifying everything. The label is due to the fact that, subsequent to the Sáenz Peña Law, the political forces that were the mainstay of these years were self-described as or were called by others "conservative," and they constituted the foundation of the conservative parties that were to come into being later on.*

# The belle epoque

Throughout these three decades, the rest of the world was also going through a very special time, which posterity has named the *Belle Epoque* and which was characterized by the peace which prevailed in Europe at that time. The last war that had occurred had been the Franco-Prussian War, in 1870, and already in 1880, France —which, almost by accident, had elected a republican system instead of returning to a monarchy— asserted its economic strength and its political stability and placed itself once again at the head of Europe. The German empire, which in fact had been created out of the defeat of France, tended toward a very centralized regime under the empire. Bismarck had already disappeared, but his theories on the strengthening of the empire continued to be applied. The emperor William II, who had bellicose whims, converted his country in no time into something that inspired a fair amount of fear in the rest of the European continent.

Great Britain, also, had secured its power, and after the Boer War it completed the coloring of the planisphere with its vast overseas possessions. It was, undoubtedly, the most important power in the world, with its enormous fleet, huge trade, massive industry, and noteworthy institutional stability.

As for the United States, it began to reveal its strength, something which it did spectacularly in the war against Spain in 1898. In this war, which had the island of Cuba as its stage, the Spanish fleet was sunk in an almost pathetic way by a North American fleet whose superiority was overwhelming.

On the one hand, this meant that the United States was beginning to show itself partial to an imperialist style policy, which led it to virtually occupy Cuba, the Philippines, and Puerto Rico, and to adopt a meddling attitude in American affairs, with a sense of hegemonic power in the region. On the other hand, Spain, who at that time was enjoying a stable political system (of parties) for the first time in a century, felt the defeat of Cuba as a sort of national failure. This brought about a series of consequences, most of all of a literary and cultural nature, by way of the so-called Generation of 1898, who generated self-criticism regarding the events in Cuba.

Except for these two wars, that of Cuba and that of the Boers, in the south of Africa, the world lived basically in peace during this period and, consequently, stability was absolute; the availability of capital, very great; and the European immigration movement to different parts of America continued or increased. In these beginning years of the century, moreover, a sort of optimistic mood prevailed.

The idea of undefined universal progress, the elimination of nationalisms, the lesser importance that religious ideologies were apparently to have, the standardization of political and economic regimes throughout the world (where interchangeable coins practically were used and where the international commercial system had no sort of barriers or interferences) gave rise during this period to reasonable optimism. We have seen it in books, novels, works of theater, cinematographic films. It was believed that definitive world stability had been attained. This state of affairs, obviously, collapsed in 1914 with the First World War, but regardless, the Conservative Order in Argentina occurred within the context of a world with these very special characteristics.

## A project of nationhood

This period of thirty years bore witness to the birth of modern Argentina. To state it in graphic terms: if an average Argentine, who in 1880 or in 1879 might have been twenty years old, would have taken a look at the country, he would have seen a rather promissory project, endowed with interesting natural resources, but which lacked a capital and a National State; a country where a third of the territory was occupied by Indians and which had no money of its own nor presence in world trade. This is to say, that at some point it could function well, but that, for the time being, it had many stages to go through.

Thirty years later, this same Argentine, barely fifty years old, would have seen the most advanced country of South

America; one that had a perfectly logical and revenue-yielding insertion in international circles of investment, production, and consumption; one with the biggest railway network in Latin America and one of the biggest in the world; one with an admirable education system; one that distinguished itself from other nations of America because of its large middle class; and one that enjoyed political and institutional stability, which it had not known during its entire history. That is, that this Argentine, who at twenty had seen an Argentina in search of its maturation point, in 1910, during the celebration of the Centennial, could be proud of this truly successful country, where there was perhaps only one unfortunate aspect, about which we shall speak later.

Chronologically, this period began in 1880 with the first presidency of Julio Roca. The city of Buenos Aires had already been converted into the capital of the Republic by the laws of the Legislature of the province of Buenos Aires and of the National Congress. The National State had been structured in such a way that, in the words of the president himself, it would have to be above any disturbance or revolution. That is, it must possess the necessary authority so as to truly be the arbiter of conflicting interests in the life of the Nation.

Between 1880 and the sanction of the Sáenz Peña Law, we can block off three quite separate periods, politically speaking. The first began precisely in 1880 with the presidency of Roca, when the National Autonomist Party was in power, that is, the former Alsinaist party —or, at least a fraction— plus provincial groups which had supported Roca and became the main force of the governmental party by antonomasia. The hegemony of the Autonomist Party continued during the presidency (1886-1890) of Roca's brother-in-law, Miguel Juárez Celman, who accentuated the exclusivist character of officialism [the party in office] by declaring that the chief of the National Executive Power would also be the sole head of the officialist party. There were practically no other important parties in the country —although the word *parties* may be considered almost abusive in defining what were

Citizens swear loyalty to the National Constitution.
View of Plaza de la Victoria, daguerreotype of 1854.

European immigrants heading to America, circa 1862.

The Conquest of the Desert allowed the colonization of the pampa.

Buenos Aires harbour, circa 1860.

cliques of a sort, where the president of the Republic, the legislators, and the governors of the provinces —that is, those who were really governing and permitting the ideology in force to work— formed a tight mesh of political interests.

In 1890 this system suffered a grave setback with the Park Revolution and with the appearance of an opposition party, the Civic Union, which a year later would become the Radical Civic Union. From that moment on, Juárez Celman disappeared from the political scene and Roca returned, trying to make viable something that had been seriously called into question: the system he himself had set up years before.

Roca understood that this exclusivist form of governing, which had defined his presidency as much as it had that of Juárez Celman, had reached its end, and that henceforth the authority of the State would have to base itself on a confluence of political forces —forces that were not separated by any important concept, nor by a necessarily different proposal as regards the country, but simply by divergent interests. Thus it was that Roca sought an accord with Mitreism, which was practically excluded from official life since 1880, when it was defeated in the Tejedorist revolution.

After 1891, then, Mitreism, through different pacts, supported this system, this regime, and this order, from all of which it did not consider itself distant, despite certain nuances of differentiation. The accord managed to withstand victoriously the political problems of 1891, when radicalism launched into a very strong electoral campaign with the candidature of Bernardo de Irigoyen. It also withstood the terrible year of '93, studded with radical revolutions in almost all the country. The accord survived, then, and not only did it uphold Carlos Pellegrini in his presidency (1890-1892), but it helped him out of the economic crisis in which the country was submerged. It imposed Luis Sáenz Peña as president, as well, who resigned in 1896 and was replaced by his vice president, José Evaristo Uriburu. In 1898, Roca returned to the presidency for the second time and filled the office until 1904. Manuel Quintana, who in 1904 assumed office, died two years later, leaving his vice president, José Figueroa

Alcorta, in command. In 1910, it was Roque Sáenz Peña who assumed the presidency, only to die four years later and be replaced by his vice president, Victorino de la Plaza, who in 1915, surrendered the insignia of power to Hipólito Yrigoyen, the first president elected by the universal vote according to the new electoral law.

To summarize, let us say that during the Conservative Regime we can identify a first period that goes from '80 to '90, marked by the exclusivism of the National Autonomist Party; a second period, that begins in '91 and is characterized by a permanent accord with Mitreism, accord which permits withstanding the situation even in moments as grave as the revolutions of '93 and that of 1905; a third period, during which we can observe, from Quintana's appearance in the presidency onward, the progressive political elimination of General Roca and his replacement by those forces that in 1912 would sanction the Electoral Law. These three periods frame the development of some ideas that characterize the Conservative Regime and which we shall take a look at next.

## Ideology

In the first place, during these decades the ideology of Juan Bautista Alberdi, which we have examined in previous chapters, was put into effect: a civil society that offered all the guarantees and all the rights necessary to prosper, enrich oneself, educate one's children, etc., but in which political rights were not yet conceded, since there was no certainty that the people were capable of exercising those rights sensibly. Regarding this issue there was a pact, an accord, a permanent conciliation between forces that, although they had nuances of their own, on the whole they coincided entirely with this proposal. Be they Rocaists, Mitreists, Pellegriniists, modernists, Sáenz Peñaists, or Udaondoists, all agreed to postpone an electoral reform that would permit the unconditional surrender of the vote to the masses. They shared a policy that basically consisted in opening frontiers abroad to encourage men, ideas, goods, capital, even fashion to arrive.

This was the common ideology of those men generally called "the generation of '80," even though they were not a generation, rather a group of two hundred to three hundred personalities in the whole country. As a rule, they had been educated in the same schools and universities, they spoke the same language, they shared the same ideology and the same code of behavior, they knew one another, and they were even friends. They could compete for power fiercely, but in the end they felt the same way about the country and its destiny.

This regime, shaped by friends who, though they fought publicly, did not differ much as concerned how to run the country or the future they hoped for it; they also shared a certain understanding of the world. But this was not an affair solely of the political leadership of the time; all of Argentine society shared it, without the need to study the topic much nor to inform themselves much about what was happening. It occurred intuitively, because many tendencies that came from the past converged at that moment to find ideal conditions for development in the world and in the country.

Argentina thus succeeded in intelligently inserting itself in the circles of consumption and production through the rational exploitation of land, applying the technology of the era to achieve higher income-yield capacity. This is one of the most interesting phenomena of the era and has been much studied. It never ceases to fill one with admiration, this collective motion, this movement that, without the need for departments of planning, nor flow charts, nor seminars, nor anything of the sort, saw to it that Argentina did exactly what it had to do at the time. That is, to try to exploit the land, the great resource that it had in order to attain precisely the type of production that, at that time, could be exported and, thus, could have presence in world trade. This was achieved by introducing and applying some techniques that had become rather cheap and accessible, and whose utility was demonstrated by their experimental application.

In the first place, wire fencing, whose use was already known, but which only became widespread in the decade of 1880. Wire fencing meant that a proprietor could feel the physical materialization of his property, instead of that vague perception that orignated in colonial times, according to which John Doe's property went from that umbra tree over there to the edge of the brook. Perimetrical wiring, by contrast, indicated concretely what the property limits were and, more importantly, it made possible the division of the countryside into pasture plots. That is, the separation of pasture ground with wire fencing and rustic gates, which permitted a division between agriculture and livestock, and prevented sown land from disappearing in the course of the night, trampled on by cattle. Moreover, thanks to this new system, one approached a much more rational handling of corrals. The calves could be separated from their mothers, sending a flock of cattle to the alfalfa field so they could finish fattening themselves.

Another extremely important technological element was the mill, which meant that there would be water wherever one desired. The propietor no longer needed to look for a lagoon, a river, or a stream so that the animals could go to water. The wind was what did the work of sucking up water from subterranean water tables and emptying it into the large circular water tank from where the animals could drink. This made it possible to increase the country's exploitable land.

Furthermore, the first seeders and the first steam reapers also began to be seen (this is easy to confirm because of the advertisements in the newspapers of the period); naturally, these made work in the field much easier, and allowed for the replacement of the farm laborer and the ox-driven plow by large machines that did a more selective and profit-yielding job.

The other fundamental technological element, which was not an Argentine invention but totally changed the vision of our countryside and its image, was artificial cold. It allowed the cattle breeders of Buenos Aires to make their dream come true, they who since the era of the *vaquerías* had been racking their brains over how to preserve beef in such a way as to turn it into something tasty, and not into that salted food that only slaves could stomach.

Following 1879, when the first refrigerated ship managed to transport its merchandise successfully to Europe, cold-storage plants began to be installed and red meat improved in quality (to satisfy the European market there was a move from frozen mutton to beef). One sought a more fatty meat, tastier, from a type of animal that had a more precocious development; and thus began the crossbreeding of cattle, which until then had been lean, big horned, long-legged, and a roamer. What was wanted was an animal that roamed little and fattened signficantly and quickly.

The physiognomy of the Argentine countryside changed, as did the *estancias,* which were gradually turned into great emporiums. The former central portions of the *estancia* were replaced by French style houses or Norman castles. The production was so profitable, that in a little less than thirty years Argentina became the number one exporter of grains in the world and the number two exporter of frozen meat, following the United States. Our country had realized how to slip into world commerce, and it did so quickly and in the best way possible.

## Debts

To put up wire fencing, to create mills, to crossbreed cattle and to sow, an investment of capital was necessary and, usually, in order to do it, proprietors fell into debt. This was one of the causes of the crisis of '90, although it had been an intelligent indebtedness, because its objective was to capitalize the countryside. The proprietors would lease more or less large strips of their land to immigrants, generally, farmers who would pay in spices or cash according to the contracts that were made, and who began to bring about what James Scobie, a North American researcher, called the "Revolution of the Pampas." That is, the conversion of this land, which until then did not have rational exploitation, into an amazing source of oleaginous plants and of grains.

This feat is one of the fundamental characteristics of the thirty years that we are describing. Through exports (which are also those that counterbalanced the economic and financial problem during the crisis of '90), what had been a peripheral country inserted itself in the world, where henceforth it would have not only commercial but social presence, as well: that of the Argentine travelers, the rich *estancia* owners who settled in Paris or who traveled there to live, to undergo treatment, to die, or simply to enjoy themselves.

Within very few years one spoke of Argentina as a sort of El Dorado. This image was corroborated by almost all the travelers who visited us and who, in large part, left admiring the country and the amazing transformation that was being carried out. This also created an air of optimism, a mood not very different from that which the world at the time was experiencing, only in the case of Argentina it was materially verifiable. New cities sprung up, such as La Plata, or so many others; railways were laid there where there was no one; in the interior of the country, islets such as Mendoza or Tucumán appeared, where the protection of the grape-growing, wine-producing, and sugar industries permitted extraordinary prosperity.

These factors and, the progressive but very rapid creation of a middle class, in addition, distinguished the Argentina of these years from other countries of Latin America, where what existed was a very rich oligarchical class, generally resting firmly on the ownership of land, and an enormous magma of people who didn't live in a style very different from that of the colonial era. In Argentina, by contrast, there was a population formed mostly with white immigration, whose children received the benefits of an obligatory education, which was organized almost parallel to the policy of immigration and that of pacification.

## Immigration, education and peace

It could be said, then, that the policy of the Conservative Regime was defined by three desires of the State: in the first place, immigration, one of the most faithful continuities of the thinking of Alberdi who, as we have already said, had

proposed the need to foment it. Alberdi imagined a prefer-
ably Anglo-Saxon immigration that would go about changing
the ethnic type of our people, so as to teach them work
habits, economy, respect for authority, et cetera. Although the
immigrants that disembarked were not Anglo-Saxons —which
provoked Sarmiento's protest, when he saw Poles, Jews,
Arabs, and Syrians arrive: "These were not the immigrants we
wanted"—, it was in any event a type of immigration that in
general brought in cheap manual labor and added new elements to a population still very small compared to the enormous extension of our country.

In this sense, the immigration policy that the governments
of the Conservative Regime went ahead with was very broad
and in no way discriminatory. There were no impediments to
any type of immigration. Even Roca, during his first presidency, named a special immigration agent to try to divert toward
Argentina the tide of Russian Jews who were fleeing from the
*pogroms,* generally to the United States. Precisely in these
final years of the century, some colonies of Jews began to
settle in the city of Buenos Aires. The policy, then, was very
broad and, though at some point there were voices raised to
protest against some type of immigration that apparently
would not interest the country, at no point were restrictive
laws sanctioned.

In the second place, the State took care of education.
Undoubtedly, in this, too, the Conservative Regime was
faithful to the thinking not so much of Alberdi as of
Sarmiento. The need to educate a sovereign people, on
which Sarmiento had insisted, was progressively becoming
reality following 1882, when the National Council of Education was created and was given funds and autonomy. From
then on, primary schools —which would be the institutions
that would feed the national [high] schools, already created
by Mitre, and the two traditional universities in Argentina,
that of Córdoba and that of Buenos Aires— began to multi-
ply in the country.

The educational system at the primary school was
admirable. We must not forget above all article V of the

Constitution, which established, as one of the conditions in order that the National State respect the autonomy of the provinces, the development of primary education.

Given that some provinces, impoverished after '80 (growth had not been equal for all), could not maintain an organization of primary education on the order of what was desirable, after 1905, with the sanction of the Láinez Law, it was established that the Nation had an obligation to help those provinces that could not by themselves maintain primary education in accordance with what was needed.

The truth is, that this concern for primary education on the part of the leaders of the Regime did them honor. Because immigration plus popular education meant of necessity that ten, fifteen, twenty years later, there would be a new generation of children of immigrants who would claim their place in the sun in the political realm and who also would want to govern the country. Those men of the Regime knew that education was going to imply, in the long or short run, their displacement: nevertheless, they preferred to educate and sanctioned Law 1.420, according to which primary education was obligatory (that is, parents must send their children to school), free (it would not cost them a cent), and secular (it would not have a confessional tenor, guaranteeing the citizen, thereby, that in school his child would not be called to religious confession).

Immigration and education were two important pillars of Argentina. The third was peace, the deliberate intention to not get involved in any conflict with neighbors.

What today seems to be an antiquated postulate, in that era was quite an important decision, because there were pending border questions. Although the relationship with Brazil had been fairly well established, the same was not true for Chile nor for Bolivia; nevertheless, the resolution of border problems, most of all with Chile, in order to avoid an arms race that could be ruinous, was a constant concern of the leaders of the time: not only of Roca and of Pellegrini, but also of Mitre himself.

After several peaks of tension and several treaties, in 1902,

Argentina and Chile accepted the arbitration of Her British Majesty and, through the famous Pacts of May, a sort of *statu quo* was affirmed that would last many years. There were also moments of tension in relations with Brazil: the policy of Estanislao Zeballos under Figueroa Alcorta could have taken things to a rather disquieting state of risk that, finally, was dissolved by the action of men such as Roca, who postulated the need for Argentina to maintain a pacifistic position. Not only on principle, but also because it was thought that peace was something which in the end produced revenue, whereas war, though one might be triumphant, destroyed countries.

## The national state

Apart from the policy of immigration, education, peace, and the opening of the borders, apart from a system that avoided conflict through pacts, apart from the optimism, there existed a National State that worked. Until 1880, we said, there was no National State; only a government that lived on loan in the city of Buenos Aires and directed a national army forged during the War of the Triple Alliance, but without the power to avoid the challenges, including armed, that the provincial governments or political forces provoked, as in 1874.

After 1880, the National State not only had a capital, but also asserted itself through the creation of important organisms such as the National Council of Education, the *Banco Hipotecario Nacional,* and the ministries in force in the entire country, such as Public Works, for example, or that of Public Education. And with the formation of a national army, moreover, which really had strength after the law of compulsory conscription. So much so, that in the civil-military disturbances of 1890, 1893, and 1905, in which no small amount of individual soldiers participated, the army remained loyal to the government in power and to the established institutions.

It is risky to say that the Conservative Regime was liberal. It was indeed in thought, in its belief in the need to respect freedom of speech and freedom of the press, to maintain the dignity of institutions. In a certain sense, even, its thinking was liberal as regards the fact that the economic order was helped overall by an opening of the borders. But those men had a clear conscience that the State should exist; it should be strong, authoritarian, and should arbitrate constantly the interplay of interests within the community; it had duties and functions which it could not abandon.

When Juárez Celman, plagued by the economic crisis, put 24,000 leagues of fiscal land up for sale in Europe in 1889-90 (a sale which never materialized); when he put up for lease the health works of the city of Buenos Aires, that is, *Obras Sanitarias* [water and sewage system]; when he sold a few national railroads, Roca, obvious artificer of the Conservative Order, complained bitterly to a certain friend and said that if it were true that governments were bad administrators, then we should put a For Sale flag outside the barracks, the post offices, the telegraph offices, the income collection offices, the customhouses, and all that constitutes, portrays "the duties and functions of the State." In other words, these men, advocates in general of liberal thought, knew that a country that was becoming defined, as Argentina was during that era, needed a State that clearly assumed its duties. Not in order to interfere in private initiative, but to mark the limits that this latter should have and to promote the development of areas in which individual interest had no part.

## Challenges

At the same time that the country received immigration, that a certain industrial infrastructure was created, that a proletariat was established, ideas of social revindication arrived, as well, incarnated in the anarchistic or socialist leaders; these ideas permeated deep within the underprivileged classes. Above all, after 1904 and 1905, this system, which in many aspects had been so progressive, began to acquire a repressive character and sanctioned the Law of Residency. Some men of the Regime were frightened that disturbances could occur whose final phase would be the overthrow or tearing down of the order of things which had been created.

The reasons for alarm, in reality, were not so serious. There were some strikes, some unrest, but at no point in the decade of 1900 to 1910 could one have justified this repression, indicative more of a fear that had not been within the spirit of the founders of the Conservative Order. Neither Roca; nor Pellegrini; nor Mitre himself; nor the two Sáenz Peñas, the elder and the younger, slackened the optimistic tone that they had had with respect to the destiny of the country and the character of its people, but the latter epigones of the Regime, men like Marcelino Ugarte and other minor figures who are not worth mentioning because they have been practically forgotten, were terrified by what could happen with these anarchistic and socialist agitators. The repressive laws and the police action revealed a point of inflection in a policy which until then had been generous.

In any case, toward 1910 or 1912, the conservative experiment had achieved complete success. The country, designed by the thinking of Alberdi and still on the road toward development in 1880, in 1910, had already reached the absolute vanguard in Latin America. It was the most brilliant transplant of European civilization that had been seen up to that time.

One aspect had yet to be reformed. An unfortunate aspect, which provoked not only the criticism of those who were impartial, but also the continual protest of the political force that radicalism was. It was that aspect of politics based fundamentally in the pact, in the covenant, in the accord, as has already been said. Although obviously it fulfilled a certain purpose —it avoided conflicts and confrontations—, this policy permitted nevertheless a totally fictitious as well as a profoundly immoral electoral system. The distribution of power, which had characterized the regime during years and years, was a reality that undoubtedly demoralized public life, dissuaded the best people from political life, made it so that the spectacle of Parliament had a false foundation, and created a very vulnerable flank to this panorama of the republic which, in other areas, was really of sound judgment and successful.

It was then that Roque Sáenz Peña, pressured by a series of factors that we shall take a look at further on, promoted the sanction of those laws which carried his name and signified a drastic change in the politics of the country. The Sáenz Peña Law replaced the dishonest, fraudulent, and violent electoral system of former years with a system wherein a citizen could vote freely and where, in addition to guarantees to be able to vote, a system was established whereby the party that won the elections would not govern alone, rather it would co-govern with the party that followed it in number of votes by way of the open-ticket system.

The truth is that this law was sanctioned in order to whitewash a censurable, and therefore untenable, situation. The men who had formed the republic —Mitre, Alberdi— were dead, but their political descendants had all the right in the world to think that the electorate was going to follow along with them in this sort of homologation or ratification of its legitimacy, because the success obtained had been great. In thirty years they had converted a peripheral country, poor, fragmented, anarchic, into this grand, opulent country which stood apart from all of Latin America. And yet, the electorate turned its back on these old creative forces and fell into the arms of a new force, which was an unknown, which did not have a platform, whose leader was also unknown, and which, in the end, signified something totally new within Argentine politics.

The thirty years that elapsed between 1880 and 1910 were fundamental for the shaping of modern Argentina. In certain respects, we are the inheritors of that era. The huge public offices that can be seen in all the cities of the republic, and the large parques where we go for recreation, are from that period. The affirmation of the fundamental institutions, in which the life of a country becomes stable —from primary education to the university, including the Armed Forces—, are offshoots of that regime which, though it committed many political sins, had, on the other hand, good instinct and good intuition to discover what role Argentina should fill in the world of that period.

# The cost of progress

The prosperity of this period depended in large part on the production of the so-called *pampa húmeda* [wet pampa]; that is, of cereals, first; of oleaginous plants next; and above all, of meat. Consequently, the region that was privileged was that which encompassed a good part of the province of Buenos Aires, the south of Santa Fe, the south of Córdoba, some part of San Luis perhaps. Two islets were also privileged, grape-growing and wine-making, and sugar production.

But this type of prosperity, as much as the entire corresponding infrastructure (for example, the network of railways plopped down at the port of Buenos Aires) forgot or stayed away from some regions of the country whose production didn't arouse that much interest at the time: for example, mining production or the more or less handcrafted industries of the provinces of the north and northwest, which suffered relative backwardness during these years. Thus as the provinces of the littoral grew formidably, there were others —Catamarca, for example— that were more important during the period of the Confederation than during that of the Regime.

As for the demographic aspect, impoverishment was reflected in the censuses, and politically, through parliamentary representation, which depended on the population of each province and was adjusted after each census. As time went on, it began to be noticed that the provinces of the north and the northwest had less parliamentary representation in relation to the provinces of the littoral, all of which implied rather significant consequences: when certain public works were voted, for example, there was a preference for the provinces of the littoral, as a function of the wealth that they generated, and those other, old, founding provinces continued paralyzed in backwardness.

Social growth was also uneven. Many people got rich, and a very snobbish and prodigal class began to be created, at the same time that other social sectors suffered the consequences of a difficult and competitive process, where there was not a State which offered medical assistance nor was there any social security; where he who was dying of hunger, died and that was that; and he who was thrown out of a job ended up in the street without any type of indemnification.

There were not, therefore, social laws such as those that existed later. What there was, was a guarantee of the State that worked very well: that of money which, once the Argentine Peso was created, retained the same value during those years, something that allowed for the possibility of saving. The peso that was put away one day was going to be worth exactly the same ten, five, or twenty years later. This made it possible for those who had a bit of luck and the vision to save to be able to buy in installments, acquire land, build themselves a house; in short, create their own pension.

Uneven growth but formidable growth, which at its core also contained instruments of self-correction, such as that which made the transfer of power from an elitist system to a system of popular parties possible. The history of the shaping of modern Argentina is that of an admirable progression forward which did not happen by chance, rather it was fostered in just the right way by a lucid nucleus of leaders within the context of favorable conditions that would never again present themselves with the magnitude of that era.

*As our story moves forward in time, the topics to be treated diversify and it becomes more difficult to sum up those distinct sectors of life in society that, in previous eras, appeared indistinguishable from one another. The autonomy that these take on now demands a treatment that, in view of the available space, we shall not be able to give them. From hereon, then, the focus will be predominantly political, although there may of necessity be references to the economic, social, and cultural sectors characteristic of each phase.*

# CHAPTER VIII

# Radical democracy

The period that we shall look at in this chapter is that which begins in 1912 with the sanction of the Sáenz Peña Law and ends in 1930, a historical moment in which democracy, to which the Sáenz Peña Law contributed so much, suffered its first breach and the country entered into a phase characterized by, among other things, the active presence of the Army or of the Armed Forces in political life. Between 1912 and 1930, nevertheless, the constitutional continuity was perfect and the interplay of parties reached a reasonable level of pluralism, of coexistence, of formation and replacement of candidates. Aside from having been the most brilliant period of the Argentine Parliament in all its history, it was characterized by the predominance of or, if you prefer, the hegemony of the Radical Civic Union.

## The U.C.R.

In previous chapters we have deliberately omitted speaking about the UCR (*Unión Cívica Radical,* or Radical Civic Union), but it is now opportune to address it, insofar as it was the great protagonist of the civic movement and of the opinion that exerted pressure to obtain a law that assured a guaranteed, obligatory, universal suffrage, with an open ticket: in essence, all that the Sáenz Peña Law promoted. Radicalism was not only the grand artificer of this law, but also its grand beneficiary following the first elections and, above all, when in 1916 Hipólito Yrigoyen was elected president of the Nation.

Radicalism is a force that has suffered certain variants in its political and programmatic nature, as could only be the case given that it has already surpassed one hundred years of existence. Also in the era to which we are referring, it had endured some changes with respect to the moment of its foundation. In September of 1889, a group called the Civic Union was created; it was made up of very heterogeneous elements: Mitreists, former autonomists and republicanists, Catholics resentful of the secular laws of Roca and of Juárez Celman, or simply youth without previous political affiliation.

Under the banner of the fight against corruption, against electoral fraud, and against the personalist style government that Juárez Celman had incarnated, in July of 1890 this group — supported by several military elements— launched into a revolution, the Park Revolution, which, although defeated, provoked the resignation of Juárez Celman, his replacement by Carlos Pellegrini, and a new political situation symbolized by the presence, within the walls of the Park, of men such as Leandro Alem; Bernando de Irigoyen; Juan B. Justo, founder of the Socialist Party; or Lisandro de la Torre, founder of the Progressive Democracy party. Thus, the Park Revolution was a landmark event within the political history of Argentina.

In January of 1891, this political group, the Civic Union, proclaimed the presidential candidature of Bartolomé Mitre, accompanied by Bernardo de Irigoyen; a luxury ticket. Bartolomé Mitre was the most prestigious man of the country and Bernardo de Irigoyen did not fall far behind. But in addition, this ticket had another significance, that of symbolizing the union of the two great historical currents of Argentine politics. Mitre was adamantly *antirrosista* [against those who supported Rosas]; he was a convinced liberal. Irigoyen was a man who had served the Rosas regime in his distant youth and who came from autonomism.

These two great personalities, upon coming together in an electoral ticket, were representing the best country vis-à-vis the possibility of overturning the regime structured by Roca and carried to its most extreme form of expression by Juárez Celman.

But it happened that Roca, Minister of the Interior —with roguishness or with patriotism— conceived the idea of arriving at a grand agreement that would eliminate the elections, that would avoid the electoral struggle and the confrontation that he could tell was going to occur. He proposed then to Mitre to be a candidate not only of the Civic Union, but also of Rocaism, of the forces that he led; Mitre accepted immediately. It is likely Mitre was convinced of this solution beforehand, because although he was traveling through Europe when the Park Revolution took place, he had news through his many friends about the political situation that Roca was plotting.

The fact is that Mitre accepted to be the candidate of practically all the political forces of the country, ceding the second condition of the ticket; that is, he accepted that the Rocaists propose a candidate, in place of Bernardo de Irigoyen. This was received like a bucket of cold water in the ranks of the *cívicos,* who accused Mitre of repeating the same personalistic attitudes for which he had previously reproached his Rocaist and Juárezist adversaries.

## The revolution

After a period of rather acidic discussions, the Civic Union split up. On the one hand remained the Mitreists who, adopting diverse names and figures, lasted as a party until 1910 or 1912 and, on the other, the radicals, who followed Alem. "Radicals" inasmuch as Alem, in his speeches, would emphasize that he was radically opposed to this agreement; that he wanted the populace to be given the freedom to vote so that the populace could elect the best candidates.

In 1891 the Convention of the brand new Radical Civic Union proclaimed as its presidential candidate Bernardo de Irigoyen and carried out what could be considered the first Argentine electoral campaign. Alem traveled through almost the entire republic —only in some cases accompanied by Bernardo de Irigoyen, who was already an old man for such coming and going—, and he made a campaign tour that aroused much enthusiasm in the interior. From then on the party remained organized in most of the country and not only in the Capital, where it had had its structures up until that time.

Henceforth, radicalism was characterized by certain particularities that turned it into a rather unique party. In the first place, it was a force that raised the banners of the revolution. But not the revolution understood as an ultimate recourse to which one arrives because the political mechanisms make an acceptable electoral solution impossible; rather, revolution as

a sort of permanent objective, as a way of drastically changing the prevailing and established order of things.

Effectively, radicalism joined the revolution of 1893, when
Alem himself organized an insurrection in Rosario and uprisings occurred in the provinces of Buenos Aires (headed by
Hipólito Yrigoyen, nephew of Alem), Tucumán, San Luis, and
twice in Santa Fe. The year 1893 was very tough for the government led by Luis Sáenz Peña, who accepted the presidency after Mitre renounced his candidature —seeing that he
was not the figure of national union that he had desired.

The flag of the revolution continued to be raised by
Yrigoyen, most of all after the death of Alem, and was manifested in 1905 by way of a vast civic-military revolutionary
movement which, initially, was successful. It managed to take
control of points as important as Rosario, Bahía Blanca, Mendoza, and Córdoba (though not the Federal Capital), but after
the third day it was overcome. Despite this defeat, Yrigoyen
continued to use revolutionary rhetoric, and the activists of
radicalism would speak of the revolution as an objective
which would be ineluctably attained. As late as 1907 and
1908, there are records of speeches by radical leaders, where
at the end the listeners were invited to join in the next radical
revolution, which this time was not going to fail.

In the second place, especially after the directorship of
Yrigoyen, radicalism chose a very difficult two-way track,
very self-sacrificing, very unique within Argentine politics: it
chose the path of intransigence. "Intransigence" meant that
radicalism —as a dogma, so to speak— would not accept any
type of pact or conciliation with any party whatsoever, it
would not accept alliances of any kind; it rejected this
recourse that, within the political life of civilized nations, is
used with relative frequency when two parties that consider
themselves allied, at a given moment, join their forces to play
the power game.

Radicalism rejected all of this because it was aware that its
nature was not that of a political party, but that of a civic crusade, that of a movement which took on with historic projection the best of the Argentine past and which, at that time,

represented the good citizens who fought against the malefic Regime. Because of these characteristics, radicalism did not think itself part of the political system and disdained any alliance with another group.

The other track chosen by Yrigoyen was that of abstention; that is, lack of participation in the elections, a refusal to play the game proposed by the regime because, in his opinion —and, in reality, it was this way—, the conditions were not right for a citizen to be able to vote with liberty. Until these conditions were perfectly established, radicalism would refuse to participate in the electoral stakes which, in his opinion, were simply a farse typical of that opprobious regime which he condemned.

These three aspects —the revolution as a banner, intransigence as a characteristic form of conduct, and electoral abstention— gave radicalism an "antiestablishment" character. It was not a party incorporated into legality, but rather one that questioned everything in existence as far as official structure, putting this latter in danger with its constant revolutionary protest, with its abstention from participating in the elections, with its refusal to form alliances with the other forces.

Normally this strategy would seem to be suicidal: a party that apparently did not aspire to be in power, that did not even recognize alliances, that insisted on a revolutionary banner after it was demonstrated that the Army would not go along with it. (Although the revolution of 1905 had initial successes and compromised many young officials, in reality it did not have the massive support of the armed forces.)

Yrigoyen had to exercise very strict control to keep his party in operation under these conditions. Consider what the rare spectacle was, at the end of the first decade of the century, of a party organized throughout the country, with open councils in all the neighborhoods of the big cities; a party that had newspapers and assembled its organisms, committees, and conventions, but that did not participate in elections. For those who were politically active in this force, the situation was very strange and not very gratifying from a political point of view. Yrigoyen, on various occasions, had to apply all the harshness of his authority to withstand the rebellion of certain elements, generally of the upper class, who yearned within the party to begin the normal *cursus honorum* of the republican life.

## An undefined platform

What was radicalism trying to accomplish anyway? Its platform was a mystery: at the outset, under the direction of Alem, it limited itself to demanding public morality, electoral purity, and effective carrying out of the federal system. But these are simply prerequisites for good government. Under normal conditions, no party would demand "administrative morality," because one presumed that this should exist, in the same way that one supposedly needn't demand "electoral freedom." The objective that Alem was after, then, was not too well defined, which justified Carlos Pellegrini's statement that radicalism, more than a party, was a feeling.

The same thing occurred under the direction of Yrigoyen, who systematically refused to establish any concrete platform for his party. So much so, that in 1908 he broke off political relations with the most important radical leader of the interior, Doctor Pedro Molina, who was calling for a protectionist, radical pronouncement for the interior of the country. Yrigoyen, in a famous epistolary polemic that they maintained, suggested to him that the mission of radicalism as a civic crusade was so important that to ask him to lower himself to the level of trifles such as protectionism or free trade was tantamount to insulting the grandeur of his mission. Years later, in 1916, when the Convention of the UCR proclaimed Yrigoyen as its candidate, his friends attacked a proposal that was made to approve an extremely detailed electoral program. Thus, the party's harangue consisted simply in the fulfillment of the Constitution —this, too, was not a platform, for every party must respect the Constitution in order to enter into legality.

This force that time and time again called for revolution, that conspired constantly, that did not ally itself with other parties, that did not participate in elections, is a mystery within Argentine politics of this century. Curiously, its characteristics gave it enormous strength and an identity that differed from the rest of the parties of the system —Rocaism, Pellegrinism, modernism, Mitreism—, which distributed power among themselves using different names (one has to remember that in this period there were no laws regarding political parties; names would come into use as quickly as they would fall by the wayside).

Within this confusing political picture, radicalism stood out because of its ethical conduct, which made it attractive in the public opinion, above all as far as youth were concerned.

It did not have a clientele that could be called distinguished. There were men of the Argentine patriciate and sectors of urban workers, rural peasants and *estancia* owners: a curious sociological phenomenon, as it defied all ideas of class. When Ricardo Rojas joined in 1932, he said: "I went to radicalism and those who welcomed me were the grandchildren of our founding fathers and the children of immigrants."

It is possible that Yrigoyen might have refused to outline too detailed a platform regarding the future governmental action of radicalism, precisely because it was a force that included very heterogeneous elements. The pretext of carrying out the Constitution was an intelligent measure to avoid having to commit himself to basic principles that could later be re-claimed by one or another sector of Argentine life.

## The first elections

The hegemony of Roca having ended, José Figueroa Alcorta, a man with no political power, presided over the country (1906-1910). Pellegrini, Mitre, and Bernardo de Irigoyen had died, and Roque Sáenz Peña, who arrived from Europe with the idea of perfecting Argentine democracy —conception that carried great weight within the intellectual and ruling classes of the country—, was appointed president (1910-1914). The country functioned quite well; in thirty years it had been successful in the transference of a European civilization to an anarchic, poor country, with a third of its territory occupied by Indians, without money of its own nor a federal capital. In 1910, on the other hand, it could show itself off as the most perfect expression of European civilization in America, with a formidable education service, a middle class which set it apart from the other countries of the continent, great institutional continuity, and an important ruling class.

Notwithstanding, it maintained a totally fraudulent, dishonest system. Sáenz Peña believed that conditions were ripe for effecting some change in this respect. He convoked Yrigoyen to request that his party contribute two or three ministers to his cabinet, but the radical caudillo declined, saying that the only thing his party wanted was that one could vote. Yrigoyen's answer demonstrated his political genius, seeing that had his party entered the cabinet, it would have remained ensnared. Contrarily, it remained somewhat distant from this process, embossing the identity it had achieved through the principles of intransigence, abstention, and revolution, maintained up until this time.

Sáenz Peña created a standard civic model, supported by the law and the army, that would guarantee a citizen could vote freely; a closed voting space, so that no one might interfere; presence of the law at the polls; and, above all, an open list, to encourage the formation of the two major parties, with premiums for the winner and the runner-up, though without any incentive for a third party.

And so the pressure began within radicalism for the party to abandon abstention. Yrigoyen refused, doubting that the government's promises would be fulfilled, but he could not withstand the pressure of Santa Fe in the first elections, which took place in March of 1912. The logical thing would have been that the Argentine electorate homologate the men who, in thirty years, had achieved a transformation of the country. But the electorate had a different set of priorities and gave importance to the ethics that Yrigoyen had maintained without participating in schemes or deals of power during fifteen or twenty years, and claiming instead an electoral law such as that which was being enjoyed then.

Radicalism triumphed in Santa Fe and a week later, in the Federal Capital, with socialism winning the minority. In later years —Sáenz Peña being already dead and with Victorino de la Plaza as president—, the radical majority was secured, and radical and socialist congressmen, who questioned the previous era, entered. In 1916, Hipólito Yrigoyen was consecrated president by popular vote and a new phase began for the radical hegemony.

By contrast, the provision of the Sáenz Peña Law as to the formation of the two major parties was not respected. That radicalism might govern facing conservatism which, bringing together the old forces from before 1916, would use all its governmental experience in the diverse forums, would have been natural. But conservativism preferred to infiltrate in certain newspapers, in the Senate, in the financial sectors, in diplomacy, and it did not offer a democratic counterpoint to governing radicalism. In some cases, Yrigoyen intervened in conservative provincial governments using the argument that they had been elected fraudulently. Thus, inevitably, a radical hegemony was attained.

## Government action

Yrigoyen, on the other hand, had to confront the problems of the era. The World War, for example: Was Argentina neutral? Should relations be broken in favor of the Allies? On a different note, Should we support or repress university students? What to do with the strikes of the railroad and construction workers, which were affecting the economy of the country: put pressure on the owners or support them? In essence, there were a whole series of issues that obliged him to consider options.

Yrigoyen, who entered the government during the First World War, had to maintain Argentina's neutrality, sometimes with difficulties. Imports became scarce, as Great Britain, Germany, and France were participating in the war. Factories closed for lack of raw materials and complicated the scenario that much more. At the same time, unable to import certain goods, the country opted for manufacturing them, opening up the perspective for creating a national industry, parallel to the revaluation of agricultural products (grains, meat) needed by the countries at war.

The government of Yrigoyen, then, maintained neutrality plus the economic structure, it did not attack the landowning oligarchy; it took up the concerns of the student body, and, almost in silence, it produced an egalitarian revolution. Countless new Argentines —children of immigrants, beneficiaries of the public education law that had permitted them to go to school and to university— were incorporated, without being discriminated against, into public offices —elected as well as administrative. Thus ended the phase in which these positions were only filled by people with certain last names. Yrigoyen and the radicalism of the period constituted a force of high egalitarian content.

What's more, this politcal hegemony that maintained radicalism yielded some benefits in social, economic, and cultural spheres. In regard to the latter, one can see a sort of return to more national motifs than those that had previously inspired musicians, poets, or painters. For example, what is shown by the work of the architect Martín Noel, who began to value the beauty of some of the chapels of the Northwest and of colonial architecture. In the field of music, one began to take inspiration from folkloric compositions, and Ricardo Rojas wrote his *History of Argentine Literature*. Although radicalism promoted an interesting movement that tried to distance itself from foreign motifs, nevertheless, it did not succeed in changing the basis on which Argentine life was founded.

## Radical hegemony

Meanwhile, these achievements permitted a moderate prosperity; an increase in the quality of life of the working class; and the backing of the middle classes, flattered by the possibility that their children might hold important public offices or be socially recognized. Thus radicalism began extending its political effectiveness, until in 1922, for example, it reached the point of controlling the country in an incomparable manner. Only the Socialist Party competed against it in the Federal Capital; in the interior, small provincial parties or small dissidences.

But there is a law of political science according to which, when a party maintains hegemony and operates almost with unanimity, the opposition is hatched within the very same party. When things are done in such a way that there exists no national forum where one can express diverse currents of opinion and different nuances of thought, then the struggle occurs within the dominant party. And this is what happened in the decade of 1920, when in 1924, radicalism became divided between "antipersonalists" and Yrigoyenists.

The antipersonalists maintained that they were against the caudillo's personal politics. The Yrigoyenists countered that their internal opponents were but a disguised form of conservatism, a bias of the right, and that they, the Yrigoyenists, better interpreted the popular, revolutionary, transforming, and Americanist character of radicalism. The struggle produced a very interesting movement of intellectual radicals who —through books, pamphlets, articles, and later, during the electoral campaign of 1928— gave coherence to that which during the government of Yrigoyen had only been a series of decisions on diverse issues.

All of what Yrigoyen had done in the area of international politics and social, economic, and university policy was strung together by intellectual, Yrigoyenist youth, and presented as a sort of program that made radicalism a party not very different from others in Latin America —as the Peruvian APRA and the Institutional Revolutionary Party in Mexico—, a party of strong popular content, moderately statist, anti-imperialist. That is, a party of the center left.

In 1928, when the six-year term of Alvear concluded, a confrontation between Yrigoyenist and personalist radicalism was produced, this latter supported by the conservatives and by a schism of the socialists called the Independent Socialist Party.

It ended with a crushing victory for Yrigoyen, to which

the name The Plebiscite was given, because the radical caudillo succeeded in accumulating double the votes of all the rest of the parties put together. And this, which at the time seemed to be a huge victory, in the end signified a negative element for the government of Yrigoyen, because it made radicalism turn conformist with respect to what was happening.

That popular support that the radicals believed was never going to end, was lost very quickly within two years, not only because of Yrigoyen's advanced age and of certain errors committed, but because of the obstinately antiradical and antidemocratic action of a series of forces that saw the future displacement of radicalism through free elections as very unlikely and sought the more direct route of conspiracy. It should be remembered that in the decade of 1920, Italian fascism had had great success as a proposal between capitalism and communism; that in Spain, Primo de Rivera governed with a sort of bloodless dictatorship, relatively benign, but which had put things in order; that in Germany there was incipient Nazism....

Faced with this not too brilliant spectacle that radicalism put on, that surrounded Yrigoyen and maintained itself in a position of intellectual comfort, having faith in the inveterate support of the majorities, many forces demanded a hierarchical government, which did not depend on the masses nor on the vote and which better represented the interests of the society which the politicians of the period —in their opinion— could not represent. This takes us to the eve of the revolution of 1930, a decisive moment in Argentine history, inasmuch as it signified the beginning of the armed forces' interference in politics and of a lack of faith in democracy, a democracy that was not perfect but that had achieved civilized, pluralist, tolerant political practices, which from this moment on, begin to vanish.

It is appropriate to stop for a reflection here. Since the first chapter, we have touched upon topics that in some way have had to do with the present time. When we talked about the foundation of the city of Buenos Aires, we described in a certain way, as well, the rivalries that Buenos Aires provoked and the problems, with respect to the different cities of the interior, that a city founded at the entrance to land laid the groundwork for. When we analyzed the creation of the viceroyalty, that clash between Buenos Aires and the interior continued to be present. And when we mentioned the May Revolution, we referred to the militarization of society that began to occur.

Otto Baur, an Austrian sociologist, said that countries are solidified histories. We, the historians of Argentina, do not in general create History solely to inform ourselves of what happened in the past, but to understand the country of today a little better, to help answer some of those questions that not only do we all ask ourselves individually at a certain point in life, but also a community such as ours asks collectively. We ask where we came from, where we are going, who we are, what is our purpose, why do certain things happen to us, why do we differentiate ourselves from others, what identity do we have, what can we do in the future, where do our talents lie....

History, although it does not answer all these questions — or, if it does answer them, it does not answer all of them well— helps to understand in some way where we stand, and this is its usefulness. In the last resort, the historian does not have a magic crystal ball that permits him to tell what will happen in the future, but to the extent that he can look with a long-term perspective at the phenomena that he is living, he is in a better position to alert society.

From this point of view, the evocation of the widely democratic experience that the country lived through from the Sáenz Peña Law until 1930, just as its abrupt annulment gives rise to constant reflection regarding the fragility of our political system and the impatience that many times has thwarted the possibility of enriching it and making it better.

## CHAPTER XI

# The revolution of 1930

*The Revolution of 1930 was an important moment of our contemporary history because it marked the end of an era and the beginning of another. It signified something that had not occurred up until then in Argentine constitutional history: the overthrow of a legitimate government by a military coup —or, in any case, a military civic coup. In my opinion, it was a truly catastrophic event because of the consecuences it implied and because of the promissory possibilities it closed off. I know that in expressing this I am in some way taking sides, but there is no reason why the historian should abdicate the values upon which his beliefs are supported, his position vis-à-vis the country and vis-à-vis the world.*

# The plebiscite

When I state that the revolution of September 6 was an institutional catastrophe, I am then forced not to hide the table of values on which I base my beliefs about the country. At any rate, although it may have been a catastrophe, a revolution obeys causes, and we have the obligation to examine them. In this sense we must backtrack a few years, to 1928, date of the elections that were remembered for a long time as "the plebiscite;" that is, when Hipólito Yrigoyen was consecrated as president for the second time.

They were elections that categorically marked two positions in the area of politics: those that adhered to what Yrigoyen signified and those who rejected that significance. Yrigoyen was the indisputable leader of the radicalism that followed him, although this latter had become divided three or four years earlier. One of the fractions was called "antipersonalist" and was made up of those who atacked the supposedly personalist methods of Yrigoyen himself. Today we would define it as a fraction of the center right.

The center-rightist tendency of antipersonalism is attested to by the circumstance that in the elections of 1928, the faction was openly supported by the conservative parties of the whole country who saw in the Melo-Gallo ticket the possibility of avoiding Yriogyen's access to power for a second time. Nevertheless, the latter, at the head of the Radical Civic Union in its traditional version, won the elections in an overwhelming manner: 840,000 votes to 460,000 for the entire opposition.

Paradoxically, this election, won by such a large margin, led the opposition to seek a return to power by way of other methods, by non-electoral methods. As for Yrigoyenism, the triumph obtained signified a very dangerous tranquilizer. The idea that the plebiscite was a true national pronouncement in favor of Yrigoyen justified all possible errors or future omissions, because the results had been so overwhelming and definitive that it seemed unlikely that there might be a modification in popular adhesion. This is one of the causes that, very remotely, begins to give us an idea of why the Revolution of 1930 occurred: the electoral outcome, which they saw as the country's jump into the void, was very disillusioning for the conservative forces.

In the second place, in 1930 Argentina was already suffering the backlash of the world crisis that had begun in November of 1929, in New York, with the famous stock market crash and the financial ruin of banks in the United States and in Europe. Many governments took measures, in the sense of establishing limitations to previously unrestricted international trade —control over foreign currency, customs protections—, in order to thus save their economies and finances from catastrophe. Let us not forget that our country up to this moment was exclusively an exporter of primary commodities with a very incipient industry, that is, an economy very vulnerable to international affairs. In '29, for example, exports from Argentina suffered a substantial reduction with respect to what had been exported until then.

In the third place, 1930 was a very special moment in the history of the world, above all European history, with the appearance of political systems opposed to the traditional democratic liberalism that had been in force in Europe and in the most civilized countries from the past century up to the First World War. Fascism, for example, had created order in Italy following 1923 and sought to turn the country into a power of the first order. The charismatic figure of Mussolini never ceased to attract many admirers throughout the world, even in the countries that would be his enemies, such as Winston Churchill in the United Kingdom. In the case of Spain, fascism was transformed into the dictatorship of Primo de Rivera.

On the other hand, in the Soviet Union the regime of Bolshevism was secured, which had triumphed in the Revolution of 1917 and which, after 1925, under the iron-like control of Stalin, attempted a massive industrialization of the country (apparently successful, as his epigones proclaimed throughout the whole world). What's more, in these years, apart from the crisis that shook the United States and apparently placed the entire capitalist system throughout the world in danger, several military coups occurred in Latin America that overthrew more or less democratic civil systems.

## A very special moment

Meanwhile in Argentina, politics was passing through a moment of mediocrity. It seemed that even the significance which the first government of Yrigoyen had, had become diluted: a peaceful revolution made from the top, an attempt to better distribute national wealth, to give the State a better position to arbitrate conflicting interests in the community, to introduce a little more justice within society, and to carry out a more nationalistic policy in the economic plan. The figure of Yrigoyen himself, already on in years, was, at least, that of a statesman who had lost his reflexes a little. A public administration blockage had not been reached, but yes, a certain slowness or a certain paralysis.

At any rate, one of the enigmas of this era is why the Argentine upper classes hated Yrigoyen with so much intensity, to the point of forgetting the legalist tradition of old conservativism and embarking on a revolution, when in truth Yrigoyen never attacked the economic foundations of what we could call the oligarchy; he even respected its styles and ways of life. Nevertheless, the hatred that existed against Yrigoyen in those days was palpable, and was spread through newspapers, magazines, and the publications of the period: everything was attributed to Yrigoyen. The reproaches against him, notwithstanding, were so weak and lacking in precision that one wonders how it was possible that a step as definitive as a revolution could have come about simply on the basis of this type of accusations.

There is a very curious book by Martín Aldao, that reflects the mood of the period very well. Aldao was a gentleman from an old family from Santa Fe who lived for thirty or forty years in Paris. Very well known by the substantial Argentine community there, he had the clever idea of recording in a diary the things that happened to him, the books he read, the artistic events he attended, and of course, the talks he had with the most conspicuous people of the Argentine colony in France.

This book transcribes his diary from more or less 1928 to 1932, so that it includes the full sequence of days previous to the revolution of September 6 and what happened afterwards. Through the conversations he had with people such as Marcelo de Alvear, Fernando Saguier, and other important members of Argentine society —some settled in Paris, other just passing through— one sees that the gossip and rumors that reach France are inconsistent, yet they denote the tangle of gravest accusations: the president is brimming with contentment, he is paralyzing the public administration because he is not signing proceedings, he is surrounded by a small group of sworn followers, he is going to govern with so-and-so or such and such.

A curious aspect is that, from the beginning of 1930 or the end of 1929, Aldao records as a very natural piece of information, the possibility that a rebellion may displace Yrigoyen. Furthermore, this revolution has first names and last names; General Justo or General Uriburu is going to direct it. This gives us the idea of the irresponsibility with which things were managed, at the same time as it forces us to recognize that, as far as radicalism, there was great mediocrity and lack of initiative to adopt any attitude that might confront or even stop this, that from June or July of 1930 onward seemed unstoppable. The triumph of 1928, the famous plebiscite, had calmed all disquiet, all criticism. The interests created made it so that, for example, in the elections for deputies in March of 1930, the candidates who offered radicalism were the same ones who already occupied a seat in Congress; that is, all were reelected, which suggests an attitude little in keeping with what radicalism had sustained some years before and with what the figure of Yrigoyen had represented.

## Violence

In November of 1929 a macabre event took place that had not occurred in recent decades: the assassination of the leader Carlos Washington Lencinas, in Mendoza. Lencinas was a dissident of radicalism and had adopted a position much more advanced in economic and social matters. The Lencinases of Mendoza and the Cantonis in San Juan were like caricatures of radicalism, much more populist and distributionist as far as their thinking and action. Their position was very similar to what Peronism was later: a constant aggression against all that could be considered capital or business; support for the workers; and progressive legislation, such as that which permitted female suffrage in San Juan during the provincial elections, in 1928. At the same time, a feeling of violence and of intimidation against the opposition floated in the air. Carlos Washington Lencinas, a young man, was the son of the first radical governor of Mendoza, *el gaucho* Lencinas (for this reason they called Carlos Washington Lencinas *"el gauchito* Lencinas"). In November of 1929, following fierce campaigns against Yrigoyen, he arrived in Mendoza and was assassinated by a lowly peasant, Yrigoyenist by affiliation, to which political motivation was immediately attributed, and this inflamed the passions of the entire country. Yrigoyen was accused flat out of having prompted the assassination of Lencinas, the mere idea of which was absolute nonsense.

In reality, this situation in Cuyo [the region comprising Mendoza, San Juan, and San Luis] was in response to circumstances particular to the area which had motivated federal intervention in San Juan and in Mendoza before Yrigoyen had assumed the presidency. But the interveners also conducted themselves with extreme violence and were opposed as much by Lencinaism as by Cantoniism. As for the crime, though it was a local occurrence, it had great national repercussion.

A month later another event occurred that also had bloody implications: the attempt that Yrigoyen suffered having left his home, bound for the Government House. A man, about whom not much was ever known (perhaps mildy deranged, of a very remote history of sympathy for anarchism), fired a few shots at the official automobile which was carrying Yrigoyen, but he was immediately killed by the president's guard. This gave rise to a series of accusations and criticisms against Yrigoyen himself, who in earlier times used to go around without an escort and now did so guarded by armed police who would not hesitate to kill. These events began to create an atmosphere of oppressiveness, of intimidation that, although it did not spread throughout the whole country, was manipulated with a fair amount of skill, in view of the elections of 1930, through which deputies should be replaced, by way of newspapers and opposition organs.

## A strange election

In this election, a sort of tie occurred. The 800,000 votes that radicalism had obtained in 1928 were reduced to 600,000, and the opposition, which had had some 400,000 votes, increased to the same figure. But the outcome without precedent from an electoral standpoint was that, in the Federal Capital, radicalism lost to a party that was a minority of another minority party. It lost, in effect, to the Independent Socialist Party, a dissident faction of the old, traditional Socialist Party, much more anti-Yrigoyenist than the latter and, in time, it would ally itself with the conservatives to form what would later be called the Concordance.

The defeat of radicalism in the Federal Capital at the hands of so improvised a party, was a warning. From this moment on, military conspiracy —about which one had spoken a couple of years earlier when the victory of Yrigoyen aroused certain uneasiness— began to be put forward as a solution. General Justo, Minister of War under President Alvear, had been sounded out back then, but the officer was of the opinion that, given the recent triumph of Yrigoyen by plebiscite, all forms of revolution had been repudiated. Nevertheless, in 1930, things had already changed, and the military conspiracy was put into action, headed by General José Félix Uriburu, originally from Salta, who had been a conservative deputy in 1913.

Uriburu was pro-German, and was surrounded by small, youth core-groups without political importance but with some intellectual influence that centered around a newspaper called *La Nueva República* [*The New Republic*]. This group had introduced in our country the ideology of Italian fascism —adapted and made over with a cosmetic of nationalism—, which posed the irrelevancy of democracy as a form of running the State in order to conquer the common welfare. It invalidated elections, stating there was no reason why the popular majorities should be right; it invalidated above all the whole system of parties, and postulated a constitutional reform of a corporative nature.

## The conspiracy

Uriburu was an honest man, of good intentions, but very limited intellectually. He had let himself get involved with this group of youth, almost all of whom were of a conservative origin (many of them very brilliant thinkers, as was the case of Ernesto Palacios or the brothers Irazusta), and he became a possible leader for the conspiracy. He had been actively serving since 1928 and maintained a certain prestige in the Army. He began to converse with many people in order to carry out a revolution that, in his opinion, should have been the beginning of a new institutional phase in the country, and which should imply the reform of the Constitution, the abolition of the Sáenz Peña Law, and the creation of a sort of Chamber of *fascios*, or corporations, in place of Congress.

Soon after, General Agustín P. Justo, who had been Alvear's Minister of War, conspired on his own, with the idea of going about blocking Uriburu's proposals to reform the Constitution little by little. Justo was surrounded by traditional politicians, fundamentally by conservatives and antipersonalists —that is, anti-Yrigoyenist radicals— and independent socialists. In his opinion, Yrigoyen should have been removed from office, since he had ceased to offer any type of guarantees to run the ship of State, and thus open the way for elections that would permit the front defeated in 1928 to attain power by a means that was more or less constitutional. It is worth stating that the conspiracy, though at that time it did not clearly set forth the dissidences, was led by two totally discrepant tendencies.

Parallel to this, in the public arena, the conspiracy synchronized perfectly with a series of public acts and of demonstrations, in Congress as well as in the streets, on behalf of the opposition parties. After July 1930, the tension began to increase. All the opposition in Congress united to create a sort of front that sponsored very vibrant public acts in theaters and main squares, at the same time that it increased its criticism against the ruling system. The opposition controlled much of the media, many timbres, which allowed it to create out of its accusations a plank —constantly trodden in the patchwork of public opinion—; during the month of August, above all, this became evident.

When a revolution is created, or when one goes about creating a propitious circumstance for a revolution to break out, acts generally occur on the side of the government that one is trying to bring down, acts faced with which the opposition reacts, there being created, then, this counterpoint of opposition and government that culminates in revolution. What is curious in this case, is that the government did nothing, except generate some administrative type act or another, such as the appointment of the president of the Supreme Court or a relatively insignificant decree. Whereas in 1955 there was a series of events produced by the government of Perón that caused, in turn, a series of reactions that culminated in the revolution of September 16, none of this occurred in 1930.

The radical government gave the impression of being a sort of immobile doll, against which the most ferocious blows were dealt without it even reacting. The only response, toward the end of August, were the somewhat important demonstrations in defense of the government on the part of a fairly mysterious organization, the Radical Clan. This latter was made up of the marginalized members of the committees who paraded through the streets of the center of Buenos Aires shouting "Long live Yrigoyen!" and "Down with his opponents!," although without any major repercussion, except for a shooting skirmish here and there that did not result in casualties.

The conspiratorial intention continued to be present in the newspapers at an increasingly accelerated rhythm, with presumptions and prophecies about when the revolution would break out. Some newspapers from August and the beginning of September of 1930, in particular *Crítica* and *La Razón,* said terrible things about the president. If one compares it with the electoral campaigns or the claims of the opposition today, it can be seen to just what extent Argentine political customs have improved, because the things that were said during that era were ferocious. They even meddled in the private personality of Yrigoyen and reached a level of obscenity without there being any reaction at all on the part of the government. During the initial days of September, the Minister of War resigned, impotent to curb the conspiracy, since there existed intrigues in the government, as well.

On September 4, there was a demonstration, where a hoped-for victim happened: in a shooting exchange someone fell who, it was presumed, was a student. Although later it was discovered that he was a banker, the student body of Buenos Aires rose up in a protest strike and considered themselves at war with the government. On September 6, General Uriburu succeeded in removing the cadets from the Military College and advanced on to Buenos Aires with a very short column, very vulnerable from the military point of view.

But the atmosphere was already cast in such a way that there was no possibility of resistance. Yrigoyen, now sick, had delegated the command to his vice president, Enrique Martínez. Although it was a way of clearing the air a little, the pressures on Yrigoyen for him to resign were so great that not even this gesture sufficed. Finally, Uriburu reached the Government House after a shootout at Congress Square, and there, forced the vice president to resign and took charge of the de facto government. These were the concrete events.

## Elections with a proscription

What happened after, foreshadowed what was going to occur during the decade of the thirties. Uriburu tried to carry out his corporative designs, but he did not find an echo in the public opinion. On the other hand, Justo opposed him secretly and tried to form a sort of confederation that would support him, but he, too, was unsuccessful. Finally, Uriburu had to surrender to the conservative forces, which were the only ones that supported him. Following the advice of his Minister of the Interior, he convoked elections in the province of Buenos Aires, with the idea of gradually doing the same in the other provinces and of culminating the process with a presidential assembly.

But unexpectedly, on April 5, 1931, radicalism triumphed in the province of Buenos Aires and things began to get complicated for Uriburu. From the time that it was proven that radicalism continued to be a majority —despite the loss of prestige that it had suffered, the imprisonment of Yrigoyen, and the fact that many of its leaders were absent or imprisoned— a different methodology had to be sought, that of an electoral fraud, which tainted the entire following decade and which occurred in the form of a prohibition of the ticket presented by radicalism in September of 1931: Marcelo de Alvear - Adolfo Güemes.

Faced with this proscription, radicalism abstained, so that the forces supporting the provisional government were the old conservatism —which, baptized as the National Democratic Party, succeeded for the first time since the sanction of the Sáenz Peña Law in unifying itself as a single national party—; the antipersonalist wing of radicalism; and in the Federal Capital, independent socialism. Its ticket was Justo-Roca, and Justo-Matienzo (Justo-Roca supported by the conservatives, Justo-Matienzo by the antipersonalists). The forces that were neither radicals nor conservatives —that is, the socialists of traditional stock, the progressive democrats, and minor forces of some provinces— formed what was called the Civil Alliance, which proclaimed Lisandro De la Torre (progressive democrat) and Nicolás Repetto (socialist) as candidates.

During the elections, needless to say, the machinery of the conservative parties of the provinces succeeded in prevailing over the civil alliances, which only triumphed in the Federal Capital and in Santa Fe, where the Progressive Democratic Party was strong. In December of 1931, the National

Congress met, approved the elections despite the protests of radicalism, and on February 20, 1932, Uriburu handed over the insignia of power to General Agustín P. Justo, who then initiated his presidential mandate.

# Consequences

To summarize: in September of 1930, for the first time in Argentine constitutional history, a military coup overthrew a government that, beyond the scrutiny that it might have warranted, was a constitutional government. From then on, a system of electoral fraud, violation of the Constitution, and violation of the laws was set up, which permitted the Concordance to impose its candidates and inaugurate a phase that would last until 1943.

On a deeper level of this which seems to be merely a Latin American coup —the overthrow of a civil government by a military coup— we can perceive the anxiety of the Argentine ruling classes to situate themselves in power in order to confront the crisis without being affected by it. Upon taking power, these classes organized things in such a way that the effects of the crisis that Argentina was suffering did not jeopardize their basic interests, rather, they were distributed throughout the population.

Another consequence of the revolution of September 6 was the reconstitution of radicalism, which, now in the clear, forgot its previous antipersonalist and Yrigoyenist dissidences and became unified under the direction of Alvear. Yrigoyen, who had been incarcerated on the island of Martín García, was pardoned by the provisional government and returned to Buenos Aires. Nevertheless, he did not exercise the leadership of his party but instead limited himself to giving his blessing to the new directorship of that favorite disciple who, in his eyes, Marcelo T. de Alvear had always been.

The things that changed in the country after 1930 were many, and the majority had a negative side to them. Sixteen years after 1930, a great conservative leader from Córdoba, José Aguirre Cámara, said these words before the national committee of his party: "In 1930 we committed a big mistake due to impatience, due to the sensuality of power, due to inexperience, due to whatever. We were the ones who cleared the way for military insurrection, forgetting the great conservative tradition, and from that moment on, we the conservatives are the responsible ones or the culpable ones for what has happened in the country up to now." Some years after these words of Aguirre Cámara, Juan Perón, president at the time, said: "I was very young when I saw Yrigoyen fall and I saw him fall with a wave of calumny and of insults against which his government could do nothing. This will not happen to me..." This is to say that two men who participated in the revolution of 1930, such as Aguirre Cámara and Perón (who at that time was a captain and formed part of the military staff of Uriburu), delivered a sort of *mea culpa*.

The fact is that in the years following 1930, what happened on September 6 was remembered initially with a fair amount of pomp, then with increasing silence, and finally it was completely forgotten. Today no one remembers that date in a positive light: the general idea is that it was ominous within Argentine institutional history, because it paved the way for subsequent breaches of the Constitution and signaled the beginning of a decade that I will not call infamous, but which signified within the country a domination of the traditional classes, a nonpopulist orientation, an egoistic sense of class, and it implied a retrogression to the past.

## CHAPTER X

# The decade of 1930

*The denomination "decade of 1930" does not refer strictly to a chronological period, because really we could say that, politically, the decade began in February of 1932 when Agustín P. Justo assumed the constitutional presidency and ended in June of 1943, when the conservative government of Ramón S. Castillo was overthrown.*

*In history, as in life itself, things occur with a certain simultaneity, and to describe them, it should be kept in mind that a political concern occurs at the same time as an economic process and as a cultural event — although, to make a specific question more comprehensible, it may be necessary to separate the events into different fields or dimensions. In this sense, it is useful to outline a historical framework that permits one to grasp what was happening in the world during those years. I believe that rarely in contemporary history has there been a decade with such ominous, such pessimistic signs, as that of 1930.*

# An ominous world

In 1933 Hitler took power in Germany, and from this moment on, his racist, nationalistic, and bellicose politics permitted him to occupy the Ruhr region (which had been declared neutral), to engulf Austria, to invade territories with German minorities in Czechoslovakia (and later, Czechoslovakia in its entirety) and, finally, in September of 1939, to begin the attack on Poland with which the Second World War was unleashed.

In the Soviet Union, meanwhile, a process was unfolding that, although in general it was accompanied by the sympathy of the progressive sectors of the western world and also of Argentina, it concealed negative realities for humanity that, little by little, would begin to be known. The idea of a society without classes, where money would not have importance, where there were no privileges and everyone would work toward better standards of living, generated enthusiasm. But there existed, as well, tremendous internal repression, the physical annihilation of almost ten million peasants who opposed the agrarian policy, terrible trials in Moscow, where the most veteran leaders of the Bolshevik revolution of 1917 confessed to supposed crimes —treason against one's country, conspiracy to kill Stalin. All of this, however, was found out later. In the meantime, the Soviet Union was apparently carrying out a formidable alternative experiment to the capitalist system, which seemed to be virtually bankrupt.

In the United States there were twenty million unemployed and something more or less comparable was happening in England and France, all of which gave rise to tumult and disturbances that did not go so far as to place the systems in danger, but did alarm the leaders profoundly. The United States, for example, changed from its traditional liberal politics to another where the State set in motion large-scale public works to mitigate unemployment. The New Deal, which over time did not seem to have been that important in overcoming the crisis, gave the North American people a new feeling of confidence.

In that decade, then, things were not well in the world. Totalitarianisms advanced, the democratic system was questioned everywhere, and armed and bloody confrontations were rather common. Japan invaded China, for example. Another important event, which moved Argentine society profoundly, was the Spanish Civil War, which as a prelude to the Second World War broke out in July, 1936, and lasted until May, 1939.

The Spanish Civil War moved Argentine society for many reasons. In the first place, because the Spanish community was very large. Today perhaps, one sees the great-grandchildren of Spaniards, but at that time Spanish fathers and grandfathers were common, each of whom had taken sides because of what was occurring in the peninsula. Furthermore, there were commercial and economic links between Argentina and Spain that were much more significant than those of today: one used to eat Spanish sardines; drink Spanish *sidra* [cider containing alcohol]; people washed themselves with Spanish soap; there were large companies of public services that were Spanish, such as the one that constructed the subway going from the Plaza de Mayo to Pacífico in Buenos Aires; and CHADE (Compañía Hispano Argentina de Electricidad), the energy company with headquarters in Barcelona.

But aside from these ties, Argentine society was affected because the values that were at stake (fascism, the as yet imperfect democracy of the Spanish Republic) were very much connected to our own values. The Spanish Civil War and, subsequently, the Second World War, were the violent jolts that awoke Argentine society, which until then lived wrapped up in itself, as if it were an island detached from what was happening in the world; these events alerted it to the fact that what happened abroad had importance for the country itself.

## Justo

The decade of 1930 began with the constitutional assumption of government of Agustín P. Justo through elections where the proscription of radicalism engendered by necessity a virtual fraud that permitted the Concordance to obtain power. The Concordance was made up of the old, traditional, conservative party; antipersonalism; and the small independent socialist party that had triumphed in the Federal Capital in 1930 and introduced a group of men, among whom Antonio Di Tomasso most certainly figured prominently.

Justo, the new president, did not have the slightest personal charisma, but he did have political astuteness, and he had known how to round up support. He was let in because he was an antipersonalist radical, he was a career officer, he had been Minister of War to Alvear, but in addition, he was a civil engineer, something that was emphasized during the months of the electoral campaign as if to show that he was not a military president, but rather a man who brought together his status as a military man with his status as a civil professional.

Wherever Justo went, he was whistled at in disapproval; his was perhaps the only case of a president who gave himself the satisfaction of telling the crowd just where to go with a vulgar gesture of the forearm and opposite fist: it occurred at the racetrack in Palermo (Buenos Aires), once when he went there in the presidential carriage to witness a grand prize.

Hissed at or not, Justo achieved some important things: his government was quite prolific in public works; it is to him that the first design for a paved system of highways in Argentina is due. The roads that go from Buenos Aires to Mar del Plata, from Buenos Aires to Mendoza by way of Río Cuarto, and from Buenos Aires to Córdoba by way of Rosario are works of General Justo. During his government the Law of Highway Service was passed, by which five cents of the price of gasoline was destined to a fund that would permit the creation of paved roads.

Justo, although he considered himself an antipersonalist radical, in practice was a conservative. He believed in a scheme that had made the nation prosperous in previous decades. That is, a very close association with Great Britain; great care with the British capital invested in Argentina, with the commercial link between Argentina and the British market. But when it came time to design the Argentine highway system, Justo decided that the routes would run parallel to the railroad. That is, he helped to intensify the competition by truck, which already was beginning to be important, in relation to the British railroads. It was neither faster nor safer, but it was cheaper than the railroad tariffs.

The first years of Justo's government turned out to be facilitated by the abstention of radicalism. Banished from the elections of 1931, radicalism decided to take refuge in abstention, while some of its leaders encouraged different revolutionary attemps that inevitably failed. This posture had no way out: an electoral abstention signified remaining out of the game when the other political parties were accepting the rules set down by the government of the Concordance. It was then, for example, that thanks to the hole that radicalism had left, there were fifty some odd socialist deputies in Congress, a figure that the Socialist Party never again obtained.

# Fraud

In 1935, radicalism resolved to lift the abstention, and from that time on, one began to practice on a grand scale what was to be the most promient blemish of the decade, the most unjustifiable: electoral fraud. A fraud that, if not organized, it was at the very least endorsed by the government, and it tinged the political events of that era with illegitimacy.

It consisted in intimidating the citizen in favor of the opposition so that he would not go to vote ("you already voted, get lost..."); or in threatening poll officials even with arms so they would abandon the voting area and leave in the hands of supporters of the officialist party the possibility of overturning the registered list of voters and filling the ballot boxes with votes of whatever kind; or in permitting people to vote freely, as was done in the final course of the decade, only to exchange the ballot boxes later for others with the votes that were befitting.

The fraud included everything from these sorts of manipulation to direct aggressions and shootings. In the struggle that radicalism undertook to clean up the polling procedures —even if by gunshot—, there were many dead. Amadeo

Sabatini won the elections in Córdoba, in 1935, with eight or nine dead in a confrontation with conservative bullies. The same happened in Mendoza, where officialism killed the president of the radical block, Doctor Martons. In the province of Santa Fe, General Risso Patrón was killed.

In the province of Buenos Aires, the setting of the biggest frauds, there were events of almost epic proportions. Juan Maciel, leader of Tres Arroyos, knowing that fraud was being committed in the locality of Coronel Dorrego on the day of the election of Ortiz (whose radical opponent was Alvear), set out with the sole intention of impeding it and was sewn with bullets in the town square. This was a struggle —painful, difficult— that has yet to find who might undertake its narration. But unfortunately, the fraud that was committed in the general system of things, at times, tinged radicalism, as well.

In the final years of the decade of 1930 and during the initial years of that of 1940, there were attempts at fraud within the internal elections of radicalism. It was as if a black stain began to spread over the whole country. Of course for the Concordance, up against radicalism which in practice continued to be a majority, electoral fraud was the only means it had to maintain power —aware as it was of being a minority.

The question of fraud belongs to political philosophy: to what degree does a government have the right to exert pressure in order to maintain power. The first obligation of man is to defend his own skin, says Martín Fierro. In the same way, one could say that the first obligation of a political leader when he is governing is to keep himself in power, but what limits are there on the means he may actually use? The conservatives and their allies, the antipersonalists, did not pose this problem and, there where it was necessary, they committed fraud; the Federal Capital was the only place where this did not happen.

Fraud is the mark that defines the decade of 1930 politically, and it is what justifies the label "infamous decade" that a national journalist gave it. The qualifier cannot be applied to all aspects of governmental action in the decade of 1930, but it can be to the political arena, where infamy had to do not only with rigging elections and fixing electoral results, but also with the deep skepticism that spread in Argentine society as regarded the validity of democracy.

The spectacle of totalitarianisms that were gaining ground in Europe and that of a vernacular democracy based on electoral fraud, on trickery, on a lie, on hypocrisy (for there was always a spokesman of officialism who denied it), provoked the decline of democracy and left it defenseless when, in 1943, the at any rate constitutional government of President Ramón Castillo was overthrown.

## Ortiz

When Justo reached the end of his term, there was an attempt to renew the alliance of conservatives and antipersonalists —independent socialism had disappeared—, and in secret meetings Doctor Roberto Ortiz was chosen as the candidate for the Concordance. Radicalism, on the other hand, which by now had abandoned the idea of abstention, presented the figure of Marcelo de Alvear, whose great presidency in the previous decade still remained in the collective memory, and a man who could scare no one. Fraud was repeated and Ortiz was elected, but the new president realized that he could not govern indefinitely in this fashion.

He was a sincere democrat, who had been brought up in the ranks of radicalism only to later be active in antipersonalism, and finally, to be minister to Justo. Ortiz felt that the repetition of fraud was harmful to the country, and he proposed to eradicate it. He did this with much determination and courage, breaking with those who had put him in power, cutting his ties with the men who were his patrons, his supporters. But bad luck and health betrayed him. Ortiz was diabetic and, although he tried heroically to control his illness, he could not do so completely. During this period there was a scarceness of the resources that one finds today and there was also greater ignorance, and in July of 1940, one of the most serious consequences of diabetes, retinopathy (that is, a lesion in the retina), left him practically blind.

From that moment on, Ortiz requested a leave of absence and ceased to be the effective president (though he continued to be the president formally). Castillo, his counterpart on the ticket, took power. The conservative vice president believed, just as Justo, that it was insane to let the radicals win the elections, and he continued with the policy of upholding fraud. Perhaps the most scandalous moment was in December of 1941, when Rodolfo Moreno was elected governor of Buenos Aires by way of a huge fraud condemned by all the newspapers of the period, but which ended up somewhat diluted, as at that moment Japan attacked Pearl Harbor and the United States entered the war. Those trying to be funny said that this was an agreement between Rodolfo Moreno, who had been the Argentine ambassador to Japan, and the government of Tokyo, so that the day he would commit fraud they would bomb Pearl Harbor. From that time on, Castillo arranged things so that in the future there could be a totally conservative president.

## The crisis

The economic crisis that shook the country in that decade was at its peak when Justo assumed the presidency in 1932. It was like an international shakeup, a readjustment that could not be made in any other way than through customs restraints and barriers that began to hinder international trade. Each country tried to protect its own economy through a series of norms that previously, in an almost unrestricted commercial context between countries, had not existed. The crisis produced a great drop in the prices of raw materials that our country exported: meat, wool, wheat, oleaginous products, tannin. As its revenue decreased, the government could do less with public works, and efficacy in the State apparatus was reduced.

The conservative government declared that in order to combat the crisis, legitimate sources of wealth had to be protected. Faced with the crisis, it was not necessary to be so concerned with the suffering of the people, rather with trying to reconstitute the economy of the country, above all on the basis of the so-called "sources of wealth." But it happened that these sources were the property of men who were in the government, the large greenhouse growers, the big *estancia* owners, those who were connected with international meat trade. This, then, was one of the focal points for surmounting the economic crisis.

Another fundamental idea was the energetic intervention of the State in economic circuits through the creation of the Central Bank, which came into being as an authority that was to regulate all that transpired in matters of finance and exchange. It was set up as a consolidation of public and private banks that would have as its responsibility the direction of financial policy. In addition, a control of exchange was created, and credit policy was monitored. This meant State interference through the Central Bank, in the realm of banking and finance, which previously had been free and unrestricted. But he who took charge of the Central Bank, Raúl Prebisch, proceeded with prudence, and the entity had a respectable, moderating performance, which was one of the factors that made it possible to overcome the crisis in a relatively brief period of time. These men, whose philosophy was to save the legitimate sources of wealth, did not wager on a policy of inflation or of currency devaluation. It took a lot to obtain a peso, but he who managed to, had the security that that peso would be worth the same then as within five or ten years time, and this was the cornerstone in order for the crisis to begin to be left behind.

In the third place, the crisis was overcome through the regulatory commissions; that is, the interventionism of the State was total during the decade of 1930, despite the fact that the political sign of the government was conservative and theoretically came from old liberalism. Nevertheless, the conservatives, above all by way of the policy of Federico Pinedo, did not hesitate to intervene in a very energetic way in the production of Argentine raw materials, with the idea that only the regulation of production would keep the prices remunerative for the producers. It was then that wine was poured out in Mendoza, that areas of cultivation were reduced; the idea being that production should allow the producers of agriculture and livestock to come out ahead: the Regulatory Commission of Meat, the Regulatory Commission of Corn, the Regulatory Commission of Wheat, the Regulatory Commission of Cotton, of Wine, and so on. Something similar was occurring in other countries, as well. In Brazil, coffee was thrown into the sea in sacks so that overproduction would not make international prices fall.

It was a severe, rough crisis, which was very much felt in the popular sectors. There was unemployment, railroad unions had to accept a reduction in pay from British companies, and state employees went unpaid for a very long time. The teachers of Santiago del Estero and Corrientes were the paradigm of nonpaid state employees, as they actually did not get paid for two or three years. These types of situations were reflected in popular music: "where there is a buck, Ol' Gómez, they have cleaned it out with a pumice stone..." This popular dance tune stirred the middle class and the middle class closer to upper class. It was the period when some principal families had to sell their residences, some acquired by foreign embassies and others by the State, for public distribution, which at least permitted some very beautiful examples of architecture in Buenos Aires to be saved.

But regardless, despite the great sacrifice of the working classes and of major unemployment, the crisis —which, so they say, generates its own solutions— produced certain aspects that, in the long run, were positive.

The drop in agriculture and livestock prices made it so that unemployment in the countryside was very great and, consequently, many rural workers went to the big cities. This, plus the difficulty in importing certain types of merchandise, gave origin to hundreds or thousands of small businesses, little repairshops, small textile factories, chemical and pharmaceutical laboratories where, with the cheap manual labor of those who came from the rural areas, a rather imperfect national industry began to be set up, of expensive products that began to form the foundations of the light industry that in the decade of 1940 would have its most brilliant moment.

At the same time, this phenomenon was accompanied by a slow settlement of the areas bordering the big cities: Buenos Aires, La Plata, Rosario, places where those who came from the rural areas found a more regular possibility for wages, a better standard of living, better housing, social connections. There began to be created a class that had nothing to do with, for example, those union workers with a socialist or communist mentality. These were workers of a different type, people who did not feel attached to any kind of political loyalty.

Toward 1935, the crisis began to pass. This was when the great labor strikes began, an indication that times were prosperous. When periods are very bad, in effect, workers are not interested in striking; by contrast, when things are going a bit better, the relationships between owners and workers begin to seek their natural place. A strike by construction workers in the city of Buenos Aires lasted about six months in 1935, and ended, as strikes tend to end, with a more or less acceptable settlement.

## The treaty

This crisis, weathered with such harshness, had a very important aspect to it: the reaffirmation of the philosophy according to which the business of Argentina consisted in maintaining and accentuating its traditional ties with Great Britain; the most important expression of this being the Roca-Runciman Pact, signed in 1933. The crisis had affected the primary products of Argentina, among them, the production of frozen meat, which was the most sophisticated product of the Argentine cattle industry. It affected the owners of large *estancias* and big greenhouse growers. The delegation that Argentina sent for the talks with their counterparts in Great Britain was presided over by the vice president of the Nation, Julio Roca, who, following rather difficult negotiations, subscribed an agreement that has been known since then as the Roca-Runciman Treaty.

The agreement is very complex and entire libraries have been written in favor of or against it. I am going to simplify it a great deal, by saying that the treaty consisted of a guarantee on the part of Great Britain that it would continue to buy frozen or refrigerated meat in accordance with the historic average of 1920. In reality, it guaranteed a figure somewhat less than that of this average, but it assured continual purchasing through the greenhouse growers and *estancia* owners of the country.

In exchange for this, Argentina promised what was called "benevolent treatment" for British capital, which was translated into a control of exchange that was favorable for sending profits of the British companies to their central offices and an attempt to coordinate Argentine transportation, to prevent trucks and buses from continuing to create a ruinous competition for English railroads and tramways.

What was most surprising, what was most spectacular in the Roca-Runciman Treaty, was that phrase from Vice President Roca himself, where he expresses in a not too happy fashion the position, in reality quite intelligent, maintained by the Argentine government and the Foreign Ministry. Roca said that because of the importance of Great Britain's interests established in Argentina, our country could be considered just another British territorial possession. This, naturally, caused a stir when it was transmitted to Buenos Aires. It was highly criticized, but what Roca meant to say was that Great Britain, confronted with the world crisis and following the example of other countries, had worked out what was called the Treaty of Ottawa, by which it gave preferences to its territorial possessions. In other words, meat from Canada would have preference over meat from other countries; wool from Australia, preference over wool from other countries; threads from India, preference in the British market over threads from other countries.

This meant that Great Britain wanted to maintain its empire and that the empire was maintained not only out of fidelity to the Crown, but also because of the commercial ties, through which the British market, with significant buying power, could continue to import products from its domains. Argentina then, where the greatest amount of British investments was concentrated and which, precisely because of its commercial link, had a close bond with the islands, should receive, according to the Argentine government, the same preferential treatment that Great Britain had with its dominions.

This encouraged the Argentine negotiators to go to London to try to obtain by way of this treaty protection for a legitimate source of wealth, as was frozen or refrigerated meat for export, and in exchange for this, to promise amicable treatment for British capital, which in general terms could not be realized, as shortly thereafter the Second World War began, and the relationship between Argentina and Great Britain changed completely.

The crisis was overcome in any case, and one could say that toward 1935 and 1936, Argentina had taken up the traditional dynamic of the twenties, to which should be added the receipt of some capital from foreigners who began to flee from Europe alarmed by what was happening politically and by the possibility of a war, suggested by the bellicose attitude of Hitler, the revindications of Mussolini, the Soviet enigma, the weaknesses of France and England; a war that seemed, and truly was, almost certain. The capital that arrived, some of it from Jews, helped to give dynamic to the economic circuit.

## Society

Argentine society of the decade of 1930 produced interesting things: it was the era of *Sur* —founded by Victoria Ocampo in 1931—, which was a sort of window to the outside, pulling us out of that cultural self-absorption that had characterized us. It was the era in which Borges began to publish *A Universal History of Infamy* plus some short stories in the newspaper *Crítica* that were later compiled and included in his books. It is the period in which Eduardo Mallea also published some of his great novels, *La Bahía de Silencio*, [*The Bay of Silence*] for example. Leopoldo Lugones killed himself the same day in which Roberto Ortiz assumed the constitutional presidency, February 20, 1938. Alfonsina Storni also died, having committed suicide. Gardel had already died in 1935, although he was not yet idolized as he is now. Other impor-

tant tango orchestras were formed. There was an artistic movement of great significance, great freedom of expression, pluralism, tolerance of all types of intellectual expressions, even the
most dissident.

The exception was a law that was voted on during the
time of Justo, pushed through by Matías Sánchez Sorondo, a
conservative senator for the province of Buenos Aires; but
aside from declaring the Communist Party illegal, it was of little consequence. The Communist Party already had extensive
training in being illegal; on the other hand, it was very small.
In reality, this did not imply a retrogression in the important
tradition of respect for freedom of expression.

The stain of fraud, of course, exceeded the boundaries of
politics and tainted other aspects of Argentine life as a reflection of the enormous theft that the electoral sleight of hand
signified. Some episodes occurring in the decade of 1930
were truly serious in terms of the credibility of democracy of
the era. There were some shady deals that today we could
look at even with a smile, but which in those years shook
society and gave encouragement to those who questioned
democracy, maintaining that a fraudulent system did not have
capacity to avoid these types of things.

The illicit deal of the CHADE was the first in which a
transnational company bought a legislative organism to
achieve its commercial objectives. CHADE provided electric
power to the city of Buenos Aires; its concession expired
some ten years later and, through a gigantic operation, bribed
a fair amount of people, not only councilors but also journal-
ists, leaders, and important functionaries, with an aim to
obtaining an extension on the concession and prolonging it
practically until the end of the century.

Alvear had something to do in the affair: he did not take a
bribe, but he advised the radical councilors to vote in favor
of CHADE's request. This was a scandal that was condemned
at the time, although without proof, and later, with the revolution of 1943, investigated in depth. The results were published in books that were destroyed at the order of Perón;
only a few copies survived showing the finesse of the opera-

tion teledirected from Brussels, where this company had its headquarters, and in which important figures in Argentine life had an attitude of complicity.

Another illicit deal that in 1940 occurred contemporaneously with President Ortiz's request for a leave of absence due to illness, was that of the land in Palomar. Today, this, too, seems a joke to us. There was some land in Palomar —Greater Buenos Aires— that the Minister of War wanted to buy to construct a military academy. A few crafty ones, some congressmen among them, bought this land from several elderly ladies who were the owners; after, they sold it to the State, making a profit. What is curious is that in the same book of proceedings where the notarized agreement was signed in favor of the Nation, one finds the sale of land by the elderly ladies to the shrewd bunch, and the sale, in turn, by these latter to the Nation. In the same notary's office and on the same day: there could be no greater impudence. It was inquired into, and everything was so obvious that the responsible parties were immediately apparent. And strange as it may seem, a radical deputy who had received ten thousand pesos —in reality, he did not receive the money, rather a mysterious woman collected it at some point— shot himself. There was still this type of sensitivity when one did something foolish....

## A good decade?

Overall, it was a good decade, had it not been for the stain of fraud that tarnished all that took place. It was a good decade once the worst years were overcome, those of the crisis, during which people took a pessimistic stance, as Argentina had never experienced a moment like this, except in 1890. But the memories of 1890 had been left behind — half a century had passed—, and when the crisis arrived, the tone of Argentine society exuded the conviction that "God is *criollo*" and that a couple of good harvests would set everything straight, since Argentina was destined to be prosperous.

It did not turn out that way, and the crisis hit hard within this sensitivity. When it gradually began to pass and one saw that it lay behind, this jubilant and optimistic tone that the country had was restored and people continued to live a very conventional life, very misoneistic, very adverse to change, and stratified in social classes, but at the same time, retaining the best characteristics that the earlier years had had: great social fluidity, where the foreigner was received as well as he who with a bit of luck or talent might be able to begin to climb the different strata of society. A life in which there was a place for work but also for entertainment; where people had only one job —no one thought of having two—, ate the midday meal at home, and took a siesta before returning to the yoke. One could view this decade with a certain nostalgia. It is a shame the blemish it had, which tainted all aspects of life during that era and made vulnerable a democracy that, even with its faults, was promissory.

In those years the political parties were few and important: radicalism, which considered itself to be a majority, and it was —led at the time by Marcelo de Alvear, a figure who was truly an illustrious national leader, respected by all—; conservatism, which had unified as late as 1931, but which had important, capable men, good administrators; the Socialist Party, which although it only had force in the Capital, included first-rate names on its staff —Alfredo Palacios, Enrique Dickman, Nicolás Repetto, Mario Bravo—; and the small Progressive Democratic Party of Santa Fe, which came into power with Luciano Molinas, between 1932 and 1935, a government whose intervention by Justo was one of the most unjustifiable events of the decade.

In this political context an improvement of civic practices could be hoped for and, probably, greater participation of the forces that, without being conservative (that is, without having a commitment to the ruling classes), could take on some of the claims of the popular classes. This possibility was not accomplished: fraud, stubbornness, and the blindness of the ruling classes impeded it. The consequences would be seen in 1943, the year in which the decade of 1930 really ended.

## CHAPTER XIII

# The revolution of '43

*It was an unexpected occurrence; it happened like a flash of lightning on a clear day. One morning, the inhabitants of the city awoke to the news that the troops of Campo de Mayo had advanced on the Government House, President Castillo was heading for Colonia, and the conservative government had been overthrown. The revolution, notwithstanding, had really been a foreseeable, inevitable event. This, which seems to be a contradiction, is not. The revolution of '43 —although it came about due to a banal, almost courtly, rather absurd event— responded to a series of factors that had been brewing in the country for some years, and that now, with a historical perspective, can be seen with greater clarity, a vantage point not possible during that period.*

# Totalitarianism

To understand the events of that time, one has to keep in mind the advance of totalitarianism, which since 1933 began to win positions in political or military battles and which at that time practically governed all aspects of life in Europe. In reality, seeing things with a historical perspective, we could say that toward the middle of 1943, the "mainspring" of the war had reversed and the final triumph of the Allied cause was inevitable, although this could not yet be discerned with clarity. Toward the end of 1942, the first great defeat of the totalitarian regimes took place, the Battle of Stalingrad, where the Germans lost more than 600,000 soldiers not easily replaced; furthermore, they could not reach the Suez Canal. Although the war between Japan and the United States, which was waged in the Pacific, had had an initial stage of major Japanese victories, it was ineluctably lost by Japan, a country without raw materials, that had to extend its lines of defense over too large a war zone.

In any case, the apparent triumph of totalitarianism was encouraging to many in Argentina who believed that the defeat of England and the United States could be advantageous to a country whose dependence on Great Britain was historic. According to them, the triumph of totalitarianism in the war could signify a key position in South America for Argentina. We have already said, as well, that the policy of electoral fraud that was being committed —more brazenly following the death of Ortiz and his replacement by Vice President Castillo, of conservative origin— had degraded the idea of democracy.

The idea of defending democracy made no sense for those who saw that elections were rigged, fraudulent, dishonest... The grand hypocritical statements of those in power, who tried to justify these events by saying that they were minor episodes, had lowered the defenses of those who sincerely believed in the democratic system as a way of life for Argentina. Nor was there much desire to defend democracies on the part of the forces, sectors, or parties who considered themselves to be within the line of defense of the democratic system but who found themselves cornered between the totalitarian triumphs and the presence of certain defenders of democracy, such as for example Justo —being the one who invented electoral fraud and was the beneficiary of the first proscription of radicalism, in 1931—, who the circumstances had turned into the chief of all forces advocating the Allies in Argentina.

## Silent changes

In addition, social changes had silently begun to take place in the country. We said that the crisis of 1930 began to bring to the fringes of the big cities many workers of the countryside who, displaced by the economic crisis, were in search of factories and shops for manual labor, salaries suited more to their demands, a better lifestyle, and a sociability they did not have in rural life. This silent manual labor force had integrated itself into a sort of small and primitive industrialization, helped by the particular conditions of the crisis, which made it difficult to import certain kinds of goods.

After 1939, these circumstances were accentuated due to the large amount of products that could not be imported from Europe, and for better or for worse, they started to be manufactured in our country. Manual labor began to have special value, high salaries, and a state of total employment as had occurred few times in Argentina. This social change, then, which did not yet have an entirely definite mark to it, was produced by people who had worked in rural jobs up to then and had brought into the collective spirit modifications in existing beliefs and expectations, though these were not the same modifications as those that had defined the society of the mid 1930's.

Finally, there existed a nationalistic ideology that no party in particular represented, but that had a preponderance in the military sectors and in the upper classes of Argentina. A vague nationalism, which nevertheless expressed in a way the need to defend the national industry, to decrease the dependence on Great Britain, to feel more the masters of what was theirs. This also occurred within intellectual sectors backed by the intense propaganda that had been organized, after the triumph of Franco, from Spain —a sort of mother of Latin American nations who was linked to countries such as Argentina because of historical and emotional ties. These sectors sympathized with the idea of a Hispanic stock opposed to any association with the United States or Great Britain.

Most of all, the nationalist idea was important in the Armed Forces, pampered by President Castillo, and through this body some industrial organisms were created that were dependent on the Army and Navy and were entering a stage other than pure military action. The protagonists of this type of production, where the Army was the vector of industrial activities, were Mosconi and, above all, Savio. The Armed Forces paid close attention to what was happening in Europe; they viewed with disdain the unstable politicking of fraud and hypocrisy, and concurred with the idea of a puri- fying rupture, where politics were absent and there existed other types of higher values, of a hierarchical nature, that could elevate Argentina to the position they desired, a posi- tion that the democratic system, with its burden of fraud, violence, and political corruption, apparently could not attain.

In essence there were many reasons to think that some- thing had to happen toward the middle of 1943.

Nevertheless, it was a trivial event that which precipitated the revolution. Radicalism had lost its greatest leader, Marcelo T. de Alvear, and could not find anyone with his charisma. Justo, also, had passed away in January of 1943, unsettling the front that was envisioned. The radicals were looking for a common front with the socialists and the progressive democrats, a sort of Democratic Union to demonstrate to the government of Ramón Castillo that fraud could not be com- mitted against civility in its entirety.

Castillo always justified himself by saying that fraud had been necessary to avoid handing power over to the radicals, who would have governed the country disastrously. The excuse would not have had validity in the face of a front formed by radicals, the progressive democrats (a very respected party, even with Lisandro de la Torre dead), and the Socialist Party. The front also counted on the implicit support of the Communist Party —declared illegal, but still active. The parties indicated, then, met in search of a program and a common ticket in order to contend for power in the elections that were to take place in September of 1943.

In February of 1943, Castillo —a stubborn, intractable man— imposed his own choice for the future presidential candidate, the name of Robustiano Patrón Costa, and, despite the fact that it produced uneasiness within conservatism, above all in the province of Buenos Aires, his name was accepted. He was an industrialist from Salta whose sympathies oddly enough lay with the Allied countries and whose lack of neutrality was not what one might have expected from a man designated by Castillo.

The electoral game then that would be played out, was more or less arranged thus: on the one hand, the democratic front, which had not yet found its candidate but which would be composed of the traditional parties of the country. On the other, conservatism and antipersonalism, once again united in the Concordance, wielding the name of the conservative Patrón Costa.

This was all going on, when a group of radicals had a brilliant idea: to offer the presidential candidacy of the Democratic Front to the Minister of War, General Pedro Pablo Ramírez. They speculated that fraud could not be committed against an active officer; much less, if he was the Minister of War. As a result, radicalism would win the elections and would be in government once again. They spoke then with General Ramírez, who did not appear displeased by the possibility. The president found out and demanded a public explanation. General Ramírez issued a rather ambiguous communiqué and Castillo warned him that he'd better disaffirm his candidacy. It was then that Campo de Mayo rose up in arms and on June 4, 1943, overthrew the president.

## The G.O.U.

It happened that the Army operated a lodge, the GOU, created in March of that year. It was made up of nationalistic officials and a young colonel named Juan Perón, who had been on an academic trip in Europe until a short time before and held a certain amount of esteem within the lodge. It was the GOU that set in motion this military coup that, in reality, did not have either a platform or a leader. The military commander of the revolution was General Rawson, who, as such, should have assumed the de facto presidency, but his very advocates impeded it because they did not agree with some of the names he proposed as ministers.

So, the beginning of the Revolution of '43 and of the government that arose out of it was almost grotesque: a revolution that broke out because of a trivial event; a movement of the regiments of Campo de Mayo to the Government House without a concrete platform and with a chief who could not assume command. Finally, the ex Minister of War of the overthrown president took charge, which in itself suggests the presence of treason and measures that from the beginning were contradictory, and it shows that the Army —or, better yet, the garrison of Campo de Mayo— had set out without knowing what to do. Not only among the military but also in the public opinion of the era, there existed an idea of what was not wanted, but there was not a very clear idea of what was wanted.

Thus began the de facto government that from the outset was very suspicious to the Allied countries, fundamentally to the United States. Precisely because of the lack of a plan, the military leaders of '43 surrendered certain important positions to some of the nationalistic sectors with which they had had dealings. They were the only ones who at least had a libretto and could give the government of the revolution content. And basically they gave it that, but in such a way that it provoked rejection from the democratic, intellectual, university, and academic sectors. The first measures of this nationalistic phase of the de facto government were to impose the teaching of the Catholic religion in the schools, for example, to dissolve —naturally, also by decree— political parties, to repress a series of intellectuals who had demanded that the country fulfill its international commitments.

Within a short period of time, the aversion was earned of all the sectors who had initially viewed the overthrow of Castillo with a fair amount of sympathy, for he was not popular, was grounded in the illegitimacy of his origin, and, aside from his unquestionable patriotism, began to lean toward a nationalism rather similar to the programmatic content of the men of the de facto government that succeeded him. This was expressed, above all, in an obstinate maintenance of neutrality.

Toward the end of 1943, the fate of the World War was quite clear. Nevertheless, the military of the garrison of Campo de Mayo turned the maintenance of neutrality into a question of principles, of jealous defense of sovereignty. In January of 1944, a tragicomic episode occurred. An Argentine honorary consul was arrested by the Allies during a trip he was making to Europe; it was discovered that his mission was to buy arms in Germany for the Argentine Army. The State Department of the United States presented the de facto Argentine government then with a sort of ultimatum and Ramírez had to break relations with Germany and Japan, in short, with the Axis countries.

This caused so great an impression that the Army deposed de facto President Ramírez, replacing him with his Minister of War, General Farrell, a man who though not too bright, was more conciliatory and put up less resistance. From then on, the de facto government tried to make out as best it could in an international context that was increasingly adverse to it and in the framework of an inter-American policy, inspired by the United States, which isolated it progressively; all the American countries withdrew their ambassadors from Buenos

Aires, as a criticism to the neutrality that by then no country in Latin America maintained.

None of this had direct bearing on the economy or on the standard of living of the Argentines. The economic period was at its height and was prosperous, in the first place, due to the impossibility of importing what was manufactured here. Secondly, because the exportable remnants of raw materials from Argentina were well situated in European markets. And in fact, the politics of isolation that the United States was carrying out against Argentina had an objector: none other than Winston Churchill, prime minister of England, who asked Roosevelt on various occasions not to take things too far, because Great Britain needed Argentine meat, plus one could not be too insistent on principles with a country that maintained neutrality when Great Britain was respecting the neutrality of Ireland, for example.

Isolation continued regardless, without direct effect on the economy of the country. On the contrary, it was one of the most brilliant moments in Argentine economy as far as the standard of living; gainful employment; and exports that entered the market at insane prices, transforming Argentina into Great Britain's creditor. To be certain, some things were missing (stockings for women, cosmetics, tires, fuel), which showed the vulnerability of the Argentine economy though they were replaceable things (trains burned cornstalks, for example, instead of coal), and the country did not become paralyzed. There arose, on the contrary, countless small industries, forming an electorate from which Perón benefited. Essentially, it was he who amidst such entangled and contradictory politics began to justify this provisional government —integrated by civilians as different as the nationalists of the first phase and those who came later, of the radical style— by emphasizing a policy of social justice.

In March of 1945, with the war ending in Europe, the Argentine government found that it had to declare war against Germany and Japan, under penalty of not being able to enter the UN (in order for which having declared war against the Axis countries was an indispensable requisite). March of 1945 was perhaps the lowest moment of prestige for the military government. War was declared against two already defeated countries. Universities were normalized and henceforth were bastions of antiofficialism. In Buenos Aires the man arrived who would coordinate activities against the government, Mr. Spruille Braden, ambassador of the Unites States.

Braden was a diplomat who had been in various countries of Latin America and also in Argentina, and was in contact with people of the upper classes of Buenos Aires, but he had an obsession which the State Department quickly endorsed. His thesis was that the United States had engaged in a gigantic struggle to eradicate totalitarian systems from the world and that it had won this war, in Europe at least; in Asia, it would end during the month of August, but it was absurd — in his opinion— to permit Nazi-Fascist focal points such as Spain and Argentina, countries whose governments should have been overturned on the grounds that they helped the opposition.

So that Braden came to Argentina to set up an opposition front that would oblige the military government to call for free elections and to surrender power to the democratic traditional forces. Throughout 1945, Braden undertook practically an electoral campaign, in which he traveled to diverse points of the country, delivered speeches that were reproduced in the major newspapers and unified all the sectors that were already against the military government. Martial law having been lifted by the government in August, the month of September was taken advantage of to hold the march of the Constitution and Liberty, a protest of great magnitude that traversed the streets of Buenos Aires demanding an end to the de facto government, which, for its part, was very disconcerted.

## Perón

The government had one saving grace: the work of Juan Perón in the Department of Labor. Perón had taken charge of it in November of 1943, some few months after the revolution, and from there he approached the traditional labor unions. He found the CGT, *Confederación General del Trabajo* [General Confederation of Labor], divided into two central offices; he allied himself with one of them, forcing out the other; he persecuted the socialist and communist leaders and aided those who were neither; he created new labor unions, prescribed new statutes for diverse trade unions, established increases in salaries; he projected some important norms —approved later—, such as fair labor, paid vacations and a Christmas bonus, and some other measures of a permanent nature. But what Perón fundamentally did in the Department of Labor was to organize a series of trade unions without a union tradition.

Many people who had come from the rural sector to work in the city were ignorant of the concept of syndication, which on the other hand prevailed among the workers of the communist, socialist, anarchist tradition, and so on. But the sugar workers in Tucumán, for example; or those workers in big cities where there was no unionization, or where communists and socialists had not been able to bring together the totality of the union, these did not know what a syndicate was. From the Labor Department Perón dictated statutes for them, organized meetings for them, provided them with locales, facilitated for them in every way the possibility of recognition, and thus created a movement in which loyalties, lacking up until then, were centered on his figure. He made several very intelligent moves, such as the intervention of the railroad unions, to which he sent an intervener, Domingo Mercante, son of a railroad employee, who succeeded in turning these generally socialist unions around in support of Perón.

Throughout 1945 and faced with a sudden attack by the opposition, the government sought a contact with radicalism in order to contrive a way out so the military that had taken part in the government would not be prosecuted. Coincidences regarding specifically the social policy of Perón — sole justification for what was done in two years by the de facto government— were sought. But these negotiations did not materialize. The direction of radicalism was more akin to Alvearism and the intransigent nuclei, inheritors of Yrigoyen, had no interest in reaching an agreement with Perón.

Despite everything, the de facto government managed to assemble three or four radical leaders to be ministers. They took office in August, 1945; martial law was lifted, the life of political parties was reestablished, and it was then that the march of the Constitution and Liberty was held, a very important act, followed by an attempt at a military coup in Córdoba, which was put down.

## October 17th

Finally, the government reinstated martial law, massive arrests of opposition leaders were carried out, and on October 8, the situation being very tense, a decisive event occurred. The garrison of Campo de Mayo requested that President Farrell call for the resignation of Perón. Although it was the same garrison that had carried forth the revolution of '43 and had been the military support of Perón, it was now under the pressure of public opinion, the opposition, the North American embassy, and university intellectuals. A sort of weariness in the support of Perón had occurred. The latter resigned without resistance. There were days of great chaos, in which the opposition did not manage to fill the void of power that had been created. On the other hand, Perón's friends were working subterraneanly to produce an insurrection by the CGT and some unions.

General Avalos, commanding officer of Campo de Mayo and author of the movement against Perón, offered Sabatini, governor of Córdoba and leader of the intransigent wings of radicalism, to put his men in the cabinet and to create the conditions for a clean electoral solution, out of which Sabatini himself would end up a beneficiary. There were sectors within radicalism that opposed these types of deals and asked that the power be given over to the Supreme Court of Justice. This was unacceptable to the Army because it was equivalent to conceding their total defeat, but there was no other rallying cry capable of bringing together sectors so disparate as conservatism, communism, radicalism, socialism, etcetera.

The 17 of October was truly a very important day. In general terms, it had to do with a popular reaction where thousands of workers concentrated in Plaza de Mayo demanded the release of Perón, who at that time was detained in prison on Martín García Island and later in the Military Hospital. This event, supported by the Army (or, at least, by its passivity), gave rise to a new political scheme, which reigned over the next ten years: a trade union movement that backed a government whose support was maintained by the Armed Forces. And the entrance into Argentine political life of the masses, not linked to any traditional party but loyal to a man who had given them various conquests. October 17 marked the end of an old policy. This had to have electoral consequences.

Perón requested his retirement from the Army and from then on he began to create a political front whose backbone was the recently created Labor Party, formed by union leaders with a center-leftist orientation. His platform was very similar to that of the English Labor Party, which a short while before had won the first elections after the war and had displaced the conservative tendency of Churchill. Furthermore, Perón looked for radical leaders with an Yrigoyenist orientation (with whom he formed the Radical Civic Union-Junta of Renewal), who, though removed from their origin in common, maintained nevertheless their political know how. What also appeared were Colonel Perón Civic Centers, which represented groups that had been conservative and now gave their sympathies over to the new leader.

Around Perón, then, a front was organized on the basis of these three groups —labor, radicals of renewal, and independent civic centers—, as well as the invisible but important support of the nationalist sectors, which dreamed of a caudillo who would permit direct communication between leader and people, and of the sympathy of the Church for this Catholic military man, devoted to the Virgin of Luján, to whom he had donated his sword.

The anti-Peronism front was formed by radicalism, whose candidates, Tamborini and Mosca, honorable representatives of traditional politics, were voted in by the Socialist Party, by the Progressive Democratic Party, and implicitly, by the conservatives. It was the front that in 1943 could not be formed, and now came to the fore to curb the presidential ambitions of Perón.

## Campaign and election

A rather violent campaign developed. In December, the government launched the Christmas bonus decree, which was opposed by impresarios and rejected by the Democratic Union, something that would be, along with the Blue Book published in Washington in February of 1945, a determining factor in the narrow triumph of Perón on February 24, 1946. This confrontation and the subsequent triumph signified that with Perón there appeared the hope of a new Argentina, an idea very much present during those electoral months.

This country that had emerged from the war unharmed, that was not alligned with the United States, that had maintained a position of dignity and of sovereignty; this country whose products were needed by starving Europe and where new immigrants arrived fleeing the horrors and the misery of the postwar period; this country wanted to have something that the old political parties could no longer give it. At the same time, the Democratic Union, even physically, represented, with all the good and bad that it had encompassed, the traditional, old Argentina.

Perón's activity was a leap into something new, which could or could not be the void. He was a man who had no political programming, except for social planning, and whose background was rather suspect as far as his sympathy for totalitarian regimes; but at the same time, he ushered in a new and barely conventional language, he would speak in shirtsleeves and stood out in a crowd, the company of his wife, a radio-theater actress that the whole country knew. He drew together a series of ideas that were in keeping with the mood of the times: the idea that the State should have greater insertion in economic life, the idea of the commitment of the

State to the less fortunate, the idea of social justice, the idea of sovereignty; a man who could quote, among others, Pope Leo XIII as much as Lenin or Yrigoyen, and who had a versatility characteristic of youth, for he had just turned fifty years old.

On the other hand there was an Argentina stained by the vices of fraud that, although it had men who had fought against this as much as against fascism, they had been soiled nevertheless with the corruption of the old country.

Perón was linked to happy moments such as those which the people experienced, with gainful employment, high salaries, an absence of inflation, and a series of social and cultural benefits to which one had access only then. The people embraced the new proposal. It was a very narrow triumph, 52% against 47 or 48% for the Democratic Union, but the system of the Sáenz Peña Law permitted Perón to rise to power with thirteen of the fourteen provinces (the only one with an opposition government was Corrientes), two-thirds of the Chamber of Deputies of the Nation, and almost the entire Senate.

One could say, that when Perón assumed the presidency on June 4, 1946, the practically absurd movement of 1943 was left justified. In reality, it was the only de facto process in Argentina that had electoral success; all the rest failed.

Although within the country and abroad, piles of books, articles, monographic works, and research papers have been written that try to explain, with varying degrees of success, what Peronism was, in my opinion none manage to hit on an accurate definition of that so curious and Argentine a phenomenon. Some speak of populism or of Third Worldism; others of an attenuated fascist system characteristic of Latin American countries where the army would have hegemony through one single party. But these definitions, useful for political theoreticians, do not have much importance for us, for whom what now matters is addressing concrete things, to try in some way to besiege this political experiment that the first phase of Peronism was, so original within Argentine history. In this chapter, then, we shall dispense with theories.

## CHAPTER XII

# Apogee of the peronist regime

We should remember that Juan Domingo Perón assumed the constitutional presidency of the Argentine Republic on June 4, 1946, a term that ended on June 4, 1952, but that same day, by virtue of the reelection established by the constitutional reform of 1949, he assumed the presidency for a second time, though without completing it, as he was overthrown in September of 1955.

The two presidencies of Perón had similar characteristics, but certain nuances distinguished one from the another. In this installment, we are mainly going to speak about the first presidency, treating the topic from different points of view, insofar as it is very difficult to make a global appraisal. For the time being, we can see aspects related to economics —which was perhaps the most original undertaking of the government—, to politics, to the opposition, and to the world during those years that occurred between 1946 and 1952, period in which, what's more, a presence such as that of Evita added very unique characteristics.

## Economics

The economics of the Peronist system, initially, were nationalist, statist, and autarchic. Nationalist, because there was an attempt at nationalization, that is, at transferring to the country a series of activities and services that until then were in the hands of foreign countries or foreign companies. The repatriation of the foreign debt is an example of this. Argentina had a foreign debt whose total was not very significant. One of the measures that Perón undertook upon assuming command was to repatriate the country; that is, to buy titles that were abroad and on which little interest was being produced, thereby converting this foreign debt into an internal debt. Some criticized this operation a great deal, maintaining that the amounts that were paid to foreign creditors in the form of interest and amortization were in reality very small, while the quantity of money necessary to acquire that debt had been very great.

It should be recalled that during the Second World War,

Argentina had accumulated important reserves of money in Great Britain, and these in turn, for the first time in its history, converted it from an indebted country to a creditor country. It found itself in a very special position, strengthened by its being a provider of raw materials (above all, of grains and oleaginous products) in a world that was just beginning to reconstruct its economies and its systems of production following the war. Perón and his economic policy, then, were to a certain extent an expression of that Argentina that I described in the previous chapter; a triumphalist Argentina, which had passed through all the avatars of the world war unscathed and, what's more, felt itself a part of the most important nations of the world, its production being needed by European countries and the country itself being spoiled, even flattered by the United States, despite the differences that had existed with the previous de facto governments.

As far as the statism of the first presidency of Perón, it was due to the very signficant position that the State acquired in the economic life of the country. The National State up until then, even with the interventionism established by the conservative governments of the thirties, had a relatively secondary position. The State was not in charge of any of the public services of importance, except for a small part of the Argentine railroad network; apart from this, it did not carry out practically any public service.

Following 1946 —and to summarize— the National State had under its control: all railroad transportation, through the purchase of the English railroads realized in 1948 (and preceded by the purchase of the French railroads, which were much less important but which formed part of the national railroad network); the supplying of gas throughout the whole country, through the purchase of the *Compañia Primitiva de Gas,* which was of British origin; and the distribution of energy throughout the country, through the purchase of power plants in the interior. In Buenos Aires and in the Greater Buenos Aires area, the distribution of energy, by contrast, continued in the hands of CHADE, that international holding company, protagonist of a scandal during the decade of 1930 and which, due to a mysterious circumstance, was absolutely respected by Perón. Perhaps the circumstance is not so mysterious if we consider that, according to what has been proven, the board of directors of CHADE, at the time, helped Perón with money for his electoral campaign and that this favor was returned by Perón's allowing CHADE to continue to administer service in the Capital —though without renovating its utilities, a detail which would mean serious problems later.

But let us continue with the enumeration. The National State was also in control of: river transport, through the purchase of the *Compañía Dodero;* air transportation, domestic and international, through the creation of four companies that afterwards merged into Aerolíneas Argentinas; foreign commerce, in all that was related to the exportation of oleaginous products, grains, meats, and other important categories. The State, essentially, would buy from the farmer at a specific price, substituting what firms such as Bunge and Born or Dreyfus had done during many years, and after, it would sell the products abroad, generally setting a price with a rather healthy markup. Through the IAPI *(Instituto Argentino de Promoción de Intercambio),* which made these transactions, the State would acquire from abroad those elements —manufactured or not— that it presumed the country needed so that the circuit continued functioning. This was not always done properly and many times a huge amount of materials were received that served no purpose or that ended up rotting away in the depositories of the Customhouse.

The state presence in public services and foreign service was developed in the context of great intervention of the State in credit, economic, and financial policy, carried into effect through the nationalization of the Central Bank. The board of directors of the Central Bank, which as we know was created during the management of the conservatives in the thirties, was made up of representatives of the banks both of the public sector as well as the private sector. One of the measures that Perón requested of the de facto government before taking charge of the presidency in June, 1946, was the nationalization of the Central Bank, which consisted in returning to private banks the contributions they had made and, consequently, to make of the Central Bank an entity representative only of the official bank.

But aside from this, the financial policy of this time consisted in a very ingenious maneuver: the guarantee of all financial deposits on the part of the National State, in exchange for which, the State confiscated all the money that was in the national ambit. All of this on paper, of course, but as a counterpresentation of this guarantee, it would be the Central Bank who gave directives to all the banks —private as well as state owned— for lines of credit and rediscount. This is to say that, from this moment on, the credit and financial policy of the country was firmly in the hands of the Central Bank, dependent on the government.

Other State activities that of course had nothing to do with the lending of public services were connected to German companies, confiscated in relation to the declaration of war, in March of 1945. This development meant, in the final analysis, that the State was the patron of a series of enterprises in which everything from medicinal products to cosmetics were manufactured.

In essence the State had enormous involvement in the economic life of the country. The number of public agents increased considerably and the regulations became more and more oppressive as the economic policy suffered some difficulties. Campaigns began to be made for a decrease in the cost of living, for price regulation, for subsidies for specific activities such as bakeries or cold storage companies, or for the punishment of "unscrupulous" merchants who increased prices. It is evident, then, that the State had so great a presence in economic life that it would not be an exaggeration to say that the policy of Perón was purely statist.

As for the autarchic character of Peronist economics, this was fundamentally due to the idea that Argentina had sufficient entities and a type of production so varied as to be able to virtually provide for itself. All of which meant customs barriers to subsidize, above all, industry. And combining this with the policy of the IAPI, that is, the purchase of agrarian production to sell it afterwards abroad, signified an enormous transference of resources from the rural areas to the industrial sector.

All of this had an explanation: the favorable situation with which Argentina had come out of the Second World War. But it also carried with it the burden that, at some point, it would have to come to an end. When the international economic circuits began to be reconstructed —something that occurred quite rapidly—, when the agreements of Bretton Woods began to be put into practice, agreements that tried to liberalize international commerce and that were against restrictive policies or subsidies of different countries, our country —which by then ceased to be a creditor because it had used up the accumulated reserves by, for example, purchasing the railroads, repatriating the foreign debt, paying for capital assets of foreign companies that had settled in the country and had been acquired— was obviously to find that its policy was increasingly difficult to maintain. This policy —interventionist, statist, autarchic, and nationalist— could not, in effect, continue for much longer, unless two conditions were met, true wagers that Perón made at the time. One, very concrete; the other, a bit more vague. Wagers that failed, that did not turn out.

## Changes of direction

The first gamble was that a third world war would break out. Perón was convinced that at any moment the United States and the Soviet Union would be locked in a nonatomic confrontation that would benefit Argentina as the first and second world wars had, when its primary products obtained high prices, were easily placed, and the country attained a certain autonomy. Although the third world war did not occur, Perón was not so far off-track, for in 1950 there occurred a bellicose confrontation in Korea that, in the end, the United States and the Soviet Union were the protagonists of and that could have spread and become uncontrollable, but finally was confined to Korean territory during some three years, without producing that world conflagration that Perón presaged in articles published in the newspaper *Democracia* under a transparent pseudonym: Descartes.

The other wager, more vague, was that of predicting the existence of a national bourgeoisie with sufficient economic means so as to create new sources of work, to establish an industry that did not need to be so subsidized and protected. Perón calculated that, in an alliance with the bourgeoisie, the State and this new economic start could once again open a phase of prosperity in the life of the country. The fact of the matter is, the bourgeoisie did not exist or was timid and cowardly, or it did not have sufficient guarantees so that its surplus could be channeled into other types of activities outside the traditional ones.

And so this situation of good fortune, which in 1946 caused Perón to exclaim that one could not walk through the Central Bank due to the quantity of gold that was accumulated, in 1951 or 1952, became very worrisome. Argentine money, the Argentine peso, which in 1946 was backed 130 percent by foreign currency and gold, in 1952, was backed at -15 percent, that is to say, it did not have total coverage. Our foreign currency, the reserves of gold and dollars that the country had accumulated as a consequence of the war, had evaporated. And therefore there was a need to begin to change direction, something that Perón did from his second presidency onward, after winning the elections of 1951.

In this sense, what is also important to point out is that the economic policy of Perón, which was audacious, risky, and nourished by strong speculation, had as its central figure, in large part, a man with a very original personality: Miguel Miranda, a tin manufacturing industrialist who could have flashes of brilliance as well as some major improvisations that, unfortunately, the country had to pay for, just as at other times it was able to reap the benefits of his good ideas.

In his capacity as president of the Central Bank, Miranda was czar of the economy, since, although there was a Ministry of Finance, a Department of Commerce, etc., it was he who really managed the economy. This state of affairs lasted until January, 1949. On this date Miranda had to resign and Perón slowly initiated a change in the economic policy, whose protagonist was to be not a strongman, but teams of technical functionaries, among whom Alfredo Gómez Morales, at the outset, and Antonio Cafiero, a very young man at the time, distinguished themselves.

The politics of Perón, which today, viewed retrospectively, seem to us to be rather crazy, had its explanation not only because Argentina had come out of the war unscathed and strong, but also because the thinking of the central countries during the postwar period coincided largely with this idea of a strong State with economic intervention and a design for social engineering that would be extended to the best distribution of wealth; with the idea of nationalizing essential public services, banks, and large industries —as occurred in England after 1945, with the triumph of the Labor Party, or as in France after Liberation, when the government headed by De Gaulle nationalized some large companies, even those in automobile manufacturing. This is to say that statist thinking was rather prevalent in the world of that era.

In Argentina the wing of radicalism that responded to the Movement of Intransigence, which after 1948 took command of the party, also upheld this line of thought. The Declaration of Avellaneda, subscribed in 1945, expanded in 1946, and turned into the law of the party following 1948, also postulated a series of measures not too different from those that Perón had adopted, with the same nationalist, autarchic, statist tendency. What was occurring was that these measures, which could be necessary, were destined to become debilitated after a time. Perón did not have this possibility in mind, or he only realized it when making the corresponding rectifications had too high a cost.

What is certain, is that toward 1951 or 1952, the economic policy of the government began to lose strength, a phenomenon which in no way signified that the people might have sensed this. In general, people were living a fuller, more content life; their money went further than during other years: with a cost of living index of 100 in 1943, in 1950, an average blue-collar worker, of construction for example, earned a cost of living index of 120. That is, his buying power had increased significantly and this latter was spent fundamentally on clothes and food. People lived better, ate better, and had a better time.

Shortly after continuing with this type of policy, the standard of living would also deteriorate, because it was increasingly more difficult to carry forth an economy that needed foreign currency, dollars basically, to be able to continue supporting itself. Fuel was needed for example. *Yacimientos Petrolíferos Fiscales* (YPF) had not increased its production during these years, nor had private petroleum companies, and consequently, the fuel that was needed for the Argentine economy to continue functioning cost the country three hundred million dollars in that era, which was a lot of money and, what's more, the country did not have it. Industrial costs also, which required a lot of money and were needed to maintain in operation this in large part subsidized and protected industry were high, and money was also needed to pay royalties or to pay the remittance of profits of foreign companies established here.

All of this was very difficult to continue maintaining with a policy such as that which Perón was carrying out, added to which were the droughts of 1950 and 1951 (which were significant and undermined the country's grain export capacity), plus the reluctance of rural producers vis-à-vis a policy that subjected them to extortion. During the times when the prices in Europe were high and in which our exports were needed, there was a third (the State, through the IAPI) that bought the rural production for very little money and sold it abroad making a fabulous profit. On the other hand, the same lack of foreign currency made rural mechanization difficult, which stagnated this type of production. What is certain is that in 1951 and 1952, the area of sown land in Argentina plummeted catastrophically. But the consequences of all this only began to be noticed after the reelection of Perón in 1952.

## Political aspects

The Peronist system was also original as far as its political side. It was obviously authoritarian and populist and tended toward a one-party system. There was an official movement, composed of the Men's Peronist Party, and following 1949, from the time that the vote was granted to women, of the Women's Peronist Party; the third branch of the Peronist Movement was the *Confederación General del Trabajo* (CGT).

From the outset, even before having taken charge of the government, Perón was concerned with organizing the political instruments that he should have at hand to exercise power. Thus, before assuming the constitutional presidency in 1946, he decided to dissolve the political forces that had voted for his name in February and constituted with the rest of these forces a party that at first had no name, was later called the *Partido Unico de la Revolución Nacional* [Sole Party of the National Revolution], and finally, was called the Peronist Party.

The Peronist Party, consequently, was the direct political organ through which officialism operated. A party naturally formed by adherents and enthusiasts, but also by many tokens of obligatory affiliation on the part of public employees; a party that enjoyed obvious official patronage, evidenced in different ways. The most blatant was how the officialist party participated in the management of the State, along with the third branch, the CGT, which in a session of Congress in 1950 had declared that it formed part of the *Movimiento Justicialista*.

This must be viewed from the perspective of the authoritarianism of the government of Perón, who from the beginning had a very hostile attitude with respect to his opponents. In the previous chapter we said that the Argentine electoral system of this era gave to Peronism, despite the small difference with which he triumphed in the elections of 1946, virtual unanimity in the Senate, a two-thirds majority in the Chamber of Deputies, and practically all the provincial governments, except that of Corrientes, which was placed under government control a year later. This then meant that it had virtual unanimity in the whole country.

But as if he were not content with all of this, Perón was preoccupied with buying all the private radios in the country, establishing a chain of officialist newspapers and magazines, and applying a policy of constant pressure on the opposition parties that, as clearly follows from the above, had meager parliamentary representation and practically zero capacity to oppose the governmental policies of Perón. Nevertheless, the manner in which the opposition was treated suggested that officialism believed the latter was conspiring constantly.

The idea of "movement" was actually a very negative idea within Argentine political history, because it established a priori the conception that in that movement the national will, the popular will, history itself was incarnated, and consequently, those who were against him were practically traitors against their own country. The treatment of the opposition therefore was very harsh. Radical deputies were often prevented from speaking; some of them were expelled, others, such as Ricardo Balbín, were encarcerated. And there were those who had to go into exile.

The political parties led an active life but full of pressures, of persecutions, of risks even. The electoral campaigns were not easy, there was no access to any radio, basically there existed only two independent newspapers of national significance, *La Nación* and *La Prensa,* and this latter was silenced in 1951, when under a union pretext it was shut down and, finally, the government expropriated it in order to hand it over to the CGT. Propaganda and publicity were handled by an organism dependent on the State, which attained great perfection in the sense of not letting any news or commentary filter through that might be displeasing to the government.

It was an atmosphere in which the opposition was interpreted as if it were a negative shadow in the country, a sector that, because it did not share the ideals of the majority, should be left on the margins of the political process. Nothing similar to tolerance or pluralism existed during those years of government. On the contrary, a hostile attitude prevailed nourished by Perón himself, who in many speeches had very harsh and even demented expressions with respect to the opposition, threatening to hang them, threatening that he himself would deliver baling wire in order to kill those who would disturb a government that was enjoying the support of the popular majority. This undoubtedly made it so that Argentine politics of those years were very primitive, very harsh, dreadful, and so that the opposition also had an unloyal attitude toward the government. Many were the conspiracies that began to be plotted, almost all of them completely insane and without the slightest possibility of coming true, but which in any case gave an indication that on the part of the opposition, as well, the idea of a fair game did not exist.

Who was to blame for all of this? I believe that in these cases the governments are always mostly to blame; they should in general have a dose of patience and greater tolerance than the oppositions. Perón was not a model of patience and tolerance. And here we have to name then an element that had much importance in this sort of fanaticism that he aroused and in the submissiveness that was deliberately encouraged from the officialist circles: the personality of Evita (Eva Duarte, wife of Juan Perón).

# Evita

It is unjust to speak of Evita in so small a space. Her figure would require a more detailed analysis —it has already been done; she is an individual that has aroused the curiosity of many observers in Argentina and abroad—, but it could be said in any case that the presence of Evita in the Peronist government fulfilled various functions.

In the first place, to establish a contact between the government and the worker's movement, the trade unions. In the second place, to be the head of the Women's Peronist Party; that is, the born leader of a new electorate that had joined the national scene and that had enormous numerical importance. And in the third place, in a certain sense it was Evita who, through her disheveled oratory and her fanaticism, infused the Peronist ranks with a mystique difficult to maintain over so long a period of time. Six years, in effect, is a long time to maintain a mystique, and notwithstanding, Evita managed it until her health betrayed her.

So these three functions, plus that of directing a sort of informal Ministry of Social Welfare as she did from the Foundation that bore her name, gave Evita very outstanding and very original characteristics. Undoubtedly, this woman, who lacked education and culture, had very fine intuition; she knew how to make her way, she found out how to adjust the instruments of her proselytism, and, in the later years of her life, she began to fine-tune her militant side —even physically.

Personally, I respect Evita greatly; I respect her as a very authentic woman. But I would not like for that archetype to be repeated in Argentina, because it signified a regression in every sense of the political life of the country. It added a tremendous element of fanaticism, a demand for unconditional adhesion to Perón, which did not do the republican system any good —although within the Peronist system it might have been something inevitable. She died, as we all know, few days after Perón assumed his second presidency.

## The constitution of 1949

The other element to keep in mind as far as politics during the time of Perón goes is the sanction of the Constitution of 1949. The authoritarian idea of constructing a hegemonic political force began to manifest itself in Peronism from the moment Perón took charge of the constitutional presidency —and this despite the speech with which he inaugurated his term, stating that he was going to be president of all Argentines and promising tolerance and comprehension for those who did not think as he did. Perón's first concern was to organize a scheme of power that would permit him to first realize his objectives and later, to the extent that it was possible, to become known throughout time. In order to achieve this he tried to eliminate all institutional obstacles that could be in the way.

The first episode in this respect was the trial of the Supreme Court. In 1948, all of the Supreme Court justices, excepting only one, were brought to trial and were dismissed on account of bad conduct. In reality, no concrete charge was attributed to them because they might have fulfilled their duties poorly. The charges that were made against them were of a political nature, and the purpose of displacing the Court was to appoint another that would not cause problems.

It was a very tough, very abrupt event; it was the first time in Argentine political life that it was done —and I hope, the last. In addition, it was a very unjust and offensive episode as for the values of justice, but surely to Perón and to his circle it seemed indispensable that there not be a possible obstacle of this kind for the legislation that was going to be sanctioned. And in practice, really, it was not in any way so revolutionary as to not be able to be homologated by this Court, composed of gentlemen who came from the conservative era but who had demonstrated sufficient ductility so as to accept a large amount of changes in legislation.

From this moment on, a sort of race toward the reelection of Perón occurred. The Constitution of 1853 prohibited the immediate reelection of the president; the idea of its reform, therefore, was launched. What is curious is that Perón, in a paragraph of the inauguration speech of the Legislative Assembly of 1948 gave the best arguments possible against presidential reelection. They were very sensible arguments and already customary in political and constitutional science, according to which reelection in a certain way signified the opportunity for permanent arbitrariness, for the perpetuation of a person's power.

Nevertheless, several months later Perón accepted the idea of the reform of the Constitution, an idea that was voted incorrectly in the Chamber of Deputies, with a majority that was not what was stipulated by the Constitution and without having established, in accordance with constitutional practice, which points of the text were to be reformed. At any rate, the mechanism of reform was set in motion; elections were held; the Peronist Party triumphed overwhelmingly, as always; and the Constitutional Convention, which met some few times between January and April of 1949, was realized.

Despite the fact that additions of a rhetorical nature were made, the base itself of the Constitution of 1853 was untouched. What was added, because in the end it was the purpose of the reform, was the possibility of reelecting the president indefinitely. And this was made clear when during a decisive session, the president of the radical block, Moisés Lebensohn, hounded the majority speaker and the latter confessed that in reality the entire reform was being made solely to be able to reelect Perón.

The Constitution of 1949 then, established a new scheme of power and the possibility for Perón to be reelected in 1952 for six more years. That is, for his hegemony to last twelve years, with the possibility of prolonging it indefinitely.

But the Constitution of 1949 also established a series of aspects that escaped Perón's control and that did not turn out to be too agreeable to him. For example, article 40, which stipulates a very rigid policy regarding the rendering of public services and the ownership of mineral deposits, waterfalls, and sources of hydroelectric energy. Perón himself was practically imprisoned and impeded from carrying out possible reforms to his economic policy.

As we saw previously, Miranda had resigned in January of 1949, just when the Convention began to meet. This signaled, in some way, advance notice that the economic policy of Perón was going to be reformed. And it is at this time when a small sector of Peronist conventionalists of nationalist extraction succeeded in introducing article 40, which would lock Perón in to a very rigid program of an economic policy. As we shall see further on, this would have importance later, in 1955.

# The international context

The Peronist system, with its political and economic peculiarities, was taking place in the context of the increasingly pronounced Cold War, in a world in which the United States needed allies and could find an important one in Argentina. In 1949, Perón launched the so-called Third Position: he announced to the world that Argentina was neither with the Soviet Union nor with the United States, but that it adhered to a different position. It was a sort of presage of what later would be the Nonaligned Movement, from which only a short while ago our country removed itself due to a decision —paradoxically— by a Peronist government.

The Third Position was more rhetorical than anything else. In practice, it was not carried out. In reality, in large international forums such as the United Nations, the Argentine delegation almost always voted along with the United States. But it did not adhere to the International Monetary Fund (IMF), nor to the United Nations Educational, Sciencific and Cultural Organization (UNESCO), nor to the Food and Agricultural Organization of the United Nations (FAO). That is, it maintained itself in isolation, which basically responded to the autarchical idea of the economic policy that the Peronist government carried forth.

In any case, the Third Position, rhetorical as it was, helped to infuse the Argentine people with an even more nationalistic feeling, giving them the idea that our country could place itself above the contingencies and affairs of international politics and maintain a position that, in the last resort, was none other than the neutralism upheld by Hipólito Yrigoyen during the First World War and, during the Second World War, by a conservative president such as Castillo and by the military of the de facto government of 1943-1946.

What is certain is that the idea that endorsed the Third Position was the possibility of a third world war, which did not come about. Perón nevertheless, had sufficient ability so as to color his Third Position speech with the assumption of specific attitudes, above all as concerned his relationship with the United States, which around 1953 was evolving toward almost total agreement. Meanwhile, it is appropriate to analyze what the oppositional backdrop was during these six years of the first presidency of Perón.

## The opposition

In the first place, the traditional parties, those who had received a beating in the election of 1946, opposed Perón. The only party that had come out of the election with certain vigor, so as to be able to lead the institutional opposition of Perón, was radicalism. With its 44 deputies in the Chamber, it constituted a very solid block, very homogeneous, composed of personalities that in many cases would later have a lasting importance in the politics of the country, as is the case of Arturo Frondizi, Ricardo Balbín, and many others. It was a block that in some cases formed a very high-quality opposition and established very respectable positions. In other cases, it let itself be carried away by the logical reaction of feeling so pressured, so antagonized, that its opposition diminished and turned simply into a fight for survival.

But around the block —whose sign was intransigent and therefore nonunionist; that is, more connected to the tradition of Yrigoyen than to that of Alvear— a movement of reconstruction of radicalism began to be realized. In 1948, as we pointed out earlier, this movement attained the direction of the party and established as partisan documents those that the Intransigent Movement had elaborated, with a tendency as statist as Perón's, as much or more neutralist, and more antioligarchical, more antiimperialist. More revolutionary, in essence. It was the thinking of the era, but was strengthened by a party that, as it did not have the slightest possibility of attaining power, could consequently play with ideas in a, shall we say, unpunished manner.

Next to radicalism, conservativism had practically broken up, had shown itself to have an almost nonexistent electorate. For the first time since the Sáenz Peña Law socialism had not obtained a single representative in the Chamber of Deputies. Communism remained clandestine or illegal. This did not mean though that the opposition to Perón materialized only at the political level, in parties such as the radical or socialist party.

There was a loose and dispersed opposition, which at times was manifested along class lines, as was the case of the Argentine upper classes, who were bothered by this egalitarian sense that Peronism had, at times vulgar and aggressive. The fact that people could go to summer resorts that previously were the pleasure of the elite irritated and displeased many people. Several of the country's traditional institutions, such as the Jockey Club or the Twentieth of February Club, were an essential part of the opposition and were harassed by the Peronist government. The Jockey Club was burned down; the Twentieth of February, expropriated, something that happened to several other traditional institutions, as well.

In some centers of business there was a hushed opposition against Perón, although it was not made manifest in too clear a fashion. Nevertheless, it did exist, above all in rural environments, which were the most levied against by Perón's economic policy. But in any event, this opposition was rather individual, loose —similar to what Gastón Boissier describes in referring to the time of the Caesars, when in reality, more than an opposition, there existed some individual voices that, inaudibly and not all too clearly, showed themselves to be against what was happening and pointed out those acts that in their opinion were condemnable.

The institutional opposition, then, was incarnated in radicalism, which with many difficulties in carrying out its proselytizing action, with many problems in maintaining its organization throughout the country, nevertheless sustained a spirited position that permitted it, in 1951, to give 32 percent of the votes of the electorate to the Balbín-Frondizi ticket. It is true that Perón got more than 62 percent of the vote; but actually, if one considers the conditions under which a political campaign could progress at the time, having obtained this proportion was quite a feat.

There existed opposition in the Armed Forces, as well. There was a position of repudiation, or at least, of nonadhesion to Perón, despite the fact that he —general of the Nation himself— took advantage of the economic situation of the country and pushed for the modernization and reoutfitting of the Armed Forces, above all of the Air Force, which was his baby. Nonetheless, there were many reasons for resentment within the army, because undoubtedly there was a policy of encouraging those commanders and officials who were followers of the Peronist regime, and of marginalizing those who were not.

Although this was of course not the only reason for the revolution of Menéndez of 1951, in a certain way it constituted the background of this military coup, a coup occurring in a void, because if one views it with a historical perspective, it had not the slightest possibility of succeeding. It took place in September of 1951, and with barely two months remaining until the presidential elections, it had no repercussion in the rest of the country. It simply consisted in the success of several retired and several active officers —among them, Lanusse, at the time captain— in removing some fragments of units of Campo de Mayo and, when they saw that they did not have the slightest possibility of triumphing, they dispersed. At any rate, this revolution indicated that within the army there were certain opposition nuclei, and naturally, from this point on, the activity of the Minister of War was to clean out the anti-Peronists from the Armed Forces.

In reality, Peronism, during its first presidency, had the allure that new things do. With a Perón still young —he had assumed power at the age of fifty—, introducing a phraseology and several slogans that easily reached the heart of the people, and within a national and international context that permitted him to sustain a social policy with a direct effect on raising the average standard of living of the people. But it was based on an economic policy that could not function for too long. And this was apparent after 1952, upon Evita's death. When Perón took over the presidency for a second time there began a series of disquieting phenomena, such as inflation, the shortage of foreign currency, and the need to turn around the economic and governmental policies completely.

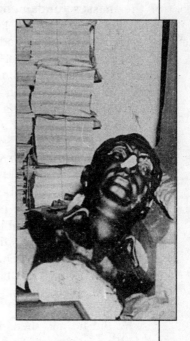

The second government of Juan Domingo Perón began on June 4, 1952 and should have continued through to the same day of 1958, but it terminated abruptly in September of 1955. This interruption of his second presidency poses one of the most burning questions relative to the era: Why did Perón fall?

# CHAPTER XIII

# The fall of the peronist regime

# The organized community

It was not power he might have lacked. On the contrary, at the time that his system began to fail, he had succeeded in establishing what he called the Organized Community, where specific functions were ascribed to each one of the organisms that represented the fundamental activities in the life of the country, such as the General Confederation of Labor (CGT), the Economic General Confederation (CGE), the Universitary General Confederation (CGU), the Armed Forces, the security forces, education, sports, and of course, a chain of newspapers and magazines that, along with the radio stations, created an almost invincible force of promotion and propaganda.

Furthermore, the Peronist regime counted on the support of the masses fundamentally. A support that had been expressed in 1951, when Perón was elected with more than 60 percent of the vote, and that had been reiterated in April of 1954 on the occasion of the election of the vice president, which yielded a figure almost equal to the previous one: 62 percent in favor of Perón and 32 percent for the principle candidate of the opposition, the radical Crisólogo Larralde.

To the organization of all the important sectors of Argentine life, then, which in some way found themselves connected to the *justicialista* State, we must add the support of the masses, which not only had been revealed through the elections but also could be perceived, without the need for an electoral poll, by the presence of the multitudes in the regime's liturgical assemblies, on May 1, October 17, and even on some new dates that began to be established, such as August 31, "Day of Renunciation," which was celebrated in honor of Evita, who had passed away a month and a half after the second presidential assumption of her husband.

Why did he fall, then? Perhaps his economic policy had reached an intolerable limit? By no means. At the time of the fall of the Peronist regime, the economic policy had been rectified and it had put aside some of the most daring iniciatives of the first era. We said already that this first phase, which could be called that of euphoria and dissipation, had given aid to interesting initiatives, but with a limited life span, a limited way out.

Nevertheless, after 1950, when this type of politics hit bottom; when it became evident that one could not forge ahead with an autarchical, nationalist, statist tendency because it meant a complete lack of foreign currency and, as a result, difficulty in importing certain essential, expendable materials for the life of the country; and when this translated into an inflation that reached 30 percent in 1951 (which was scandalous and outrageous for life in Argentina); at that moment, the government initiated a change of direction.

## Rectifications

After 1951, following the triumphant election of Perón in November, measures began to be adopted that were put into effect in February of the next year according to what at the time was called an austerity program and what, in present-day terms, would be called a price-fixing program. The program indicated the need to control certain types of expenditures and, above all, the need to once again encourage farming and animal husbandry, which had been almost discontinued subsequent to the policies of the IAPI, which as we explained earlier was the obligatory purchaser of agriculture's primary products and the vender and intermediary vis-à-vis the European markets.

Perón rectified this policy severely and fixed rather remunerative prices for the producers, aside from taking other measures such as control of prices and salaries and control of communal agreements (which were frozen for two years after 1952), and in this way he succeeded in reducing the rate of inflation to a significant degree: the year 1952 was at four percent annual and the following year, barely three percent. The economic policy, therefore, was not what precipitated the fall of the regime.

On the other hand, after 1952 there were a series of initiatives of an economic nature that made it clear that Perón had left the audacious phase behind him, only to take up once again what could be called classic economics. Already in January of 1949, Miguel Miranda —author of the Peronist economic policy during the beginning years; at times brilliant, at times mistaken, as we pointed out earlier— had been defenestrated and replaced by less imaginative and spectacular but more technical teams, with an orthodox conception of economy. It was then that some measures that truly signified a step backward in all that had been done were sanctioned. Among these, the law of foreign investments could be cited.

Until this time, Peronism had not shown much interest in the investments from abroad. On the contrary, it had contemplated them with a certain disdain, departing from the premise of the existence of a national bourgeoisie with sufficient capital so as to be able to put new undertakings into operation and to create new sources of work. But this did not occur, and so in 1951, a law of foreign investments was sanctioned; a good law, one could say; moderate, where the right was recognized for foreign principals to send remittances to their countries of origin; certain guarantees were given them and they were placed within the legal framework where Argentine companies functioned or could function. It was certainly an acknowledgment of the need for new capital to arrive so as to create new sources of work, which already were beginning to fail.

In the second place, an apparently nonofficial event —the Congress of Productivity—, which occurred in April of 1955, also demonstrated that the economic policy had varied substantially. This Congress, which had as its stage the palace of the Congress of the Nation, was led by the Economic General Confederation and the General Confederation of Labor. The State —in theory— had nothing to do with it. In practice, it was the government that encouraged the dialogue between these two forces that represented businessmen and workers.

And in this dialogue the necessity arose for an increase in productivity from the economic circuits, even at the cost of

Government House just inaugurated.

The Golden Years in a tango club, a caricature of Medrano.

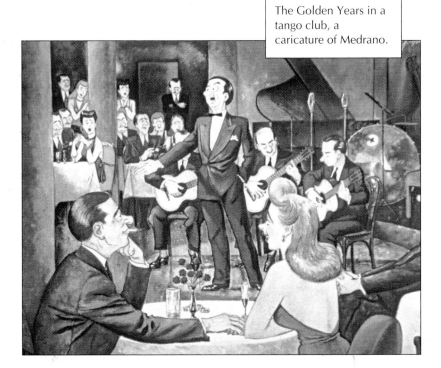

The romantic affair between the actress Eva Duarte and Juan Domingo Perón.

The unions celebrate May 1, Labor's Day, in front of the Government House in 1950.

some norms, conquests, and forms that prevailed until then in the work environment. Whenever one speaks of productivity —throughout the world, and during all eras— the labor unions began to worry. It was the same in this case, and there was even a certain resistance on the part of some trade organizations that, aside from their formally Peronist affiliation, had bases that did not depend strictly on the official party. But regardless, the Congress of Productivity recommended doing away with certain courses of action, such as the so-called "layoff industry," which during the first few years of the regime had been transformed into a major abuse, just as the abuse of overtime.

Finally, the other aspect that showed to what extent the Peronist regime had altered its economic policy throughout 1954, and above all after 1955, was the possible contract for exploitation of oil with California, a North American petroleum company with which the government entered into negotiations ceding it almost the entirety of the present-day province of Santa Cruz so that prospecting and the exploitation of oil could be carried out there. One of the most serious problems that Perón had to face as a consequence of his earlier economic policy was precisely the shortage of fuel and the scarcity of what it should have been importing: the importation of liquid fuel, required by the country's industry in order to continue functioning, cost 300 million dollars at that time. And this was an increasingly difficult expenditure to confront.

The decision of Perón, then, to make a contract with California, with all that this could connotate as far as being a concession that went totally against the nationalist policy he had preached, was an expression of to what extent the system found itself against the wire in certain respects, to what extent the economic policy had failed in certain areas. And, in effect, this was one of them, because the political cost that Perón had to pay for going forward with the contract with California was, obviously, very high. All the nationalistic sectors that supported him bristled immediately, while the opposition began to denounce what seemed to be a serious inconsistency of the government that from its early petroleum policy, which was based on the need to give YPF the monopoly on oil exploitation and commercialization, had ended up ceding half of a division of national Argentine territory for it to be exploited by a North American company.

## Farewell to the third position

Nevertheless, several more things had changed, not only the economic policy: the position of the Peronist government with respect to the United States had been modified, as well. At the beginning of his government, in 1946, the effects of the confrontation between the ex ambassador Braden and Perón still dragged on, but afterward relations began to be repaired. The issue of Guatemala, in 1953, demonstrated to what extent Perón was determined to align himself behind the United States in matters of international politics.

Since 1950, Guatemala, a small country in Central America, had a government with socialist tendencies, and naturally, it was denounced in Washington as infiltrated by communists. It had a rather firm social policy; it had applied agrarian reform and expropriated some properties of the United Fruit, the North American fruit company that had interests in other countries in Central America, for which reason denunciations rained down immediately upon that regime.

The situation was such that the United States succeeded in assembling in Caracas a conference of American ministers of foreign affairs for the express purpose of condemning the Guatemalan regime as a virtually communist regime, infiltrated within the American community. It was a sort of prefiguration of what would happen later with Cuba. When the Argentine representation had to vote on this condemnation, it limited itself to abstaining. Obviously, some years earlier the attitude would have been very different in a similar situation. But, what's more, when an internal Guatemalan group overthrew the regime of Jacobo Arbenz with the help of the United States, and the majority of its functionaries had to take asylum —some of them in the Argentine embassy until finally they succeeded in getting an airplane that would take them to Buenos Aires—, the upshot was that the Peronist government threw them in prison in Villa Devoto. This is to say that the Guatemalan functionaries who, communist or not, had believed in the possibility of better distributing the wealth of their country, suddenly discovered that the leader who had been the precursor of this type of politics in Latin America, he who in a certain way had stood as an important point of reference for those who desired a slightly more fair distribution, was throwing them in jail for more than a year.

The changes, then, were important in every sense. But they did not take place solely because Perón wanted them to, but also because the circumstances were beginning to impose them. And this had begun throughout the course of 1952 and became more pronounced in the year 1953, when Perón tried the most spectacular measure of his politics: opening the markets in Latin America. He left for Chile and there tried to sign an agreement with the government of General Ibáñez that practically amounted to almost total economic union with our country. The Chileans were opposed and the pact that was signed was much less important in the end. But regardless, Perón had great success in that country, where he was repeatedly acclaimed by the multitude.

## Toughening

Upon returning to Argentina, in April of 1953, he was met by a rather unpleasant surprise. A sudden conflict due to the supplying of meat in Buenos Aires seemed to show that there existed a network of privileged interests detrimental to consumers. Perón had the matter investigated by General León Bengoa, a very honest and very energetic military man, who believed that behind these speculative manipulations were none other than the interests of Juan Duarte, Perón's personal secretary and the brother of the deceased Evita.

This being so or not, what is certain is that around this time Perón launched a very violent speech —the one where he said he was "surrounded by thieves and panderers" and that he was going to proceed with the investigation even if his own father should fall in the process— and a day later the resounding resignation of Juan Duarte ensued. And, three days after his resignation, his suicide. It was one of the few incidents that the regime's official apparatus could not hide, and naturally it caused a great stir. That the personal secretary and brother-in-law of the president should shoot himself, leaving behind a letter —quite infantile in composition— that allowed his great personal anxiety to become known, was something that sullied the most important circles of the regime.

Faced with this, the CGT organized a demonstration in the Plaza de Mayo in support of the president and, as Perón was speaking, several bombs exploded at the entrance to the subway that gave on to Hipólito Yrigoyen Street. Two or three people died and several were hurt, and as a result of this and of some imprudent words spoken by Perón upon realizing that what had exploded were bombs, several groups —spontaneously or not— began to set fire to the *Casa del Pueblo* (of the Socialist Party), the *Casa Radical,* the Jockey Club, the Committee of the Conservative Party, the Petit Café, and other lairs of the opposition. At the same time a roundup occurred, a very intense arrest of opponents, which brought several thousand political leaders to the prisons of Villa Devoto and the National Penitentiary.

Suddenly, a rather marked tension began to grow. Things continued this way for a couple of months, until it was established who was responsible for the attack —or, at least, it was reported thus officially—: a group of youths from families more of the upper class had become organized in order to plant bombs in places from time to time, trying not to produce victims, but with the purpose of showing that there was a nucleus of opposition to Perón, at a time in which nothing organic existed that could oppose the Peronist regime.

These occurrences were unfortunate but, to a certain extent, they responded to a certain logic. What on the other hand does not seem so logical is that two months after these events had come to pass (the oppositional bombs, the fires, the arrests) Perón should have taken the initiative in pacification, in conciliating with the opposition forces. Several negotiations were carried out with leaders of the opposition, slowly some of the arrested began to be freed, and finally, in December of that year, a law of amnesty —rather arbitrary, however— was promulgated: amnesty was granted to those persons that the Executive Power considered to be eligible for amnesty, which meant that several dozens of political leaders were released from prison, but that others remained under arrest, such as Cipriano Reyes, who had been in jail since 1948, just as the protagonists of the uprising led by General Menéndez, in September of 1951, and some conspirators that had been taken as prisoners while they were conspiring under the direction of Colonel José Francisco Suárez. In any case, it was an important development that Perón should admit that not all of his opponents were sellouts of their own country, conspirators, or terrorists; rather, that there were among them people with whom he could have dealings.

Thus ended the year 1953, with this amnesty that although it was not too significant, in some way brought about a modicum of peace and of tolerance to the national political climate. It was then, in April of 1954, that elections were held, and as has been said, the Peronist Party triumphed comfortably by 62 percent. But in May of 1954, labor strikes began to go into effect that the regime's propaganda apparatus concealed. For today's researcher, it is true martyrdom to establish which strikes occurred and with what intensity during the month of May, 1954, because in the newspapers of the era absolutely no news to this effect appears. One has to deduce them from some newspapers of the interior where news of the strikes filtered through, or from bulletins of organizations of resistance that still existed. Some of these strikes were quite forceful, such as those of the metallurgic workers, who made a march on the Federal Capital that was repressed by the police and where there was at least one death.

Nevertheless, toward the middle of 1954 the panorama that Perón could contemplate was truly encouraging. On the economic front, the inflationary outbreak of 1951 and 1952 had come to an end, prices and salaries were operating within rather satisfactory stability. One was already speaking of some investments that could arrive (and in fact they did arrive, such as the automobile factories of Córdoba and some metallurgic factories in the vicinity of Buenos Aires) and of the possibility that petroleum companies might establish themselves in the south of Argentine territory.

From the political point of view, there were no problems in sight. The opposition had been pulverized. The presence of radicalism in Congress was minimal: a mere twelve deputies out of more than two hundred, in accordance with the crafty law of elections, which had permitted that in 1954 in the Federal Capital thirteen seats be given to Peronism with 650,000 votes, and only one seat to radicalism with 500,000.

So the panorama that Perón had before him was truly calm. There were no great problems, his party had permitted rectifications of an economic nature, some of the more radicalized collaborators had been forgotten, with the result that the future could be viewed with optimism. Perón, what's more, was an optimist and, although he had forgotten by now his old wager on the third world war, the new friendship cultivated with the United States on the other hand could promise him many satisfactions.

## Conflicts with the Church

Suddenly, toward the end of 1954 (in November, to be exact), Perón did something that, in the light of political logic, is absolutely incomprehensible. Less than a year later, he would be overthrown. I am referring to the speech that he pronounced before the governors of the Argentine provinces and before union and female leaders of his party, where he denounced a part of the Argentine Church as the most important focal point against which one should have been fighting at that time.

It is rather difficult to know why he did it. Personally, I think that it was a problem of omnipotence. Perón had everything. As was said earlier, he controlled the worker's, the businessman's, the journalist's world; the Armed Forces; education. Someplace there had to be something that did not respond in such an absolute form to his policies. That something was the Church, which by its very nature could not commit itself to a specific policy, although many of its members might have been grateful to Perón for obligatory religious teaching in schools and other attitudes favorable to Catholicism that he had upheld throughout the course of his government. But that Perón, in a speech that furthermore had a very vulgar tone, should name priests and bishops who were *"contreras"* [political adversaries to Perón] —these were his actual words—, could not but provoke the reaction of the Church, which in any case was very prudent and limited itself to trying to remain distant rather than breaking off relations.

All of a sudden, Perón found himself wrapped up in a dynamic that he could not stop. Some of the men who accompanied him, above all of the second or third rank, came remotely from the left and this confrontation with the Church, this anticlerical tone that Perón began to give his political preaching, brought them back to their youthful struggles. Thus, the newspapers that formed part of the Peronist propaganda apparatus launched into an extremely violent anticlerical tone. There were sections, which did not fail to contain a certain amount of humor, written by men such as Jorge Abelardo Ramos; for example, the one called *The Disorderly Bishop,* where the worst pieces of gossip about the behavior of priests and bishops were published. And this was done practically every day, with the aim of hammering the public opinion.

The Church, in turn, began to react. On December 8, when the Immaculate Conception of the Virgin was celebrated, there was an impressive demonstration, instead of the habitually inoffensive procession that usually was no more than the passing of a few devout women and a few gentlemen around an image of the Virgin. The Church was beginning to turn into the bulwark that unified the opposition, dispersed up until then.

The Peronist government accentuated its offensive and in the final days of December of 1954, Congress approved a law that repealed that of obligatory religious teaching; another, authorizing the opening of brothels; another, removing all aid or subsidy to private educational institutes —in general religious—; and finally, a fourth law, which instituted divorce. That is, Perón had approved in Congress several of the measures that could most irritate the Church. He did it at the cost of the resistance of some legislators and, above all, some Peronist legislators. Some —very few— resigned, but in any event many were authentically Catholic legislators who, although they opted for obeying the orders that came from above, did so while internally it tore them apart.

The conflict continued. Although it calmed down in summer —as tends to happen in this country—, after April it gained new virulence. In June, after other anticlerical laws began to be sanctioned, the procession of Corpus Christi took place and an enormous multitude marched, despite the police prohibition, from the Plaza de Mayo to Congress Square. And there Perón, who in all of these situations had played the role of arbiter, committed another one of those errors of his that seem incredible. Until then, he had not headed the hostility against the Church, although obviously he was in agreement with these measures that annoyed it. On occasion he seemed willing to conciliate, but suddenly he would take up some initiative or a measure that would turn things into a red-hot situation. And, naturally, the ecclesiastical sectors, above all the nonreligious Catholic sectors, became more and more worked up around a cause that was not political but rather of a religious bent, which gave much more force to their convictions.

The tremendous error that Perón committed was to attribute the burning of a flag to the demonstrators of Corpus Christi. It was discovered immediately after that it had not been they and that in reality it had been burned in a police station in the area, and this made groups from Aeronautics and from the marines resolved to hasten a coup d'état that already was being prepared.

The rest is known history: the bombing of the Plaza de Mayo and the resulting massacre of two hundred to three hundred persons who were walking around in the area, when what was intended was the killing of Perón, who was in the Ministry of War. That night all hell broke loose in the city of

Buenos Aires and in other cities of the interior. Churches were burned and looted and Perón was incapable of putting an end to the excesses, thereby causing what had happened at mid-day in the Plaza de Mayo —the desperate homicide attempt of the bombing that had provoked hundreds of deaths— to be annulled or overlaid with the burning of churches, which occurred at night, at a time when there was no movement in the country that the government did not know about. If the incendiaries had not been sent by the official party, they at least counted on its complicity, on that of the police, on that of the firemen; that is, on that of the repressive forces.

From this time on, the attitude that Perón had adopted in the year 1953 reappeared. After having undertaken measures of extreme harshness against his opponents, an initiative of amnesty. Shortly after this, when the country was waiting for the repressive measures that the government was going to take against these men who had attempted to assassinate the president, who had killed so many people, who had bombarded the Plaza de Mayo, Perón launched a peace offensive. He once again offered a conciliation: he offered his opponents the possibility of turning themselves into part of the political whole, something which up until then had not been legal; he offered to resign from the leadership of the Revolution —he phrased it thusly— and to be President of the Nation; and, as a concrete measure, he permitted his opponents for the first time to express themselves by way of radio stations. The first voice was that of Frondizi, on July 31, 1955.

A great writer of the past century, Tocqueville, said something very applicable in many situations: the most difficult moment of bad governments is when they begin to reform. It is not that the regime of Perón had been bad *always,* nor in everything, but on a political level, elements such as omnipotence, harassment of his opponents, not admitting that an opponent could be an adversary and not an enemy had been intensely present. When he began to change, when he freed himself of some of the most hated functionaries, when he gave the opposition leaders the possibility that they be listened to, at that moment his system began to totter.

The opposition accepted the offering of conciliation without any enthusiasm. It took what could be advantageous to it, in the sense of making themselves heard throughout the country, but it did not have the slightest conviction that this was a sincere attitude. Nevertheless, Perón changed his team. He divested himself of Angel Borlenghi, Minister of the Interior; of Raúl Apold, czar of the press and chief of propaganda; of the chief of police... In essence, the fuses of his regime. The brief summer of pacification lasted almost two months, until on August 31 all the radio stations of the country announced that Perón was resigning from the Presidency of the Republic.

This was apparently the moment when he pulled the curtain down over the conciliation offensive.

Before the multitude gathered at the Plaza de Mayo, he gave a totally disheveled speech, another of those errors that one does not know what to attribute them to. I spoke with some of the protagonists of the era. Oscar Albrieu, who was Minister of the Interior, says that he had conversed with Perón at noon and that he was very serene, very calm; that after lunch he found him completely changed. He was already in position to launch his speech where he threatened all of his enemies with death, when he said "five against one;" that famous discourse still in the memory of Argentines and that at that time pushed a small group of conspirators, after the purge made in the Armed Forces, to rush headlong into the street, because they believed there was no other possibility. Or they expected death or cast themselves into the street to try to overthrow the regime.

And, in effect, on September 16, General Lonardi rebelled in Córdoba, and here I have to pose several considerations. It is very curious what occurred: General Lonardi, retired, with no troops at his command, was convinced that it would suffice to establish an anti-Peronist bulwark and to maintain it during two or three days in order for the military situation to be overturned. If one thinks carefully, outside the fleet, which was unanimously in rebellion against Perón, in the Armed Forces there existed parity of forces: in the Army, at least, almost all of the units supported the government and in

Aeronautics there were also many units that supported it. Nevertheless, it sufficed that a bulwark be set up in Córdoba and that it spread its message of encouragement and hope to its sympathizers throughout the entire country, for the regime to begin to collapse on its own.

Another observation to make is that no one came out to defend the government of Perón —nor did he, it is true, impel his defense. He alleged that he had wanted to give arms to the workers, but his minister, General Humberto Sosa Molinas, had been opposed. According to other statements he made, already in exile by then, he had not wanted to fight so as to not cause irremediable damage.

What also calls one's attention is the decision with which these men acted —they baptized the movement "Liberating Revolution"—, the coolness or the ambiguity of the forces that one presumed should support Perón and the manner in which Perón himself acted, at first setting himself up in the Ministry of War, trying to carry out alone the command of operations, later shutting himself up in his presidential residence, and finally, sending a very contradictory resignation, very ambiguous, that was analyzed by the generals of the army until a group of younger officers threatened them that they had better consider the document a resignation.

Here one should consider many elements that I am not going to delve deeply into. In the first place, because they are not pleasant; in the second, because neither are there too many proofs. I am referring to the personal conduct of Perón during the final years of his presidency. It was as if the absence of Evita had deprived him of some fundamental spring. Perón could be detested by his opponents, but he could not cease to be respected: he was a man with a sober life, a worker, who obviously enjoyed his charge, but of whom nothing could be said regarding his private side. After the death of Evita, he began to frequent a group of girls from the secondary school of the UES and, subsequently, his *liaison* was notorious with a young girl fourteen years old (he was almost sixty), who he installed in the presidential residence and whom he treated like a mistress, taking her even to events such as the Film Festival in Mar del Plata, in April of '54, or to boxing matches. Just as his relationship with her was notorious, so too were those rounds on the motor scooter that he made with his little cap.

I think these attitudes caused the love of the masses for Perón to cool. I am not saying that the people had stopped liking him, but they had stopped respecting him and this is why they did not take a step forward to defend all his social conquests and a system that was so connected to their own quality of life. It should be noted that the Argentine workers lived noticeably better toward the end of the government of Perón than ten years earlier. The buying power of his salary had obviously improved, the work of the labor unions with their social, medical, and touristic aspects made themselves felt. The system of pensions, which toward the end of '54 benefited very few unions, had been extended. It is true that Perón had financed his Second Five-Year Plan by stealing from the Pension Fund, but it is also true that this situation could have held out for a few more years. The people, undoubtedly, lived better in the era of Perón and, nevertheless, in those days in which the danger of the collapse of the government was evident, this living better did not translate into gratitude toward he who had made possible this state of things. What is certain is that on September 20, the generals of the army accepted the resignation of Perón and shortly after, the latter took refuge in the Paraguayan Embassy. Already, this phase of Peronism had ended.

A last marginal note: when Perón had to take refuge in Paraguay, he was probably the most discredited man in Argentina, even among his own partisans, who accused him of not having defended the system, he, an active general. His personal relationships had become known, as well; they had revealed unpleasant aspects of the government or of the regime; and, notwithstanding, eighteen years later Perón returned. All of which indicated that, in politics, things that at one point seem secure, are never completely so.

*The expression* Liberating Revolution, *commonly used by historians and political analysts, tends to elicit different reactions according to the position that each one may have with respect to Perón and his regime. Beyond the feelings it may arouse in whatever sense, here we have to distinguish between the revolutionary movement of 1955 that was self-described as a* Liberating Revolution *and the subsequent government, which was also known, and continues to be, as the* government of the Liberating Revolution.

## CHAPTER XIV

# The Liberating Revolution

This will be the last strictly historical chapter of the present volume, for I intend to dedicate the next and last one to a sort of review of all that we have seen. But I must say that the content of this chapter is very complex, very risky, because it is full of subjective cross-purposes. I shall try to be as honest as I can, since to ask absolute objectivity of a historian, moreover of a contemporary historian, is a request impossible to fulfill.

We shall try to examine these events, then, with perspective, without passions or commitments, leaving aside even those commitments and passions that one may have had at the time. Because, this I say right off, I formed part of that half of the country that greeted the revolution of '55 as a liberation, as the end to a nightmare. But I have also tried, with the passage of time, to forget the personal aspect and to place myself in a position that would permit me to understand in a comprehensive way what happened within the other half, without prejudices or blinders, looking at these processes with the distance and honesty with which a remote historical event, detached from our own lives, could be treated.

## September of 1955

A mystery of our contemporary history is the following: How could Lonardi, with the meager means he had available, triumph so quickly? And correlativley: How could Perón, seemingly in the prime of his power, fall so quickly? I believe it is necessary to seek the answer within the realm of the spirit, though it may seem strange: Perón was mentally defeated in September of 1955, whereas Lonardi and his group were resolved to triumph at whatever cost.

Lonardi counted on the totality of the Navy, but this arm was never decisive in resolving an issue of force. His conception departed from a base that the facts proved correct: it would be sufficient to establish a rebel bulwark in an important point of the country, in order for the entire structure of the Peronist regime to topple. Perón for his part, who in the weeks previous had offered peace and war at the same time, found that the armed columns he was sending to Córdoba were proceeding reluctantly, the planes were turning around (the famous pancakes), and he distrusted his generals. He did not arm the unions, as he had said countless times, he remained in silence and virtually did not direct the operations of the repression.

The son of Lonardi, in his book *God is Just,* recounts that the rallying cry imparted by his father upon starting the movement was that of "act with maximum brutality." It's that the rebels had the sensation, justified or not, that they were risking their lives: the rash words of Perón on August 1 assured them this was so. On the side of official- ism, on the other hand, the secretary of the CGT asked for calm.

All of this was the result, in my opinion, of the long hege- mony of Perón. He had inevitably committed errors, he had isolated himself from huge sectors of society, his cause had lost animation and faith. It is indubitable that half the country continued to support him, but it is also undeniable that no one took to the street to defend him and the statements of the officialist sector did not spur any resistance.

Thus the Peronist power, seemingly inexorable, collapsed in four days in the face of the advance of several warships that at worst could fire some cannon shot but that were not in a condition to decide anything, and in the face of a Lonar- di besieged in the center of Córdoba. This is, in my opinion, a lesson in the weariness of power and in the need for every political venture to be held aloft by a spiritual motion that carries it forward.

We shall not enter into details. On September 16, at day- break, the retired general Lonardi, surrounded by a small group of young officers, installed himself in a regiment situat- ed in the vicinity of the city of Córdoba, while some units of the ocean fleet set sail from Puerto Belgrano in the direction of Río de la Plata. And on the 21 of the same month, also at daybreak, General Juan Perón took refuge in the Paraguayan Embassy. The Liberating Revolution had triumphed, almost without a struggle, and the decade of the Peronist experience was brought to a close.

One further note, and this, totally personal. With the perspective that age provides, I believe that the Liberating Revolution was a negative development. If it had not occurred, Perón would have had to reform his regime, expanding the opening initiated in July, and it is probable that his mandate would have ended with the electoral defeat of his party. Overthrown revolutionarily, the parable of his rectifications did not conclude and the matter of force opened an extended phase of weak and conditional constitutional governments, and of de facto regimes invariably concluding in failure. But this is what we can appreciate today. At the time, the thing was presented in terms of all or nothing, and the half of the country that celebrated the fall of Perón, such as myself, could not think that the overthrow of a constitutional government is never positive.

Before closing this topic, I want to briefly add two points that have to do with our political civilization. One is the fact that Perón asked for asylum, that is, he admitted his defeat, practically without having fought. His enemies said that he did so out of cowardice; he explained later that he had not wanted blood to be spilled nor for the assets of the Nation to be destroyed. Be that as it may, the attitude of Perón saved the Argentines much suffering, for the revolutionary movement could have led to a true civil war.

The other point also refers to Perón, by now given refuge in the Paraguayan embrasure. I am certain that there were projects between the most fanatical *"gorilas"* ["gorillas": violent opponents of Perón] to take the small ship by force or to sink it with its principal occupant inside. These crazy ideas were firmly discarded by the authorities of the de facto government and the Chancellor Mario Amadeo personally helped the ex-president so that the right of asylum was respected in its full reach. What I wish to say, then, is that even in the middle of the tremendous hatreds of those days, there was sufficient good

Reinaldo Bignone, the last dictator of the *Proceso,* hands the presidential power to democratically elected Raul Alfonsín.

Carlos Saúl Menem during his first presidency.

The *Cabildo* and the Government House.

The National Congress.

sense or sufficient luck so as to put certain limits on the confrontations and to maintain respect for the norms of law that are above the struggles and passions of men.

## Lonardi, a failed project

On September 22, General Eduardo Lonardi was sworn in with the charge of provisional president. A fairly heterogeneous cabinet was accompanying him, a faithful reflection of the forces that had accompanied him: from pure liberals to nationalistic Catholics that had come face to face with Perón because of his conflict with the Church. Lonardi was a retired general, without political experience nor civil relations to speak of, but he had a project that he clearly expounded to his closest associates: his provisional charge should be brief, there would be no victors nor vanquished, and solutions that would not damage Peronism would be sought.

It was a program impossible to fulfill. Many people who nourished affronts —legitimate or not— against the fallen regime and clamored for justice, supported the government of the Liberating Revolution. There existed, furthermore, a state and parastate apparatus that Peronism had gone about putting together during almost ten years: it was not logical that it should last. The military men discharged and incarcerated because of the coup of 1951 demanded their reincorporation in the ranks; the former owners of the newspaper *La Prensa* claimed the return of their property; employees dismissed from the public administration for political reasons asked to return. And the hardest lines of anti-Peronism pressed for the intervention of the Peronist party, the CGT, and the principal labor unions —pressures repeatedly resisted by Lonardi.

Lonardi would have had to bring together in his persona the abilities of Roca, Yrigoyen, and Perón, in order to lead his well-intentioned objectives to a safe port. But he was simply a man of good will who did not have major support, neither in the anti-Peronist political parties, nor in the forces that had made the victory of the Liberating Revolution possible.

Furthermore, he committed some errors in the appointment of intimate collaborators, some of whom had almost pro-fascist-right backgrounds.

Toward the beginning of November, his Minister of War had to resign, being beside himself with the pressure of his comrades, who demanded energetic measures to de-Peronize the country. Lonardi was then urged to share the power with the generals of the army. He refused and was overthrown without offering resistance, in a splendid coup that surprised many but that was, in reality, inevitable. Months later, retired from all public activity, Lonardi passed away; he was already seriously ill when he assumed power, although his energetic will allowed him to make it through those fatiguing phases without demonstrating the increasing deterioration of his health.

## Aramburu, or the end of ambiguities

The new provisional president, General Pedro E. Aramburu, had been chief of the conspiracy that was to overthrow Perón; toward the beginning of September, he determined that he did not have sufficient forces for the attempt and he declined the chieftainship, which Lonardi took up immediately, with the result described. He played a rather undistinguished role in the process of the Liberating Revolution, and upon its triumph, he occupied the charge of Chief of Staff of the Army, from which he was brought over to the chief magistracy with the support of the most revengeful military sectors and the liberal elements of the civil forces.

With Aramburu the ambiguities ended. There were victors and there were vanquished: it was fateful that it be this way. The Peronist party and the CGT were placed under government control, as were the majority of the unions; the work of the investigative commissions was activated, which had to examine the legal actions taken by the Peronist regime in order to bring to justice those responsible; the use of symbols relative to the deposed regime was prohibited; and, of course, many political and labor leaders were arrested. Without a doubt, from November of 1955 onward, those who had been partisans of Perón felt keenly their condition as the defeated.

As for the institutional way out of the de facto regime, Aramburu limited himself to affirming that there would be elections "neither a minute before nor a minute after," and this vague commitment was sufficient for public opinion to eliminate any ambition in Aramburu to continue indefinitely in power.

Those who surrounded Aramburu thought that the Argentine political equation was relatively easy: it involved proving to the Peronist country the immense deceit, the enormous lie of the *justicialista* regime. After a prudential lapse, the people would cease to be Peronist and elections could then be called with the reasonable certainty that the future constitutional president would be a friend of the Liberating Revolution and a custodian of its values.

But it happened that the Peronist populace did not decrease its adhesion to the exiled leader. It disdained all that was said about illicit transactions, orgies, and errors, and preferred to remember the conquests obtained during the captaincy of Perón; the assistance of the Eva Perón Foundation; the times of contentment lived in the enjoyment of gains to which it did not previously have access, such as vacation, union health and benefits programs; the improvement of the quality of their lives.

Some activists of Peronism tried to set up a network of resistance without much success; in the unions under government control a new generation of leaders replaced the opportunists who had enjoyed the fringe benefits of power alongside of Perón but had not defended him when the moment came to do so. The ex-president, himself, from Caracas and afterward in Santo Domingo, sent demential instructions about armed resistance, sabotage, and attacks against the de facto government. None of this moved the simple folk to externalize a massive repudiation against the government of the Liberating Revolution, but nor did it move them at all in their faithfulness to Perón. Progressively, the *gorila* advisors of Aramburu could think that the process of de-Peronization would be successful.

In any event, the decision to erradicate Peronist sentiments in everything possible was expressed on two occasions in the course of 1956. The first was during the month of May, when the provisional government annulled by decree the validity of the Constitution of 1949 and reintroduced that of 1853, promising to convoke in due time a constituent assembly to update it.

The other moment was not juridical and is associated with one of the most tragic moments of our contemporary history. In June of 1956, a group of retired military men of Peronist filiation attempted a coup in different points of the country. They had only very partial success and within a few hours the movement was repressed. The provisional government imposed martial law and decreed the execution of those who might be found with arms in hand. And despite the fact that the attempt had been completely defeated, more than thirty Argentines, military men and civilians, were executed, among them the chief of the movement, General Juan J. Valle.

It had been more than one hundred years since an execution occurred in Argentina for political reasons, and the tragic incident moved the citizens. There were those who applauded the measure, but in general, the extremity of the punishment provoked a reaction of condemnation and rejection that, although it had almost no concrete expression in the press, was perceived at all levels of opinion. Nevertheless, for the leaders of the Liberating Revolution this cost of blood signified the evidence of an irrevocable commitment to their final objectives.

# The big issues

Meanwhile, some significant phenomena began to occur at the heart of society. One of the most important was the outburst of freedom of speech, with its sequels of power over polemics and debates. The Peronist regime, as all authoritarian systems, did not facilitate the bringing under discussion of the problems of the country; its implicit thesis was that everything was going well and, if something was going poorly, Perón would set about fixing it. The control of the media permitted this conception to be maintained for as long as the Peronist regime was in effect.

The government of the Liberating Revolution opened the game of discussion upon handing over the newspapers and magazines of the official chains and networks to diverse political and ideological sectors, naturally, excluding Peronism. Rather quickly some of the big issues that the country had to face were posed: the future role of the State in the economic scheme of things, the supplying of petroleum, the role of foreign principals, education, industrial and agrarian policy, the situating of the country in the international context, etc.

I'll point out that the government of the Liberating Revolution did not have a very defined course under most of these headings. It could not have one; in the first place, because of the different tendencies that were causing internal tension, but in addition, because of its very character, which was precarious. Thus, it had approved the Prebisch Report, but had not carried out its recommendations. It dissolved several organisms of the previous system that had been seriously questioned, such as the IAPI, but it practically left untouched the state apparatus set up by Perón. It adhered to the International Monetary Fund, but its international policy was very contradictory. It created a duty free zone in Patagonia that was very criticized. It was in sympathy with the Yadarola Plan to turn YPF into a contractor of foreign petroleum companies, but it did not go forward on this path.

The open discussions on the principal questions that were made regarding the future of the country constituted one of the most positive aspects of the presidency of Aramburu and progressed at the same rhythm as the processes contemporaneously experienced by almost all the political parties. For while Peronism, persecuted and silenced, seemed nonexistent, the remaining partisan forces were suffering dissensions that in some cases ended in division.

It was logical. During the ten years of Perón, the opposition parties had had to survive maintaining their unity at all costs; any other attitude would have been suicidal. Perón having been removed from the picture, internal confrontations, different points of view, and even personal ambitions exploded with the same virulence as did the anxiety to debate and discuss all that was repressed during the overthrown regime.

Socialism split up into two fractions; conservativism, into three; and the UCR, the principal oppositional force, which until then had maintained an apparent unity, though artificial, toward the beginning of 1957 separated irremediably into two parties: that which Ricardo Balbín led, with a tendency to support the government of the Liberating Revolution, and that which Arturo Frondizi directed, increasingly at odds with the de facto government, drawing increasingly close to banished Peronism, and with programmatic flags of the advanced guard that seduced youth, intellectuals, and the progressive sectors.

## Globular re-count and presidential election

Toward the beginning of 1957, the government of Aramburu convoked elections of the constituent assembly members, to be realized in July of the same year. The election served two purposes: one institutional, the other political. At the time it was essential to homologate, by way of the representation of the citizenship, the annulment of the effectiveness of the Constitution of 1949, disposed by a simple decree. On the other hand, it would be a cautious survey of opinion, a "globular recount" —as was said at the time—, to establish the preference of the electorate with a view to the future general elections, to take place at an as yet undetermined date.

The counting of votes was disappointing for the leaders of the government of the Liberating Revolution. Perón, from Caracas, had ordered his loyal followers to vote with unmarked ballots, and in effect, this suffrage of rejection obtained 24 percent of the public's will. Peronism continued to be a majority. Radicalism of the People (Balbín) followed it with a volume almost equal, and Intransigent Radicalism (Frondizi) cleared 21 percent of the vote. As the electoral system was proportional, the Constituent Convention would have to reflect the pluralism of the partisan panorama of the country —naturally, however, Peronism was to be left to the side, despite the several assembly members of Peronist origin, though removed from the orthodoxy of his movement.

The Convention met in Santa Fe and the representatives devoted to Frondizi impugned the meeting and withdrew, leaving the body with a strict quorum; the decision was agreeable to Peronism, which with their blank ballots had also impugned the meeting. Notwithstanding, the assembly managed to ratify the effectiveness of the Constitution of 1853, to whose text the so-called article 14 bis was added, with norms of a social nature. It then dissolved. Preludes of the important electoral campaign began, the one that for several years would define the future of the country: the general elections for president and vice president, governors, senators, deputies, etc., which the government of Aramburu set for February 23, 1958.

At few times was such intense political activity seen in Argentina. Frondizi continually hastened to court Peronism in order to obtain the electoral support that was indispensable to him, and parallel to this he embossed a program capable of satisfying the most diverse sectors: lay persons and Catholics, industrialists and liberals, partisans of an international pro-Western position, and sympathizers of the left. His figure, unknown in Argentine politics, was that of a professor who vaticinated a program of development "for twenty million Argentines."

Balbín, by contrast, had to travel a very narrow road, circumscribed by his support for the de facto government and his electoral needs. There were a half dozen more candidates, but it was unquestionable that the option lay between those two leaders of radical origin who seven years earlier had made up the ticket of their party against the reelection of Perón and now confronted one another rancorously.

Perón, meanwhile, found himself in a difficult situation. It was uncertain whether his loyal followers would vote with unmarked ballots again: now at hand was the election of constitutional authorities who would steer the country for six years, with thousands of candidates at stake, at every level. To be left out could signify for him an enormous weakening of his influence. Furthermore, it was increasingly evident that the average Peronist felt inclined to vote for Frondizi, who criticized the government of Aramburu harshly and promised to respect the unity of the worker's movement and to put an end to the phase of hatred and revenge.

Was there really a pact between Perón and Frondizi? The latter always emphatically denied having signed any electoral agreement. But it is undeniable that conversations existed between intimate collaborators of the candidate of the UCRI and the exile in Santo Domingo. And it is also indisputable that two weeks before the elections Perón ordered, through diverse means, that people vote for Frondizi. The historical enigma, in any case, is irrelevant. Without the order of Perón, Frondizi would have won anyway, although certainly in a less devastating fashion.

For on February 23, 1958, 49 percent of the electorate anointed Frondizi as president, while his principal rival obtained 29 percent, and the blank vote was barely expressed with 8 percent. Frondizi's party had obtained all the governorships, the entire Senate, and two thirds of the deputies. Never had a triumph of such magnitude been seen in Argentina. But the starting vice —the support of banished Peronism— would mean a heavy burden for him in the future.

Naturally, this could not be perceived in the days that followed, in the middle of the euphoria of the triumphant party and the generalized sentiment in the public opinion, in the sense that, finally, the country had entered the path of definitive normalization. Although within the government of the Liberating Revolution there was, according to what was asserted at that time, some intention to disavow the results of the elections, Aramburu hastened to greet Frondizi as the president elect and to reaffirm his clear disposition to surrender power.

And, effectively, on May 1, 1958, Arturo Frondizi received the insignia of command and readied himself to assume his responsibilities. And at this moment I must bring to a close the telling of our history.

## An onerous inheritance

Allow me now several reflections to close this chapter.

The Liberating Revolution (and the provisional government that followed it), beyond the intentions of its animators, paved the way for very negative consequences. I said at the beginning that the outburst of the revolution of September of 1955 had saved Perón from making important rectifications in emblematic aspects of his politics. Which Perón, then, was the genuine one? He who nationalized the railroads or he who negotiated an enormous petroleum concession in Patagonia? He who proposed a third position or he who desperately sought the support of the United States? The one of social justice or he who reduced social conquests in the Congress of Productivity? He who spoke of conciliation or he who promised "five against one"? The Revolution saved Perón from falling into increasingly more profound declinations and inconsistencies. But it is clear that the rebels were not in the mood for such considerations: for them, overturning Perón was a question of life or death that did not admit holding back.

Nevertheless, the worst toll of the Liberating Revolution resided in the attitude assumed by the Armed Forces, in the sense that they saw themselves as the custodians of a closed anti-Peronist vigilance. This was the principal reason for the innumerable proposals that Frondizi had to put up with during his administration, and was also the reason for his overthrow, in 1962. Anti-Peronism led them to outfit Guido so that the election presided over by this modest patriot would guarantee a government without even the most minimal Peronist participation. And the danger of a new Peronist triumph impelled the overthrow of Illia, since the conception of Onganía's de facto regime was also that of freezing politics until "the damned matter" of Peronism was weakened.

In other words: from the Liberating Revolution arose an Armed Forces prepared to not allow the slightest hint of a reappearance of Peronism, in any form nor in any context. This determination distorted the entire process of Argentine democracy because it engendered a series of weak constitutional governments, conditioned or marked by an illegitimacy of origin, and military regimes that invariably failed.

At the same time, Peronism —banished and lacking a partisan political channel that represented it—, sought alternative forms to continue having a presence on the national scene. Naturally, it found this channel in the organized union movement and it is thus that the CGT or the 62 Organizations turned into the Peronist party that the legislation dictated by the Liberating Revolution had abolished. The union movement exerted pressure, attacked, harassed, and conducted itself in the same way in which a political opposition would have behaved, but without the institutional control that limited and conditioned the actions of the parties. And this, too, was a serious distortion that debilitated the governments of Frondizi and of Illia, as well as a source of conflicts for the de facto regime of Onganía. That is to say, the institutional game was completely altered by the Liberating Revolution, with the Armed Forces turned into gendarmes of Peronism and a worker's movement transformed into Peronism activists.

This schema, perhaps, is a bit simplistic, but in general terms I believe that it is correct. *"Gorilismo"* darkened Argentine life and led to the lack of faith in democracy for the sake of a mythic national revolution, a socialist country, or so many other destructive utopias. I am of course not disavowing the responsibility of Perón, who from his exile encouraged a *"gorilismo"* in reverse. But what is certain and true is that following the Liberating Revolution, one could not govern with Peronism; but the stubborn facts demonstrated that neither could one govern without Peronism, nor, much less, against Peronism.

When one looks back at those years, one notes that hatred and yearning for vengeance were common and prevalent sentiments. Peronism in power had sown these feelings in abundance with its arrogance and its authoritarianism; the liberators gave back their resentments, justified or not, generously. Nothing positive was acknowledged in the enemy (because really they were enemies, not adversaries), and this left a black and lasting period of germination in Argentine society. Only time could begin to heal these exhausting and sterilizing infections. Time and the healthy spiritual condition of the majority of the Argentines, a condition which tends to prevail when the latter are not artificially incited toward violence and intolerance.

## CHAPTER XV

# The lessons of history

*On beginning this book I said that to try to amalgamate Argentine history in fifteen chapters is almost an irreverence, because the historical process is always complex and interrelated. Tendencies and factors exist that act upon one another, and all attempts to simplify them betray in a certain sense the intention of accuracy that should animate all historians. But it is also true that history is infinite and ungraspable by definition: never can the whole story be told; important segments, significant elements will always be missing. So that our intention of summarizing, synthesizing, showing some aspects of what seemed fundamental to us —though many others may have remained in the inkwell— is also valid.*

Thus in these pages we have tried to put forth some tendencies that have to do with the very substance of our founding processes and with that of other, subsequent ones, which have also shaped the Argentina that we are living. We began by recalling the most remote events, in the first place the foundation of the city of Buenos Aires, and considered our story over until we reached the point in which our own lives became confused with what was being related; it seemed prudent to us to put the final period here.

This is the last chapter, then. And it would seem appropriate to speak about what we could call "the lessons of history," although I know that history does not instruct, history is not the teacher of life, as Cicero might have said twenty centuries ago with a phrase that many —including Cervantes— repeated later on. But we know it is a compassionate lie, a courtesy toward our discipline. For if history were really the teacher of life, it would not commit the errors that societies and its leaders tend to commit, and we, the historians, would be not only counselors but infallible priests of the rulers and the ruled... So, I am entitling this last chapter "The Lessons of History" though its content be much more modest, less pretentious. What you are going to read, simply, will be that which a historian gathers as the remains of the chronicle he has provided.

## Federalism

We said that historical processes are composed of fractures (that is, ruptures, sudden cuts), but also of continuities (that is, tendencies and contents that remain through time; sometimes in a silent way, at others, in a more notable way). This interplay of fractures and continuities is, shall we say, a counterpoint that articulates the great symphony of Argentine history —of universal history, we should add.

So far so good: Within the more notable continuities, we should point out what indicates the will of the peoples of this country in the sense of giving themselves a federal organization. And not only a federal political organization but also a type of society where neighboring, provincial, and local identities may remain pronounced, may have an effect on the life of the community at large.

This we have seen in our expositions from the beginning, for as has been reiterated, since the founding of Buenos Aires one notes a struggle, sometimes muted and almost clandestine and at other times violent and devastating, between those two Argentinas: the one that grows along the shores of the River Plate and its region of influence, and the other, the Mediterranean, that of the North, Northwest, Cuyo, and then, Patagonian Argentina, as well. If a dialectic exists in our history, it is that which is composed of the confrontations and the understandings between Buenos Aires and the rest of the country.

And here a very curious circumstance must be pointed out: Argentina is a federal country. It is so because of its constitutional organization, but also because of the communal vocation we spoke of earlier. And in spite of this, the geographic configuration of Argentina condemns it to being centralist, to depending on one center alone —obviously, Buenos Aires. For how can a nation that has one single outlet to the outside world develop into autonomous entities? That gateway to land that Buenos Aires was in the conception of judge Matienzo turned into a toll office, and its occupant, the people or the ruling classes of the city of Buenos Aires, charged a lot for keeping the door open, half-open, or closing it completely....

Rosas was not that mistaken when he asserted, in his Letter from Hacienda de Figueroa, that the cases of United States and Argentina were very different, for there the federal system had been established with naturalness because the thirteen founding colonies, all of them, had maritime ports; here, on the other hand, only Buenos Aires is a port. Despite this geographic fatality, history shows us the vocation, the federalist genius of the Argentine people; and this genius, in documents, in the laws, in the constitution, has prevailed over geographic determinants.

But in practice, our country is a centralized country. Buenos Aires constrains and frees from constraint; Buenos Aires orders, imposes, collects, apportions, consecrates, overturns. "This is Castille, which doth make and unmake men," states the old Balladeer. Buenos Aires makes and unmakes prestige, governments, and economic and political proposals. The Park Revolution —as we already saw— or those of 1930 and 1943, were exclusively *porteño* movements, and notwithstanding, their effects cut across the entire country.

Will this tendency some day be reverted? The lesson of history (I continue to refer to this artifice) shows that true federalism, increasingly, is a utopia. But it also shows that men can, with imagination and audacity, pose partial remedies to an increasingly more asphyxiating centralism. I have been an ardent advocate, for example, of the Federal Capital's move: I said this at the beginning of 1982, explaining the pertinent reasons in my book *Buenos Aires y el país* [*Buenos Aires and the Country*]. I believe President Alfonsín proposed the move of the capital to Viedma in an incomplete and mistaken manner, all of which caused society and even his own party to accept this issue with a great deal of indifference, until it fell by the wayside on its own. But I continue to believe that the move of the three powers of the National State to another city —existent or yet to be built— is a necessity that is going to become more and more imperative. It will not remedy the problem of centralism completely but it will be an important palliative.

Meanwhile, it is necessary to continue to keep in mind that the federalist vocation is authentic, has profound historical roots, and has allowed for moments in which the conflict began to surpass the basis of intelligent and realistic formulas. It seems to me that if there is any lesson that the knowledge of our history offers us, it is this: that of federalism; that is, the issue that makes for the singularity of our regions, for their right to grow according to their own guidelines, for the need that their physical wealth and human resources do not end up absorbed by that almost monstrous element of seduction that is our beloved Buenos Aires; this issue, is paramount and makes for our essence as a Nation.

# Democracy

Next I would like to bring up another vector, another constant that flows through the course of our entire history: I am referring to the tendency toward a better political democracy, which goes hand in hand with the tendency toward a truer social egalitarianism. One might be able to point out this current at a given moment during the colonial era, but it began to show itself in an unavoidable way after 1810.

We said at the time, that the movement of the May Revolution brought about a great change in ideas, among them, the replacement of the scholastic conception of the common welfare for the principle of popular sovereignty. This principle took a long time to have practical applications. At one point democracy simply consisted in the caudillo's capacity to head his town: "each lance, a vote..."

But as the country began to evolve, juridical and political formulas were found so that this democratic vocation, which existed above all in the popular sectors, would be channeled pacifically. It is a process that culminated with the sanction of the Sáenz Peña Law although that did not automatically signify the establishment of a perfect political democracy. Moveover: the Sáenz Peña Law was eluded often and the legitimacy that arose from the popular will, peacefully expressed at the polls, was at times destroyed by military experiences that we have all known.

But without a doubt this is a nation made for democracy. It is, in a historical perspective, because the human type that arose from colonial times was free, autonomous, poorly subject to hierarchies or authorities; Buenos Aires, we already saw, was a plebeian city and without aristocracy, and the interior, where caste societies prevailed, soon began to modify its structures, largely from the middle of the previous century onward. Later on, the great immigrations contributed in accentuating this tone, because these people came to accomplish something for themselves according to their personal capability and they depended solely on their strength and their luck; and what's more, their children, brought up on the type of education set up by the men of '80, soon claimed their place in the sun.

History, then, shows us a tendency toward democracy that is undeniable. It is true that during some contemporary phases a certain consent to authoritarian solutions or to those removed from popular opinions could have existed; but these interregna were always taken as provisional, as painful remedies —although, according to some, necessary. And always, when one voted anew, the Argentine electorates did so massively, I would say with delight. There is a political democracy, then, with which we are historically consubstantiated.

Something similar occurred with the egalitarian sense that characterizes our society. It also comes from way back, like the democratic vocation. Travelers of the 19th century admired the simplicity with which laborers treated those who employed them, a very different attitude from the servility and humility that they saw in other countries of America. An Italian immigrant settled in Colonia Caroya (province of Córdoba), toward 1870, wrote to his relatives from his *paese* explaining what surprised him most in his new country, and one of these novelties was the fact that to speak with a rich person it was not necessary to reveal onself, to remove one's hat.

Egalitarianism does not mean that we all consider ourselves equal, but that all should have equal opportunity to face self-fulfillment in life. This is to say that no one should be left out because he did not have the education he deserved, that no one be treated with disdain because he may lack wealth, that a minimum of dignity be acknowledged for all. Perhaps because of this a conception such as that of social justice raised by Perón was accepted by all after the first confrontations, and the operative norms that were prescribed in the application of the principle that the State could not be indifferent to the fate of the less fortunate, continued to be in effect after his overthrow.

Democracy and egalitarianism, two sides of the same conception, they are invariable vectors of our history. Their development may have had stumbling blocks or interruptions but it has never been expunged. To do so, within our society, is to act against nature. Not all the countries of Latin America can say the same. And this is a toll of the historical processes that we have lived, a clear lesson of history. But there are still a few more tendencies to underscore.

## Conflicts and harmonies

Also visible in our history is a dual process of confrontations and agreements, confrontations that can be quite harsh but also agreements that reveal political intelligence, tolerance, and pluralism. In a book that I wrote some years ago I called this dual series *Conficts and Harmonies,* borrowing the title from a work that Sarmiento wrote in his old age.

It is true that in our country, luckily, those terrible and heart-rending struggles that have stained many brother nations of America with blood have not occurred —or have occurred in a very circumstantial way. But our political struggles have also been harsh, at times: in the previous century the unitarians and federalists; after, the radicals and conservatives or the Peronists and the anti-Peronists.

There were moments in which the Argentines felt that they were divided; and they felt that those divisions were not artificial but rather real, and that it was worthwhile to adhere to one or the other of the terms of the game. Suddenly, important values appeared and a profound conflict was raised thereof. I do want to say that I am not invalidating the legitimacy of conflicts and that I do respect those who give themselves over to them wholeheartedly. But there has to be something at stake that truly matters. A supporter of Yrigoyen at the beginning of the century was willing to die in the revolution that his leader organized, because he was fighting for popular sovereignty, for his right to vote. This is respectable and Pellegrini, no less, declared it thus when amnesty was being discussed for the revolutionaries of 1905.

These types of confrontations serve to clarify things, to define values. What is ideal is that they conclude in compliance with the only arbitration that a democracy should respect: the will of the people, peacefully and freely expressed at the polls. Sometimes it does happen this way, sometimes it does not... And then the other series comes to pass: that of pacts, agreements, conciliations, alliances. And this, which is orchestrated in varying ways, consists basically in reducing slightly one's own positions, one's own ambitions, one's own compromises, to settle situations that, otherwise, can become uncontrollable.

The Constitution of 1853 was a covenant of this sort: a formula of compromise between provinces that had been in confrontation with one another. The Sáenz Peña Law also, in a certain way, was a pact: the Regime told the radicals: "Renounce the revolution, forget abstention, and vote; we shall guarantee free suffrage, we shall acknowledge your victory if you win and we shall cogovern with you if you lose." Political alliances exist, as well, which are made with the understanding that the parties are a part of a whole, and consequently, faced with certain circumstances, can strengthen or make their affinities with other parties possible.

This dual series of conflicts and harmonies marks our history throughout and one has to admire the men who knew how to head or lead confrontations —the case of Alem, the case of De la Torre—, as well as those who implemented accords and conciliations —the case of Roca, the case of Ortiz. With both series, the plot of our political history is woven. To live solely on confrontations is impossible: every society at some point seeks to lie back in peace, in fraternity. "Every Nation is a daily plebiscite," said Renán, and this plebiscite can only express itself in the acknowledgment of the validity of the other, of what is alien or of the adversary.

But nor can one live on the basis of constant understandings and this is the lesson that the trajectory of Roca's regime leaves, which began to degenerate in the dealing out of power and in the immorality of a constant pact. There are times then for civilized confrontations. And there are also times for honorable accords. But this should be kept in mind: the best accord is respect for the Constitution and fundamental laws. This is the basic accord, the norm that establishes limits and checks, inviolable rules of the game, procedures that in their reiteration acquire a sacred respect.

We needn't fear confrontations; we should, however, keep them from getting out of control. But nor should we repudiate harmonies, because society is but one great list of harmonies: of codes and customs, of languages and gestures, of fears and prides, of legends and fantasies, of myths and realities. Certainly, the wisdom of nations consists in knowing how to ration the doses of their conflicts when it is necessary to clarify something that is obscure, and to administer their accords so that they be fructiferous and lasting.

Perhaps this seems to you too theoretical, too rhetorical. Neverthess, throughout these pages you have read we have often referred to conflicts, to confrontations; but to pacts, accords, and covenants, as well. This is to say that there is a lot of Argentine experience in this area, and history too, in this sense, shows us lessons that we should take advantage of.

## America and Europe

Let us examine now one of the most persistent as well as coherent tendencies followed in these parts since the time of Spanish domination, probably until the present day. I am referring to the vocation of forming part of the European world, of being connected to Europe.

You will recall what we related in the beginning chapters: the struggle of Buenos Aires and of the inhabitants of the region of the River Plate, in general, to have this territory function as a crossing point for the goods that were traveling to Potosí by way of an absurd itinerary, quite long and expensive. It was a struggle of two centuries before the imports that were supplying the internal market of Buenos

Aires, Tucumán, and Upper Peru succeeded in entering through the estuary, that is, in arriving by way of the South Atlantic. This meant a greater connection with Spain and, owing to this, with Europe.

The tendency became more pronounced with the creation of the Viceroyalty, with the Free Trade Regulation, and much more intensely later, following 1810. With some ups and downs, the tendency continued, and subsequent to Caseros, turned into the official policy of Argentine governments. Up until now I have not spoken of the significance of the Elizalde Memorandum. It was a document issued by Rufino de Elizalde, Mitre's Minister of Foreign Relations, responding to an invitation on behalf of his Peruvian colleague to participate in a meeting or congress to be held in Lima with the purpose of preventing hostilities that some powers were perpetrating —we are speaking of 1864 and 1865— against American nations. In his answer, of almost brutal frankness, Elizalde said that Argentina had little to do with the rest of America; that on the other hand it had great expectations regarding its relationship with Europe. He added that our country, save for exceptional circumstances, had not had problems with the nations of the Old World, that on the contrary, it had received immigrants and capital from them; moreover, it hoped that these contributions were to become more and more plentiful.

The Elizalde Memorandum defined a policy that lasted almost a century, with different governments and in different international circumstances. It should be recognized that, at the time, it was an intelligent policy. There were Argentine regions —Cuyo, the North, the Northwest— that maintained an age-old commercial link with the rest of America, or at least, with the neighboring countries. But as our country began to become an exporter of products coming from the wet pampa, this American link weakened until it practically disappeared and the bet was on Europe.

I repeat, it was an intelligent policy, the only one that could yield immediate revenue. Europe constituted a good market for our production —above all Great Britain, France,

Belgium, and Germany—, but in addition, these and other countries of the old continent brought us men, capital, technologies, merchandise, ideas that enriched us in every sense. What could the American continent offer us? What exchange could there be with these countries, many of them unstable and involved in conflicts?

Everything began to slowly change following the Second World War. Our business associate and principal client, Great Britain, lost its status. Europe began to shut itself in, it put obstacles in the way of our production. Other markets had to be sought. But regardless, our country continued to feel more European than American. Perhaps because of this old tradition of economic, commercial, and financial connections; perhaps because of its ethnic composition: Carlos Fuentes, the Mexican novelist, says that the Mexicans descend from the Aztecs, the Peruvians from the Incas, and the Argentines... from ships. Almost all of us have a grandfather or great-grandfather who came off the ships, and this is the root that one does not forget.

Let us state it with complete frankness: we Argentines, in general, are not very Americanist. The American element begins to appear right around Córdoba and on up through the north, when a chapel, a face, a song, takes us back to pre-Hispanic origins. But the Argentines have only experienced one moment of authentic Americanism, when San Martín crossed the Andes to help emancipate the Chileans and the Peruvians. All the rest is rhetoric, except perhaps, in 1982, during the Falkland Islands War: at that time (and beyond the madness of the episode itself) we could note that the only voices of encouragement that accompanied us were those of Latin Americans. The countries of Europe, with whom we had a more intense emotional closeness, turned their backs on us essentially. Careful: I believe that they had all the reason in the world to do so. But I have the impression that what happened to me, happened to many compatriots: I perceived that the only solidarities came from this continent of ours to which we were indifferent for so long.

And now? I am not an expert nor a politician. There is no

reason why I should state what the position, the opening is, what course the country has in the international context; I do not know if we should trust less in Europe and expand on the other hand some mechanisms of integration with neighboring countries, as MERCOSUR (Common Market of South American Countries) would propose. What I do wish to indicate is that, historically, one of our constants is the vocation of being close to Europe in all fields. Perhaps the moment has arrived to accentuate this closeness, perhaps it is a question of opening up other roads; maybe this multipolar and rare world requires of the imagination other efforts, efforts that I am not in a position to make nor do I have reason to try. I limit myself to pointing out a tendency, a continuity, a vocation. Which is, moreover, an experience. If in the physical world, "nothing is lost, everything is transformed," in the world of societies all experiences, positive or negative, are useful. Though it be merely to avoid their own repetition...

We can refer to other tendencies, other constants that offer us knowledge of our history. But I cannot resist the temptation to speak about one of them, because it has always called my attention: Argentina's getting into debt.

Fourteen years after the movement of 1810, our country, one of the United Provinces of the River Plate, had already acquired its first foreign loan, the famous Baring Brothers, which has passed into history as a paradigm of an expensive and useless loan. Since then and excepting the era of Rosas, Argentina constantly got into financial commitments abroad. Urquiza did it, to save from ruin the government of Paraná over which he presided; Sarmiento did it in a superlative way; and later, Roca and those who came after him. Perón, who in 1946 gave himself the pleasure of repatriating the foreign debt, four years later had to ask the United States for a special credit. Let us not explore the topic in depth: it is enough to recall the monstrous increase in debt during the Military Process between 1976 and 1983.

What I should like to say is that Argentina was, almost constantly, a debtor nation, and this also characterizes our nature fairly well. But one can get into good debts and bad debts, and we have had both types. Bad debts were, for example, those that were acquired so that people could go to Miami or create apartments for themselves in Punta del Este (Uruguay). And good debts, those that the country assumed at the end of the previous century, when in order to exploit the countryside rationally, it was necessary to buy wire fencing, mills, seeds, breeders, et cetera. But what is certain is that the quip about the "great debtor of the South," which Sarmiento spoke of in parodying the National Hymn —and forgetting that he had been one of the great begetters of debt—, is something that cuts across our history, with all of its nuances.

I could also say something —and with this I end the examination— about the geographic location of our country. If we take a look at the earth, we can see that our position in the world is very peripheral; we find ourselves at a great distance from the other continents, and even in the American vicinity we are sort of hanging at the extreme south.

This planetary situation bears advantages and disadvantages that are noted throughout our history and also today. At the time, our remoteness during the period of the Hispanic domination gave rise to a certain abandonment, a certain disinterest on the part of the metropolis until things began to change with the arrival of the Bourbons. And even today we do not realize our peripheral status: the problems of the great powers affect us, but concern us little, because we feel that we are removed from the eye of political storms; this perception must have influenced, among other factors, the elaboration of neutralism that Argentina maintained during the last two world wars with governments of diverse natures. And we also perceive our remoteness when we confirm the limited quantity of tourist trends that come from Europe and the high incidence of shipments of our imports and exports to countries that may not be our neighbors.

At the same time, the form in which we are a country, the north to south stretch that encompasses more than 2,480 miles, affords us every climate and every production, that is, it equips our imagination and our effort to confront any challenge. If one hundred years ago the Argentines understood perfectly that the key to national success resided in reaping the fruits of the land, the great unoccupied resource that the country possessed, today this diversity of possibilities should demand our ingenuity in order to take us out of activities that have by now become barely income-producing and impel us onto new avenues, new productions, different exploitations, in which, naturally, advantage could be taken of an education that, despite its deterioration, continues to give our people the notable characteristics of mental quickness, capability to adapt to recent technical demands, and flexibility for all that is distinct, different.

## To get to know better

So then, we are reaching the end of this voyage that weighed anchor during the beginnings of this country, from its humble and remote origins, and has brought us up to contemporary times. Retrospectively, we have lived through stormy periods, and calm phases, as well.

I have tried to be truthful and to honorably expose the facts and the interpretations that, in my opinion, correspond to those facts. As we already know, in matters of history objectivity does not exist, because the expositor is a human being, has been born in a specific place, has a particular education, adheres to certain values. Inevitably he looks at things from his own vantage point. But we also know that there exists a possibility of being honest in the exposition of a chronicle such as this, and I assure you, I have been honest. And also, I assure you, I have enjoyed myself very much.

I do not know what these pages leave you with. For me, as a narrator, they have been very useful, because they have forced me to review and synthesize processes that I have had to simplify in order to make them comprehensible to a public that has no reason to be acquainted with them. For you as readers and, in some way, participants perhaps, too, it has been useful, this quick glide through Argentine history. For to know a little bit better the country in which one has been born or in which one lives almost always implies appreciating it a little bit more. And it also suggests the possibility that, on understanding the country better, one may be more compassionate toward its defects and its deficiencies and at the same time feel prouder of its positive notes, which maybe we would not have noticed if they had not been shown to us with the perspective of history.

For me, I must say, the study of the way in which this country was made, my country, always reinforces my innate optimism. Because I can appreciate the way that enormous difficulties began to be sidestepped, divisions, and confrontations that seemed insalvageable, problems seemingly unsolvable. Always, in the end, there were solutions. Always, one way or another, we forged ahead. For this reason, I do not much believe in any one government, but instead, I believe in my country a great deal. In its sense of justice, in its capacity for tolerance, in its noble egalitarianism, in its democratic instinct, in its intelligence.

This does not mean that I have a naive attitude. But in no way am I pessimistic. Believe me, we have a good country. And in these pages it seems to me that it has been made clear that this is so. The only thing that we, the Argentines of the end of the 20th century, are lacking is to deserve it.

# Glossary

*adelantado:* governor-commander.

**Alfonsín, Raúl:** Argentine president from 1983 to 1989.

**Alto Perú:** *Alto Perú,* or Upper Peru.

*Audiencia:* High Tribunal.

*bandeirantes:* Portuguese colonists from the southern part of San Pablo who made incursions with the purpose of enslaving Indians.

*cabildo:* town council meeting.

**Cabildo:** Town Hall.

*capitanía:* territory in colonial America governed by a captain general.

*cívicos:* supporters of the Civic Union party.

**C.G.T.:** *Confederación General del Trabajo,* or the General Confederation of Labor.

*colorados:* political party of the center right, in Uruguay.

*criollo:* born in the Americas of European ancestry (often of Spanish parentage).

*encomienda:* Indians who were awarded to Spaniards in order that they work for the latter in exchange for a certain well-being.

*estancia:* ranch where livestock is raised.

**Gardel, Carlos:** the most famous of Argentine tango singers.

**gaucho:** primitive inhabitant of the pampas.

*gorila, gorilismo:* name given to the ultra anti-Peronists.

**Guido, José María:** provisional president of Argentina from 1962-1963.

**Illia, Arturo:** Argentine president from 1963 to 1966.

*justicialista:* the party of Perón.

*Leyes de Indias:* Laws of the West Indies.

**Lugones, Leopoldo:** well-known Argentine poet, died in 1938.

**Mallea, Eduardo:** important Argentine novelist, died in 1982.

*Martín Fierro:* national poem of the *gauchesco* genre, written by José Hernández.

**May Revolution:** *Revolución de Mayo.*

**Ocampo, Victoria:** important Argentine writer, founder of the magazine *Sur.*

**officialism; officialist:** the party in office; characteristic of the party in office.

**Onganía, Juan Carlos:** de facto president from 1966 to 1970.

**pampa:** extensive plain.

*porteño:* native of the city of Buenos Aires.

*quinto:* tribute to the king of one fifth of earnings.

*real, reales:* Spanish coin equivalent to about twenty-five cents.

*realista:* royalist, one who supported the Crown of Spain and was against the patriots.

*Reconquista:* struggle by Spanish Christians to oust the Moors from Spain.

**Storni, Alfonsina:** Argentine woman poet, died in 1938.

*tertulia:* a habitual gathering of friends or colleagues to converse or discuss issues.

*vaquería:* hunting of unclaimed cattle to skin them and use the hide.

# Contents

# Humble Origins

## 13

# The Colonial Period

## 33

## Chapter III
# 1810 and Its Effects
## 53

## Chapter IV
# The Search for A Political Formula
## 73

## Chapter V
# Toward National Organization
## 93

## Chapter XV
# The Lessons of History
## 255

Esta edición
se terminó de imprimir en
Verlap S.A. Producciones Gráficas
Vieytes 1534, Buenos Aires,
en el mes de marzo de 1996.